PEOPLE OF THE
TROUBLED WATER
A Missouri River Journal

PEOPLE OF THE
TROUBLED WATER

A Missouri River Journal

Nancy Mayborn Peterson

Illustrations by Asa Battles

Nancy Mayborn Peterson

Asa Battles

RENAISSANCE
HOUSE PUBLISHERS

A Division of Jende-Hagan, Inc.
541 Oak Street • P.O. Box 177
Frederick, CO 80530

Renaissance House Publishers
A Division of Jende-Hagan, Inc.
541 Oak Street ~ P.O. Box 177
Frederick, CO   80530

First Printing October, 1988

Library of Congress Cataloging in Publication Data Pending

Peterson, Nancy M., 1934-
  People of the troubled water.

  Bibliography: p.
  Includes index.
  1. Missouri River--Description and travel.
2. Missouri River Valley--History. 3. Missouri
River Valley--Description and travel. I. Title.
F598.P44 1988   978   88-26418
ISBN 1-55838-082-5
ISBN 1-55838-083-3 (pbk.)

For Jim, my loyal chauffeur
up and down the Troubled Water.

Foreword

Nancy Peterson's *People of the Troubled Water* is a long-labored but nonetheless brilliant narrative of the successive (sometimes simultaneous) cavalcade of fearless men and women who penetrated the far west. These were the pioneers who attempted to assault the longest (2,464 miles)* if not the most treacherous river in America, for reasons ranging from monetary profit to sheer excitement and high adventure.

The Missouri is formed where the Gallatin, the Madison and the Jefferson join at Three Forks in southwestern Montana. Its tributaries include the Mussellshell, the Milk, the Yellowstone, the Grand of South Dakota, the Cheyenne, the Niobrara, the James, the Big Sioux, the Little Sioux, the Platte, the Kaw, the Grand of Iowa and Missouri, the Chariton, the Osage, and the Gasconade Rivers. The Missouri was the artery of commerce for Indians before the coming of white men-- notably the Mandan, the Arikara and the Hidatsa. Like the Missouri's tributaries, a myriad of Indian tribes were influenced by the river and its many watersheds and basins. The council fires of the Sioux -- the Teton, the Oglala, the Miniconju, the Hunkpapa, the Santee, the Brule -- as well as those of the Crow, the Shoshoni, the Blood, the Piegan, the Blackfoot, the Minatari, the Arapaho, the Cheyenne, the Nez Perce, the Sac and Fox, the Omaha, and perhaps others all shone from time to time along the Missouri's drainage.

The river was, for fur gatherers and hunters, little more than a highway to hell. The farther up stream men waded its cold waters searching for the coveted plew, the greater the danger: the bigger the chance of getting one's skull split open with a beaded war ax. As the inimitable John Colter once punned, "Alls the Injun wants to do is raise a whitemans hair."

The fur trade, perhaps more than any other single force, provided the impetus for exploring, conquering and settling not only Nancy Peterson's west, but most of the North American continent. And the fur trade remained the most vital economic occupation in the new world for many generations. Yet the ultimate fate of this vast domain and industry was settled elsewhere in the world by outside forces -- forces beyond the fur empire's control. England, France and Spain literally toyed with the continent's interior for a century or more, not really knowing its worth or the crown jewels in store...concerned only with skins and hides. It was rather late on the world political scene before wily Thomas Jefferson with his captains Meriwether Lewis and William Clark turned the historical key and revealed this gigantic treasure chest.

Peterson reassembles the wonderful cast of characters throughout the pages of her book. She ties them to the river, which was artery and soul, the life blood of the business for better or for worse. In a sense the fur trade was an enormous crap game -- the stakes a vast plains and mountains wilderness, a hinterland whose resources would eventually make possible the most powerful industrial nation in the world. The high and low rollers were the company men as well as the free and unattached fur trapper and trader.

Aspects and biographies about the fur trade and the opening of the West have been written and published with consistency, but no one has used such a strong uniting force as does Peterson. DeVoto, in his masterpiece *Across the Wide Missouri* treats his subject in classic Harvard style, by utilizing if not glamourizing the great pictorial documentary art triumvirate of the trades era: George Catlin, Karl Bodmer and Alfred Jacob Miller. Although I prize the book, in a sense the erudite DeVoto denies us the nitty gritty of the industry. We see much visually, but may or may not interpret correctly. *Across the Wide Missouri* is not a book for the beginning student. *People of the Troubled Water* is factual and offers as much for the layman as for the serious reader.

Dean Krakel
High Plains Heritage Society
Spearfish, South Dakota

---

*Source: Bernard DeVoto

Introduction

Before Spring had a name the river was there, draining the heart of the continent, committing muddy rampage as the mountain snows dripped, flowed, threw themselves toward the sea.

And the sea, at first, was the northern one its troubled waters found by way of Hudson Bay. Only after colossal ice plows rearranged the land was the river turned south to thrust its waters into the Mississippi. Indeed, it drained more land, visited far grander sights, came within a day's walk of besting in length, an eyecup of surpassing in flow, the river which claims its final segment.

But that was man's decision, just as it was a man who marked its beginning 300 miles from its true sources on the west edge of Yellowstone National Park in the Rockies. Still -- deprived of both beginning and ending -- it has fascinated man as have few other rivers.

The Fox Indians named it Missouri for the stout wooden canoes its people needed to survive its brutal waters. It was written *8emess8rit* on the map by the first white man who gaped at its force, and that designation evolved over the years to its present form. But even this first visitor had trouble settling on a name, labeling it Pekitanoui in his text. The French tried to call it the River of St. Phillip for a time in the early 1700s, but Missouri it was to those who knew it (Mahzurah, if you want to please the natives) and Missouri it remained.

Other Indians called the river Nishodse or MiniSose or Anati, most of their names translating, according to explorer William Clark, to some version of Troubled Water. Its turbid, chocolate-colored flood troubled everyone who had the questionable pleasure of its company, whether in bullboat, pirogue, keelboat or steamboat.

The Missouri's other characteristic was and is the cottonwood tree. From its source at Three Forks, across Montana, down through North and South Dakota, south between Nebraska and Iowa, past the corner of Kansas and across the state of Missouri, its course is lined with cottonwoods. And the river makes it its business to take as many of them as possible with it to the sea...or it used to.

As I researched Missouri history and got to know the river through the words of its people, I was almost afraid to take my planned trip to trace its course. I knew it could not be the same celebrated tyrant -- channeled and corseted with dikes, dammed and reservoired -- and I resigned myself to seeing a prisoner on good behavior. So it was for much of its 2,315 miles. But that October it roused itself enough to chase the steamboats to their docks, to force us onto detours to reach Daniel Boone's home, to close Interstate 70 for a time. We watched it flood cropland and breach hastily filled sandbags.

One bright day I stood on a point at Vermillion, Nebraska and watched a cottonwood log swirl downstream, retreating from the point when my companion observed it was so undercut it could join the river at any moment. For an instant I was with Lewis and Clark, Manuel Lisa and Henry Brackenridge.

The Missouri's log-laced waters and galloping sandbars inspired white men to give it many labels -- Old Misery, Hell of Waters, The River Sticks; to compare its lower waters to a hog puddle, its upper reaches to a rainwater creek. Here was a river that never chose a middle course -- or the same course two days running. It washed you from your bed one week, yet was so dry it blew sand in your eyes the next, a fact commemorated by the Omaha Indians when they called it Smoking River.

The Missouri was a barrier to some, an unwilling highway for others. It changed nearly everyone who challenged it, for it was the near shore of the West, the baptism into a land where all the canons were new, and the people who attempted coexistence found both paradise and perdition. They were as varied as the river's moods. Some -- John Colter, Hugh Glass, Sitting Bull, John Brown, Teddy Roosevelt -- created their own legends. Others -- Francis Chardon, Emily Partridge, Henry Palmer, Waheenee -- simply coped with the life the Missouri dealt them and vanished, leaving the stories of their trials and triumphs to sink or surface as they would in the current of Missouri history.

Table of Contents

Terra Incognita

The Missouri River roared out of the wilderness and made itself known to the white man in late June 1673.

The saintly and cheerful Jesuit, Father Jacques Marquette, may have thought it issued out of nether regions even darker than the wilderness, attacking as it did his frail birch-bark canoe.

"I have seen nothing more dreadful," he wrote later. "An accumulation of large and entire trees, branches and floating islands was issuing from the mouth of the river Pekitanoui with such impetuosity that we could not without great danger risk passing through. So great was the agitation that the water was very muddy and could not become clear."

He and his fellow explorer, Louis Joliet, had been warned by natives that they'd find man- and canoe-eating monsters in the river they had been riding so serenely -- the Mississippi.

Their mission, assigned by Governor Frontenac of New France (present Canada), was to explore that fabled river's connection with the sea, hoping it emptied into the California Sea. If it did, French traders could reach across that sea to the rich trade of the Orient. It was a remarkably modest expedition for so significant a goal, but the two explorers and their five voyageurs were confident and at home in the wilderness.

Father Marquette had carefully bundled his vestments, holy vessels and traveling altar in their leather bag, asked his personal saint for her blessing and set his wide-brimmed, black hat firmly on his head. Joliet, dressed like the voyageurs in the bright calico shirt, sash and breeches from their French culture and the Indian moccasins they'd found so practical, saw to their more earthly needs. He loaded the canoes with a modest supply of dried maize and pemmican, the Indians' staples, and a meager amount of trade goods to buy the good will of tribes they expected to meet. They had slid their two 20-foot canoes into the waters of the Strait of Mackinac in mid-May and been on their way.

Joliet was Canadian born, the son of a wagon maker, but he immediately decided to trade saw and adze for the more adventurous life of a *coureur de bois* and, at 22, already had a reputation as an explorer, guide and interpreter.

Marquette, in the French tradition, would represent the church on the mission. He was a short man, slight in stature and with a constitution more suited to peaceful cloisters than smoky Indian huts, but his eager, open nature and intelligence earned his black-robed figure a welcome wherever he went. The Indians had come to respect this bearded, moustached man in the flowing gown who set such store on the cross and string of beads tucked into his sash.

The youngest son of a prominent family of Laon, France, Marquette had been schooled by the Jesuits. He had felt the call to God's service and become a novitiate by age 17. Imbued with the zeal of his order, dedicated to spreading the faith to the farthest reaches of the world, Marquette was eager to be away on his life's work.

But his superiors had chosen other places for him to serve. During 12 long years of teaching in Jesuit colleges in France, he had plenty of opportunity to exercise his capacities for patience and obedience. Annually he requested missionary duty. Annually he was told to wait another year. Interested at first in serving either in China or India, he soon was devouring the letters in *Relations* which described the travails his brothers were enduring as they attempted to bring God's light to the tribes in the forests of New France.

Although he was well aware of the horrors some Jesuits had suffered at the hands of the Iroquois tribes, he gave fervent thanks to his patron saint, the Blessed Virgin Immaculate, when at last he received his assignment to the New World in 1666.

Once across the Atlantic, he'd spent more months learning the rudiments of the Indian languages, a task his facility for language made comparatively easy. Then he'd gladly accepted the dangerous assignment to push farther west, eager to carry God's word to strange and unknown peoples. He'd struggled to save Indian souls at the far western end of Lake Huron and then moved to a new mission where the waters of that lake joined those of Lake Michigan.

Luckily for Marquette's conscience, he could serve his Lord and at the same time satisfy his own need to know what lay around the bend, beyond the horizon. He questioned the Indians constantly and learned all he could about "a great river running to the western sea." He longed to "open the way to so many of our fathers, who have long awaited this happiness."

He'd filled the air with grateful prayers when he was assigned to go with Joliet to find the mouth of the Mississippi. "We are ready to do and suffer everything for so glorious an undertaking," he wrote. "I have no other thought than that of doing what God wills."

As it turned out, there was not much to suffer, if one ignores the hunger, danger, heat, hard beds, consuming insects, cloud-bursts and physical labor any trek through the wilderness entailed.

Propelled to the rhythm of the voyageurs songs, the group paddled their brightly painted canoes south through the waters of Lake Michigan, floated down Green Bay and through the spreading marshes at the mouth of the Fox River. Across a narrow portage they entered the Wisconsin, shaded by oaks and walnut trees on its banks. On June 17 they reached "with a joy I cannot express," 'The Great River' they knew must be their goal.

The Mississippi was in a gentle mood, the Indians they'd met were peaceable and the scenery beautiful as they paddled on south. The voyagers could average two leagues an hour when God kept the waters calm, even more if He blessed them with a breeze for their sail. Sometimes they had to bail a little with the big sponge, if the pine gum sealing the seams gave way. Renewing the gum and often some of the cedar binding was a nightly chore. The Father knew one had to step carefully on the cedar frame, for a foot could go through the bark bottom, it being hardly thicker than the brim of his hat. But he had traveled countless miles in the bouyant craft, and he didn't question their worth.

Marquette carefully noted descriptions of the Indians' culture, passing out medals to the savages, attempting to communicate in one of his six native tongues, and casting the seed of the Lord's word on the ground in hopes "it will bear fruit in its time." He also recorded vivid details about the countryside, the "wild cattle" and the plant life, tasting the latter with brave abandon. He celebrated his 36th birthday as they floated south, the first white men to penetrate America's heartland.

Two weeks later they were startled and then bemused by giant red, green and black scaly monsters. The Indians had painted the huge figures on the rock cliffs lining the Mississippi just above the mouth of the unexpected Missouri. Marquette pondered how they'd managed to paint the cliff face and wondered if artists in France could do as well.

Then backs straightened and paddles rested, forgotten momentarily as they listened to an incredible roar. It was water proclaiming its power. Eyebrows raised, they asked themselves, 'Is it a fall?' The Indians had said nothing. 'Is it a rapid?' If so it must be of unbelievable volume.

But there was little time to speculate and no chance to get to shore to reconnoiter. On they swept, their eyes seeking the west bank from which the roar seemed to issue.

Then they saw it was not a rapid on the Mississippi but the tremendous voice of another river giving up its wild waters. Father Marquette gasped, crossed himself and breathed the name of his patron saint. Then they were bobbing in the churning brown water, caught in the grasp of a very real monster, paddling furiously to dodge reaching branches, tangles of logs and even tree trunks uprooted whole from some distant bank. Tossing about in a welter of jagged missiles, any one of which could tear their boats to shreds, they mustered all their skills to survive.

Joliet shouted instructions; the voyageurs swore; Marquette prayed; they all paddled. Eventually, safe on the other side of the torrent, they could drop their paddles, catch their breaths, and assess the river that had almost done them in.

They hadn't even known it existed, but the Missouri -- the Pekitanoui -- the River of the Osages -- with and without a name -- had wound through the minds of Europeans for years, not as a river so much as a dream: a dream that somewhere in the midst of this great continent there must be a river that would lead them to the western sea. Already realizing the mighty river they were exploring headed too directly south, not angling to the west as they'd projected, Marquette and Joliet transferred their hopes -- midstream as it were -- to the Missouri.

"There are many villages of savages ranged along this river, and I hope, by its means, to discover the Vermillion or California sea," Marquette wrote. "From the Indians I learn that advancing up this river for five or six days, you come to a beautiful prairie 20 or 30 leagues long, which you must cross to the northwest. It terminates at another little river on which you can embark, it not being difficult to transport canoes over so beautiful a country as that prairie. This second river runs southwest for 10 or 15 leagues, after which it enters a lake, small and deep, which flows toward the West, where it empties into the sea.

"I do not despair of one day making the discovery, if God does me this favor and grants me health, in order to be able to publish the gospel to all the nations of this new world who have so long been plunged into heathen darkness."

But God did not grant Marquette the favor of exploring the Missouri and meeting the "Oumessourit" tribe which would give the river its name. He and Joliet floated on down the Mississippi for three weeks, until there could be no doubt it led to the Sea of Florida. Then, their mission accomplished, they headed home with the first accurate information about the upper reaches of 'The Great River' that white men had ever had -- and the disappointing news that it did not go where they'd hoped. Nevertheless, Pere

Marquette deemed their three and one-half month trip a success and himself well rewarded, for on the return trip he was able to baptize a dying child and thus ensure "salvation for that innocent soul."

Their return journey was uneventful, but Marquette, never a strong person, had damaged his health with his strenuous wanderings. He died on the shores of Lake Michigan less than two years later, still cheerful, brave and in his faith, thanking his Lord for the chance to die bereft of comfort in the wilderness. His tomb at St. Ignace mission became a shrine to the few Indian converts who traversed the Great Lakes wilderness.

Although his own name was memorialized in a university and a modern city in Michigan, the name he gave the Mississippi in honor of his patron saint, *Riviere de la Conception*, lived no longer than he did.

But his conception of the Pekitanoui (or the Missouri, as it would come to be called) the tantalizing, intriguing, faith-filled hope that this river would lead Frenchmen west to the rich mines of Santa Fe and on to the Gulf of California, hovered in white men's minds for decades. It was a rambunctious, rampaging, untameable river, but it sang the siren song of hope.

King Louis' Banner

On an April day nine years later, in 1682, the visionary Robert de La Salle took possession of the Mississippi Valley for "the Most High, Mighty, Invincible and Victorious Prince, Louis the Great." He named it Louisiana in honor of the Sun King and claimed only "all the nations, peoples, provinces, cities, towns, villages, mines, minerals, fisheries, streams and rivers" of the watershed -- and whatever happened to lie to the west.

But Louis XIV was too busy with the complications of European politics, and the Iroquois in the Great Lakes country remained implacably hostile; the rich colony La Salle envisioned was stillborn.

Another 17 years passed before a tiny French settlement was established near the Missouri on the Mississippi at Cahokia (across the river from present St. Louis) in 1699.

Frenchmen yearned to explore the Missouri for the next decade, and perhaps a few individuals did. The French government collected rumors, reports and wishful thoughts that had the Missouri rich with lead, or copper, or tin, or iron mines, depending on who was telling the tale. It was also, according to rumor, visited regularly by Spanish traders, their mule trains humped with supplies.

Pere Marquette must have been right.

The Missouri must be the route to Santa Fe.

The life style of the man who finally pushed up the Missouri in 1714, planted the first colonial flag and came close to reaching the vaunted trade with Santa Fe probably would have horrified the good Pere Marquette. The Jesuit fathers who did know him accused him of "scandalous" behavior.

Etienne Veniarde de Bourgmond was not known for exercising either patience or obedience, and self-denial was not high on his list of acquired character traits. Son of an old Norman family, the dashing young Bourgmond demonstrated a wild, romantic streak. He'd served as an ensign in the army of New France during its struggle against the Fox and the Iroquois in the Great Lakes country, served it well enough to be given command of Fort Detroit in 1706.

But he'd deserted his post in 1707 to elope to the wilderness with his mistress, the wife of Monsieur Tichenet, also of Fort Detroit, and a few other disenchanted French soldiers. Chased down, arrested for desertion and tried that winter, he evidently had enough charm -- or enough relatives in high places -- to be acquitted and reinstated in the army.

Madame Tichenet evidently tempted him no longer, but in 1712 another maiden beckoned him into the wilderness. He made friends with a group of Missouri Indians visiting Fort Detroit, fell in love with a daughter of the tribe and accompanied them back west to the river which carried their name.

From about 1712 to 1719 he lived with the small Siouan tribe in their village on the flood plain of the Missouri near the mouth of the Grand River (present Van Meter State Park in central Missouri). The 200 families which made up the Missouri tribe sometimes roamed the country from the Platte to Lake Erie, but their permanent home was their Missouri village.

Like many Frenchmen, Bourgmond was immediately at home in the rounded, rush-covered lodges of his Indian friends and it wasn't long before he'd discarded his officer's waistcoat and tricorne hat for more practical skin clothing. He admired the robust, muscular Missouri men who easily left him gasping in their wake when he was foolish enough to compete in one of their foot races. Just as

formidable on water, they fearlessly challenged the river's currents in heavy canoes they'd hollowed from huge logs -- vessels so notable their enemies had named the tribe for their big canoes.

Alert and proud of bearing, many Missouri men shaved their heads except for a bristling scalp lock. They often painted their faces and bodies black and vermillion. Strings of beads dangled from the rims of their ears, which were often pierced in two or three places to accommodate them, and those who were worthy hunters hung large necklaces of bear claws over their bare chests.

Bourgmond loved the freedom, the lack of constraint, after his attempts to tolerate military discipline. He felt empathy for the natives' union with nature. And he reveled in a life that called on all his resources and courage.

While his young bride and the other women tended the small garden patches outside the village, cultivating their corn and melons, he crept through the woods with the braves, seeking deer and elk. If Wakonta was not disposed to favor them with bigger game, they made do with raccoons or rabbits, or searched the rushes along the rivers' edges for ducks and geese.

In the spring, he watched his wife and the other women wade into a shallow lake to gather the first lily root, returning part of it to the water with care and ceremony to assure next year's harvest. Before long her loose deerskin dress bulged with the child she was carrying and a few months later he was the father of a fine son.

Then, when the clan of the Buffalo People said it was time, he rode west over the rolling prairies with the whole village in the celebration that was the semi-annual buffalo hunt. "These are the most beautiful countries and the most beautiful lands of the world," he wrote. "The prairies are like seas and filled with wild animals, especially with buffalo, deer and stag, which are in such large quantities that it surpasses one's imagination."

He found the Missouris to be superb horsemen, challenging him and each other to ever greater feats of daring. They amazed him with their archery skills, and with their appetites for the fallen game. But there was nearly always enough to eat, even in winter, with dried squash, corn and pumpkin to supplement the meat dried from the fall hunt.

Winters they gathered around the fire of a convenient lodge for storytelling sessions while the women sewed the skins from the Bear clans' fall hunt into clothing. One of the Missouris' favorite stories, told with a glint in the eye for Bourgmond's benefit, was of the Missouri chief who'd been outsmarted by a French trader in the early days. He had wanted the Indians to trade for gunpowder, but they protested that they already had plenty. So he advised them to sow their gunpowder in the field where it would yield a new crop. This they did, and he was able to sell them more powder. However, when the next Frenchman appeared, they were waiting for him. They took his goods and refused to pay. When the trader protested, they told him he had only to wait until the gunpowder they were growing was harvested. He could have all the furs they gathered on the ensuing hunt.

Other days, bundled in deerskin leggings and buffalo robes, the Missouris checked their traps for skins to sell the Frenchmen at the fort in the east. It was a generally idyllic life, but not without danger. The Missouris were always outnumbered by their enemies, the Sac and the Fox, and they often had to fight to keep their hunting territory. Many of the braves wore permanent scars of battle.

Bourgmond, however, had more than tribal rivalries on his mind. He could see the endless resources that France could put to use and wondered whether she could find enough settlers to claim the land. Eternally curious, he explored up the Missouri at least as far as the Niobrara, absorbing all he could about the country and the tribes who lived along the way: the Oto, Iowa, and Ponca, who were relatives of his Missouri friends, the Kansa, the powerful Pawnee and the Omaha. His face became known and welcome in the lodges of all the nearby river tribes and his voice was heeded in their councils.

But something called him -- or drove him -- back to civilization with his son in 1719 when the boy was about five. He fought again for his country in the Battle of Pensacola in 1719 and then returned to France. Bourgmond, proud of the colorful Cross of St. Louis which now decorated his chest, and apparently unencumbered by his Indian family, married a rich widow and settled in to enjoy the good life.

However, the Missouri was not finished with him. In the early 1720s the Company of the Indies, which controlled all trade in Louisiana, heard reports that the Spaniard Villasur's expedition had probed clear up to the Platte. That expedition had ended in death for most of its men. The Spanish blamed the French and they were said to be seeking revenge. Rumors flew that they planned to build a fort on the central plains to win the Indians' allegiance and gain their trade. Suddenly the neglected Missouri country was treasure to be coveted.

The Company and the Duke of Orleans, regent for young Louis XV, decided they needed a fort on the Missouri to block the Spanish threat. Even more, they needed peace and allegiance from all the tribes from the Missouri to Santa Fe so they could establish trade.

French courtiers, tucking lace handkerchiefs in gold-braided cuffs, ignored the fact that the Comanche of the western plains were fierce and dedicated enemies of the river tribes. Both factions often raided each other and captured women and children to use as slaves or to sell to French traders and Spanish mine foremen. The Comanche were also allies of the Spanish at Santa Fe, who had been teaching them to fear and hate the French for years.

The Company men were smart enough to realize only one Frenchman had a prayer of accomplishing what they wanted. They sent for Bourgmond. Would he build a fort, establish a trade route to Santa Fe and talk all the tribes into loving the French and each other? And while he was at it would he please bring back a few chiefs for a visit in order to impress them with the power of France and keep them suitably cowed.

Intrigued by the challenge of this seemingly impossible mission, and eager to see his son's people again, Bourgmond said he would try...for a price. He asked to be honored with letters of nobility if he succeeded.

It was agreed. Bourgmond sailed for New Orleans in June 1722. There he learned that the King's Council, Company directors in Paris and Company agents in New Orleans all pulled in different directions. It was February before he could cajole enough supplies from the local agents to put his expedition on the river.

Nosing their boat into the bank at his old Missouri village in early November 1723, he and his son were greeted with huzzas of delight by his Indian friends and welcomed into their dim but cozy lodges. Seated by a fire that stirred faint memories, the boy challenged the credulity of his mother's people with stories about great waters which took weeks to cross and lodges piled one atop the other until they blocked out the sun. Bourgmond the elder, without the leisure for reminiscence, moved immediately to construct his post across the river on the north bank before winter tightened its grip on the land.

And now this free spirit began to learn the cost of his noble title. He was trying to construct a fort "with every nail and tool" brought clear from New Orleans, in a half foot of snow, with the questionable help of only nine men and some Indians. The company representatives, one de Pradel and de Belisle, kept the rest of his 40 men busy on their personal quarters.

Bourgmond, the only one who could communicate with the Indians, had to supervise building the pole-sided, thatch-roofed huts, but he also had to see they all had something to eat. He needed a warehouse to protect the Company goods, a chapel and a house for the priest, a house for the gunsmith and one for the toolmaker. Already harried, he endured perhaps the first labor union problems on the Missouri when the gunsmith and the toolmaker refused to pound a nail or tote a log because it didn't directly concern their trades.

Worst of all, he had to deal with the bewigged and waistcoated de Pradel and de Belisle, who spent the winter months writing bitter letters to New Orleans about every move Bourgmond made. They accused him of housing himself first. (Until everyone else was housed, he had stayed in a leaky tent, only moving to an Indian lodge when he developed a fever.) They carped that he restricted trade. (He did. He forbade trade in slaves of the tribes he must visit to sue for peace.) They complained that he forbade them to buy horses. (He did, not wanting the price to escalate before he could buy mounts for his

expedition.) They insulted him before the Indians and tried to usurp his power. They undermined his position with the Company, urging his vital trading goods be curtailed.

In earlier years, such challenges might have roused him to direct and satisfying action. But, still wearing the veneer of civilization, he instead spent the long winter evenings pouring out his frustration in a nearly endless letter to his employers. Asking for their support of him and his already-difficult peace mission, he still wrote confidently, "Once with the Indians, nothing will be impossible to me."

Impatient with administrative chores, he made certain that the rude living quarters, chapel, warehouse, ice room and smithy were complete. Then he set off from his new Fort Orleans on July 3, 1724 on the most important part of his assignment.

He knew Indians, or thought he did. He had often joined the formality and dignity of their councils. He knew the wants and needs of the Missouri River tribes.

But of the plains Comanche, whom he called Padoucas, he knew only that they were friends of his enemies, the Spanish, and feared enemies of his friends, the Missouri River tribes. He hoped his instincts and negotiating skill were up to the test. He also made a special purchase he hoped would earn the Comanches' good will.

With him on the risky journey went 100 loyal Missouri friends and 64 neighboring Osage. Marching from 4 a.m. to 10 a.m. and from 2 p.m. to evening to avoid the worst of the muggy heat, they had reached the Kansa villages (near present Kansas City) by July 8. Greeted warmly, Bourgmond was carried in honor on a buffalo robe to each chief's lodge. With banquet and oratory, the Kansa declared, "You have never deceived us. We have no other will but yours."

Awaiting pirogues of supplies he'd sent ahead from Fort Orleans, Bourgmond battled an epidemic of fever in himself and the Indians. He worried at the loss of time and stamina, but worried more when his special purchase -- two Comanche slaves he'd bought from the river tribes to return to their homes as a goodwill gesture -- died before he could return them to their people. The Osage, fearing more would fall with fever, abandoned the expedition. More did fall sick, but Bourgmond bled them and made medicine for them. The soldiers passed the time making something more palatable -- wine from the grapes of the Kansa Indians.

The Kansa offered Bourgmond the horses he needed to cross the prairies, but at a price he knew was prairie robbery. He refused to pay it. Rather than enmity, his refusal earned him respect. The Kansa sold him the horses at his price and decided to accompany him also, promising not to leave him "till death."

Then they agreed to sell him three other Comanche captives, and he regained his bargaining chip. But they made another offer he had to refuse. They chose a 13-year-old maiden as a bride for Bourgmond's ten-year-old son. Careful not to insult them, the explorer suggested diplomatically that perhaps the ceremony could take place when the boy was older.

On Monday, July 24, the expedition finally stepped off into the cool sweetness of the prairie dawn. In battle formation with beating drum and waving flag, clad in army tricornes, breeches and knee-length gaiters, the 19 Frenchmen led the parade. In their wake, enjoying the cadence and admiring the ceremony, rode 300 warriors. Their wives, children and dogs trailed behind, equipment and supplies piled equally on the dogs and the women. The braves did, however, consider it an honor to assist the soldiers, and carried their knapsacks, helped them repair their boots and fetched them water.

West and south they moved, through valleys of grass taller than their heads, up ridges where they prayed for a little breeze, into thunderstorms building on the horizon.

But in a week, Bourgmond had to admit even to himself that he could not go on. His fever intensified until he could not sit his horse, and he knew the landscape danced before his eyes from causes other than heat waves. Frustrated and angry, he chose a delegation to carry his greetings, and the three new Comanche slaves upon whom his hopes rested, on to the Comanche villages. Then the proud man crawled on an ignominious litter for the journey back to Fort Orleans, to wait impatiently for word of their reception.

Word came in early September and it was good. The Comanche, pleased by the ransom of their people, were amenable to a council. With legs still slightly wobbly, Bourgmond packed his son, the surgeon and nine cavalry men for another journey toward Sante Fe.

He boated to the Kansa villages, paused long enough to bring Oto, Iowa, Pawnee and the Kansa together for an impressive and satisfying council, and hurried on west. Now, both the grass and the days were short. The air was crisp and frost glistened atop Bourgmond's tent in the mornings. They crossed the Kansas River (near present Topeka) October 11 and left the burnished trees behind.

Herds of buffalo soon replaced the trees, and Bourgmond impressed the soldiers by riding down a buffalo and dispatching it with his pistol. Then he introduced them to the delights of bison tongue *a l'americaine*.

A week later (near present Ellsworth, Kansas) they saw the long-awaited clouds of smoke against the blue October sky. They fired the prairie in answer. Soon 80 mounted Comanche charged through the smoke. Breaths quickened; but they waved the colors of France instead of feathered lances. With them were the Frenchmen who had been sent earlier. Bourgmond called his men to arms and galloped towards them, his own flag snapping, his hopes high.

Bourgmond's emissaries had done their work well. The Comanche were eager for friendship with the country that provided fine banners and promised plentiful trade goods. They shook hands in the white man's way and he smoked the pipe in theirs. Fifteen braves gave Bourgmond and his son another ride on a buffalo robe to meet the chief, and then it was on to the main village for feasting, oratory and distribution of the coveted trade goods.

Bourgmond piled out more rifles, sabres, axes, powder, bullets, red and blue blankets, mirrors, knives, scissors, combs, and kettles than the astounded Comanche had imagined there were in the world. Indeed, many of the items they had never imagined at all, for none of them had had contact with the French before and their annual contacts with the stingy Spanish had yielded only a few knives and axes. Many, eyes round with awe, had watched their first gun fired after Bourgmond's delegation reached their tribe a few weeks before.

Bourgmond gathered the 200 Indians around him and the trading pile and, banner in hand, let them know the price of the goods. They were to keep peace with the Missouri River tribes and they were not to molest any Frenchmen who traveled through their country to trade with the Spanish. If they agreed and kept their word, King Louis, the big chief of all nations, would defend them against their enemies.

Delighted to ally themselves with such powerful friends ("Is it true that you are really men?" one chief asked...) the Comanche promised peace and brotherhood would reign. They presented Bourgmond with seven fine horses, draped a necklace of a dozen bright blue stones around his son's neck and promised to keep the King Louis banner white.

By November 5, de Bourgmond was back at Fort Orleans. The Frenchmen fired a salute, raised the flag and sang the *Te Deum* in honor of peace on the prairie.

In September 1725, Bourgmond presented one Oto, one Osage, one Missouri, two Illinois, one Metchigamia and a "princesse de Missouris" to Paris society. Received by the Duke de Bourbon and the Duchess d'Orleans, they were presented to young King Louis on a chill November day as he returned from hunting. The chiefs performed war dances at the Opera and hunted a stag in the Bois de Boulogne. They were presented with scarlet waist coats and breeches, silver laced hats with blue feathers and ruffled shirts.

The "princess" was gowned in flame-colored damask of gold flowers with a fashionable panier around her hips, a petticoat of the same, and silk stockings. She was baptized in the gloomy cavern of Notre Dame and then married -- undoubtedly with Bourgmond's blessing and sigh of relief -- to his aide, Sergeant Dubois.

Bourgmond, back in the embrace of society, retired again to the good life. In December he had the pleasure of viewing his new coat of arms -- an Indian resting against a silver mountain on a blue field. It must have stirred his heart. He knew the Indians as brothers and the valley of the lower Missouri was as familiar to him as the road to Versailles. Although he hadn't reached the silver mountains or the adobes of Santa Fe, he probably had come as close as any Frenchman. The route he had pioneered could put the French where they had so long wished to go.

He had accomplished his mission. He'd allied all the tribes of the plains below the Platte to the French cause and opened the entire area to trade and possible settlement. If his king acted, the French could have the Missouri, the central plains of North America, and wealth and power beyond their fondest hopes.

Seekers of the Sea

But words came easier than actions in the turgid atmosphere of the court at Versailles. The fort Bourgmond and his men had struggled to build was abandoned almost before the chiefs returned from their journey across the great water.

Bourgmond's efforts went for nought. The chiefs told their tribes stories too incredible for them to accept; they refused to believe them. His Missouri friends were driven from their village by Sac and Fox who attacked from the north; the reduced tribe took shelter near an Osage village. The Comanche, Kansa, Oto and Iowa were left to war as they wished and nobody checked to see if King Louis' banners were kept white.

The Missouri's promise was left twinkling in the sun, awaiting another man, another time.

ASA BATTLES

In September 1736, Pierre Gaultier de La Verendrye stood at the lake's edge with head bowed and fists clenched, fighting to keep his emotions in check. At his feet, silent voyageurs unloaded a canoe of beaver skins. Wrapped in the skins, compliments of the Sioux, were the heads of his chaplain, 19 of his men and his oldest son, Jean Baptiste. They had been ambushed, decapitated and left on an island near his post, Fort St. Charles, on the Lake of the Woods in the Canadian wilderness.

Lieutenant La Verendrye had known much hardship and pain in his 51 years as a soldier, trader and explorer. Born in New France, the eleventh child of one of Canada's first fur traders, he had lost his father when he was four. He had enrolled as a cadet in the army at age 12, and in 1707 was called to France to join Louis XIV's forces for the War of the Spanish Succession. At 24, he had lain while blood from his five wounds soaked the battleground at Malplaquet and, left for dead, survived 15 months as an English prisoner of war.

Bearing scars of four more wounds, he had struggled, back home in New France, to support his young wife and six children, seeking furs in the forested wilderness along the St. Lawrence River. Here in the frontier posts, he learned to deal with the long night of winter, when the temperature refused to rise above -20 degrees for endless weeks. He learned to deal with a supply line that encompassed more than 1,200 torturous miles of paddling and portaging to Montreal. And he learned the delicate art of cajoling and commanding the Cree, Assiniboin and Monsoni tribes whose friendliness was essential if he were to get the furs he needed.

But nothing had been as hard as this. Nothing had ever so drained his spirit and wounded his inherent optimism. He had brought Jean Baptiste, two other sons and his nephew west to share his dream. Now both his son and his nephew were dead; his sister's son had died of illness on a wild river only four months earlier.

He had to wonder: had it been worth the cost? Would any of them ever reach the Sea of the West that had been in his dreams so long?

Eight years ago he had sought assignment to a post on the edge of the unknown west for a very particular reason. Growing up in the whitewashed village of Three Rivers on the St. Lawrence, he had heard La Salle spin stories by his grandfather's fire. He had listened as the great Duluth, convinced he had been only 20 days from the long-sought sea, voiced his frustration. And he dreamed of someday finding it himself.

Just what the sea was, nobody knew. Most thought it was an inland sea from which a river led to the Pacific Ocean. Perhaps it was an arm of that ocean, reaching far into the continent like Hudson Bay. Whatever, it held promise of an easier route to the Orient.

He'd begun in 1728 at his post on Lake Nipigon, questioning each visiting tribe, scratching maps in the ashes of the fire, collecting, comparing, mulling rumors, legends, speculations; refining all the information he could gather. And coming to a conclusion: beyond the chain of lakes the traders knew, a great river flowed west. On its banks lived a tribe of exceptional natives, probably white; at its mouth -- the sea.

He wrote to Governor-General Beauharnois and asked support for an expedition of 100 men to open trade to Lake Winnipeg and find the *Mar l'Ouest*. Beauharnois knew Verendrye and trusted his ability, but he did not have sufficient authority. Only the Minister of the Marine, Comte de Maurepas in Versailles, could help him.

Maurepas looked down his sizable nose at the proposal and said Verendrye had permission to go west to open trade -- at his own expense. He should discover the Sea of the West for the glory of France, not for profit.

Verendrye was not interested in profit, but he had no resources to fund an expedition. To get underway, he was forced to indenture himself to merchants, promising a rich return in furs.

Slowed by the necessity of building posts and conducting trade for furs, hamstrung by lack of supplies, bedeviled by creditors, Verendrye did not reach the Lake of the Woods until 1732. As he was needed at the post to supervise trade, he sent his sons to explore in his stead. He also sent word for his youngest son, Louis Joseph, to attend cartography school, and brought him west in

1735 to take part in the family's explorations.

His eldest, Jean Baptiste, had traveled west to Lake Winnipeg and built a post in 1734 -- a huge step which had given them all hope. Now he was dead, without the comfort of absolution or a Father's blessing. Verendrye hoped his brother, a priest, and his sister, a nun, would forgive him.

Sick at heart, he resisted offers by the friendly tribes to avenge his dead. He lost the better part of a year on the weary voyage to civilization and back to defend his lack of progress in exploration.

But he did not give up.

At last, in the fall of 1738, he and his sons headed west, west to meet the incredible Mandan (were they a new race, he wondered?) -- west to the sea, and the fame and satisfaction such a discovery would bring.

Traveling in canoes, the blue-coated expedition journeyed first to Fort Maurepas, which Jean Baptiste had established at the southeast corner of Lake Winnipeg. They then probed south up the marshy delta of the Red River to find the mouth of the Assiniboine, where exploration was put on hold while commerce built Fort Rouge (at present Winnipeg). Then they moved west again, up their first prairie river and into a new country.

The Red had been lined with large groves of trees. Poplars, willows and cottonwoods crowded banks that were choked with plums and other brush. At first the Assiniboine, too, was lined with trees. But beyond, it was different country. Verendrye, used to the dim and limited views of the forest, found he could now see for miles across the bright grassland. He did not have to look so far to see buffalo and deer; they grazed everywhere he looked.

It had been a dry summer and the grass waved shrunken seed heads above yellowed stalks. The wide, winding Assiniboine was marked with shallows. Progress became more and more of a struggle.

As the corps moved up river, the Indians for which it was named began to gather. They advised the Frenchmen to abandon their light canoes before they were ruined on sandbars. On October 2 Verendrye decided it was time. He stopped where a portage led north to Lake Manitoba (the present Portage le

Prairie), and erected another post in an ideal position to intercept Indian trade intended for the British on Hudson Bay. Commerce ruled for another two weeks while he built Fort la Reine, named for his queen. While Verendrye watched the fine October weather dwindle away, he thought eagerly of what he would find at the Mandan villages.

The Cree and Assiniboin said these superior people lived in seven fortified cities on the banks of the River of the West, that they raised fine crops and had horses and goats, that they were talented craftsmen who produced arts all the Indians coveted. They did not have guns or iron, but they were white like the French and had beards like them.

What's more, on down this westward flowing river, where it gave its water to the sea, there were people who had iron and cloth like the Frenchmen. Verendrye could almost taste success. "Everything they said gave us hope of making a remarkable discovery," he wrote later.

On October 16 Verendrye had the drummer beat the call to arms, reviewed his company and chose the 52 soldiers and voyageurs who would continue the journey with him, his trading partner and his sons. Francois would go, along with his youngest, Louis Joseph, the map maker. And, whether Verendrye liked it or not, so would about 300 Assiniboin who didn't want to miss all the excitement or the chance to trade.

Surrounded by savages who were naked except for moccasins and buffalo robes, dogs pulling wickerwork travois filled with firewood, lively children and basket-laden squaws, the French left the river and marched south. They turned west along the flank of Turtle Mountain, crossed the Souris River twice and turned south again. Verendrye pictured their reception by the Mandan and planned what he would say to this remarkable people.

October and most of November disappeared as the Assiniboin stopped the line of march to hunt and dress out buffalo or detoured to visit other villages. Verendrye tried to be patient with these simple people who called him Father and who shed tears of joy when he laid his hand on their heads in ceremony. Urging them to hurry had no effect.

The grass had disappeared under snow and the voyageurs had replaced their bright knitted toques with coon fur caps and mittens by the time Verendrye finally met his first Mandans, a chief and 30 men sent out to greet the visitors. Whatever grand speech he had planned stuck in his throat.

The chief was just another naked Indian in a buffalo robe. He was tattooed in black parallel stripes down his left side. He was not white and certainly not of any new race. He gave Verendrye an ear of corn and a roll of tobacco.

The shocked Frenchman tried to hide his disappointment. How many more of the grand tales he had heard were untrue, he wondered? Why had the Assiniboin and Cree told such lies?

He did notice that the Mandan easily cheated the Assiniboin in trade, vacuuming up all their European trade goods for only a few of their beautifully painted skins and colored feathers. And he was mildly amused when the Mandan chief sized up the crowd he'd be expected to feed and announced a Sioux raiding party was imminent and he would welcome the Assiniboins' help in battle. Terrified of the Sioux, the Assiniboin vacillated for a day or two while Verendrye moved on toward his first Mandan village.

As dusk fell on December 3, 1738, led by the banner of France, the Verendryes approached the first village (near present Minot,

North Dakota). Dozens of large, solid-looking round lodges were grouped within a log stockade. Smoke rose from a hole in the roof of each, to be swirled away by a brisk winter breeze.

Shouting in delight, scores of fur-cloaked Mandan raced out to greet them. Before they knew what was happening, Verendrye and his men were all hoisted on the Indians' shoulders. Laughing, protesting, they were carried inside the walls of the fort.

Verendrye had only a brief impression of scores of Indians cheering them from the dirt roofs and children running beside the procession. Then he and his sons were in front of a log-framed passageway cut into the side of one large lodge. Even on the Mandans' shoulders they had no need to duck as they were carried down the passage into the dim interior.

The room was surprisingly spacious. From a dirt floor dug a few feet into the earth, Verendrye looked up to see that the log dome of the ceiling arched nearly 20 feet over his head. His arms could not have encircled the four huge timbers supporting the structure. Above the wooden pillars a fan of smaller timbers met the square framework of the opening that served as both skylight and smoke hole.

But roomy as the lodge was, it could not hold all the braves of both tribes who tried to crowd in with them. Before the chiefs could reduce the crush, the bag of gifts he'd intended for the Mandan disappeared into some opportunist's hands.

A greater loss was in the offing. The next day, too nervous about the Sioux to remain, the Assiniboin decamped. With them, in spite of entreaties and offers of extra pay, went Verendrye's interpreter.

The explorer was devastated. He had asked a few questions the night before, but not nearly enough. The answers he'd gotten were not clear. Now he and his sons were reduced to sign language. How could they ever learn what they needed to know?

He'd been told that down river other people lived where the water was undrinkable and too wide to see across; that white people there worked in iron, wore iron armour and used lances and sabres; that their houses were of stone and their women did not work in the fields. Was this the Sea of the West? Or New Spain? With every report things got more confusing.

Embarrassed to be without gifts, Verendrye was grateful for the Mandans' warm hospitality. He couldn't help but like them, and the Mandan took immediately to the soft-spoken, tactful explorer.

The men were "big and tall, very active and, for the most part, good-looking." The women were "handsome," especially those who were fair-haired. While he did not consider them white people, he saw enough with light complexions and hair that he wondered if they were some mixture that included white blood.

The people all seemed industrious. He saw no clutter in their "spacious" lodges. Their belongings were stored in bags hung from the interior posts of their clay-covered homes. On first glance, their beds reminded him of tombs. But he noted that when several people climbed into the skin cases resting on platforms two feet above the floor, they would sleep cozily even when the winter wind howled down the smoke hole.

He sent Louis Joseph, who, as a younger son without property, carried the title Chevalier, on to see the larger Mandan villages on the river while he took stock of the one he was in.

Verendrye was impressed by the Mandans' protected village. "You may say they are impregnable to savages. Their fortification, indeed, has nothing savage about it," he wrote. He counted 130 of the buildings and estimated they were 50 feet in circumference. The Indians used the rounding rooftops as places to lounge and play games. Buffalo skulls were scattered atop some, and tall poles topped with masks and effigies reared here and there among the lodges.

Wickerwork frames stood outside many lodge doors and Verendrye learned they were used to dry the squash, pumpkin and corn the Mandan raised along with their tobacco and beans. Food did not seem to be a problem. They proudly showed him deep holes lined with straw where they stored their surplus crops.

But when he joined their nightly feasts as an honored guest, he wondered how they could have any surplus. "They are great eaters and strong on feasts," he noted. He could stomach their almost raw meat, but their favorite dish -- buffalo that had drowned and "ripened" in the Missouri floods -- was too much for him. He sometimes took his dish away from the fire and ate alone.

The Chevalier returned from his visit to the villages on the river (the Missouri at present Bismarck, North Dakota) to report that they looked much like the one they were in. "When you see one you see them all," Verendrye concluded. Louis Joseph could report that the river there ran south-southwest, but not much more. Communicating was just too difficult.

With great reluctance, Verendrye decided it was pointless to go on. He had no goods to pay a guide and he'd found promises did not go far with the Indians. Powder was low and the weather would be a gamble. The journey back to Fort la Reine in the dead of winter would be dangerous, but at least they knew the route.

He decided to leave his servant, "a prudent, God-fearing man," and another employee with the Mandan to learn their language, cannily ordering one to one village and one to the other so they'd be forced to learn more quickly. As soon as they could communicate, they were to find out what nation of whites lived at the river's mouth, what metal they worked with and if there were mines there. They should ask, too, about the country up river. More and more convinced that the mouth of this river was in Spanish territory, which held little interest for him, Verendrye speculated that it might be the headwaters which would lead him to Sea of the West. "Leave nothing undone to get all possible knowledge of the country," he stressed.

Always aware of the Indians' love of ceremony, he presented the Mandan with a French flag and a be-ribboned lead plate to keep in a "box of remembrance" which signified that Verendrye had taken possession of the land in King Louis' name. The Mandan plied them with food for their journey and begged them to return soon.

Before he could depart, Verendrye fell ill, his battered 54-year-old body protesting the strain of his demands. But he insisted on attempting the journey. They left the Mandan on January 13, 1739.

They moved as rapidly as possible over the frozen expanses, forcing numbed feet to take the next step, burying their chins in their chests as they faced into the arctic wind. The Chevalier and Francois watched their father with concerned eyes and held worried consultations. As soon as they reached the Assiniboine, the trader hurried ahead to seek help from Fort la Reine.

Verendrye, hanging on, refusing to buckle, knew he was at the edge of death. "My need was extreme. Never in my life did I endure so much misery, pain and fatigue as in that journey." Gray with pain, he thought that death alone could deliver him from such distress.

However, he was not ready to die. His visit to the Mandan had been a disappointment, but he clung to the belief that he had been close to realizing his dream of discovery -- for France, for himself, and for the Verendrye family. He endured. He made it back to Fort la Reine.

But he could surmount neither the suspicions of the court at Versailles nor the machinations of the businessmen in Montreal. Ensnared in legal and commercial tangles, bankrupt, and facing disgrace, Verendrye spent much of the next two years in Quebec, trying to salvage both his cause and his reputation.

He sent word for his older son, Pierre, to revisit the Mandan and try to make contact with the Horse Indians, known to come there for trade. They lived to the west and traded with tribes still further removed. Surely they would be a source of information.

Pierre went and waited for two months. The Horse Indians did not come.

In the spring of 1742, Verendrye asked his sons to make a final effort to achieve the goal that had become a family obsession. Daring, capable and possibly identifying most strongly with his father's dreams, 25-year-old Louis Joseph readily agreed. Francois, 27, would go with him, along with two voyageurs.

The young men reached the Mandan villages in May, to hear again about the Horse Indians who come from the setting sun, where white men live in forts of brick, pray to the Great Master of Life and sing songs out of books. Their forts are near the Great Lake, the waters of which rise and fall,

but of which one does not drink.

Tantalized, hopeful, they waited. But the Horse Indians did not come.

Finally on July 23, they despaired of waiting, concluding they would have to find these elusive Indians for themselves. They hired two Mandan guides and set out on foot.

Wandering west and south, passing from tribe to tribe, abandoned by their Mandan guides, they eventually found the Horse Indians (probably Cheyenne or Crow) on November 19. They did not know the way to the Sea of the West, they said, for their enemies, the Snake People, who had just attacked them, barred the way. The Horse People were terrified of the Snake People (possibly Kiowa), but the Bow People traded with tribes that went to the sea and they were not afraid of the Snake People.

Indeed when the Frenchmen, on horseback now, reached the Bow People (possibly Pawnee) a few days later, they were planning a raid on the Snake People. They lived, the Bow People said, on the eastern edge of some very high mountains. From the top of those mountains one could see the Great Water. Would the Verendryes like to go along?

Louis Joseph thought of his father and all the long years. Perhaps, at last...

As they traveled slowly through the cold of December -- a great rolling mass of horses, squaws, tent poles and dogs -- he was discouraged to hear the Bow People using some Spanish words. Reluctantly he decided that the sea the Snake knew must be south, not west. This trip was probably in vain. Still, no Frenchman had ever crossed to the Spanish sea. That, at least, would be something.

On New Year's Day 1743, the mountains stood before him. They were very high and wooded (probably the Black Hills). The Indians stopped, made camp for their women and children and prepared for hostilities.

The brothers agreed that Francois would remain to guard their equipment and Louis Joseph would accompany the warriors. With a hand clasp and a quick hug, he was on his way.

Twelve days later the Chevalier approached the foothills. His breath caught as he imagined what lay on the other side.

But suddenly the Indians around him erupted in pandemonium. Scouts had discovered an abandoned Snake village. That *must* mean the Snake warriors knew they were here and had circled around them to attack their women and children. There was a mad dash back in the direction of the camp.

Louis Joseph could do nothing. Nothing but go with the mob. He gave an anguished look at the spine of the mountains and all that it promised. Then he raced to join the retreat.

From now on, the brothers' goal would be simply to survive. Fighting deep snow, they headed back east, eventually joining a band of Arikara and traveling with them back to the Missouri.

There, on March 30, the four Frenchmen climbed a high, rounding grassy hill on the west side of the river (across from present Pierre, South Dakota). Louis Joseph looked at the small lead tablet in his hand and then at the hilly, tawny grasslands stretching in all directions around him. He had to smile slightly at the irony. The land crested and rolled into the distance, but it was hardly the sand beach and the breaking surf of the Sea of the West where he and his father had pictured this ceremony.

The young explorer kicked aside some of the loose black rocks that capped the prominence, dug a hole in the hard earth and lay the tablet inside. Then they gathered some larger stones and erected a small pyramid in honor of the supportive Governor Beauharnois. Turning their backs on the west and the mystery they had been unable to solve, they headed home.

Verendrye, immensely relieved to have his sons home safely after 14 months without word, but unable to produce the Sea of the West for the impatient Maurepas, retired in disgrace and in debt to two rooms in a widow's house in Montreal.

Even now accused by Maurepas of neglecting his explorations to profit in the fur trade, he attempted to answer his critics. "Money has never been my object," he wrote. "I have sacrificed myself and my sons for the service of His Majesty and the good of the Colony."

Seven years later, in September 1749, after Maurepas had toppled from power, Verendrye was granted a captaincy and awarded a Cross of St. Louis. More important, he was asked to resume his work in the west. Feeling vindi-

cated at last, he eagerly planned an exploration of the Saskatchewan River, sure now it must be this river which would lead him west.

Contemplating an expedition to western mountains "the heights of which can be reached only in the second year after leaving Montreal," he wrote, "I shall be only too happy if after all the trouble, fatigue and danger I am about to encounter in this long exploration, I could only succeed in proving to you the disinterestedness and zeal of myself and my sons for the glory of the King and the welfare of the country."

He was 64 years old.

But he did not get the chance to go west again. He died that December. The man who had done so much to establish the French fur trade, who had secured hundreds of thousands of dollars in pelts and opened new territory larger than Mother France, left an estate of a few books and $600.

His vital and energetic family did not long survive him. Pierre died in 1755. The Chevalier, leaving a journal of his 1742-43 exploration so vague it would frustrate historians for centuries, drowned with his two sisters and two nephews in a shipwreck while trying to flee New France after it fell to the British in 1761.

Only Francois lived to old age. He died, childless, in 1794.

The tablet the Chevalier had buried on the hill overlooking the Missouri lay undisturbed for 170 years. On a Sunday afternoon in February 1913, three teen-agers were out walking on the hills across the river from Pierre. Hattie May Foster saw a corner of the eight-inch gray plate and kicked it loose. Decorated with tiny fleur-de-lis, the Latin inscription still readable, it claimed the land for "our most illustrious sovereign," Louis XV. Now displayed in the Robinson Museum in Pierre, the tablet marks the only spot that can be positively identified from the Chevalier's wanderings in his final attempt to find his father's dream, the route to the Western Sea.

La hameau at the Mounds

The war that cost the Chevalier his life closed the upper Missouri to the French. The Union Jack now waved over what had been New France.

On paper, the lower Missouri was also closed to the French because, as the world discovered, all the vast stretch of land south of Canada and west of the Mississippi River had been ceded to Spain.

But pens scratching on papers in the mirrored halls of Europe were little noted in the markets and docks at the mouth of the Mississippi. French for three-quarters of a century, it would not become Spanish overnight. The French merchants in New Orleans were as eager as those in Quebec to drain North America of soft dark pelts. The richest pool of these, they were told, lay far north and west. When tapped, it would pour down the troubled waters of the Missouri River.

Hunching his shoulders against the cold February wind, the dark-eyed teenager balanced himself at the front of the barge and studied the western bank of the Mississippi River. Though his breeches had been new only months before, they were already skimpy on his lengthening form, and the gusts which flapped the skirts of his waistcoat penetrated easily. Navigation had opened only a few days before and ice chunks still swirled on the current they battled, rattling angrily against the sides of the boat.

But though the wind was chill, Auguste Chouteau could feel an undercurrent of the dampness of spring, and its promise mixed with his own excitement. They were nearly five days above Fort Chartres and the site he was looking for had to be near.

He and his stepfather, Pierre de LaClede Liguest, had climbed the bluffs and roamed the plateau with delight the December past. After nearly three months of laborious travel up river from New Orleans and another month of searching the frozen river bank, they realized they had found the site for their new trading post.

Here, curious rounded mounds suggested an earlier people might have made their home. Limestone bluffs rose high enough to be protection against both Mississippi floods and the unhealthy climate of the lower shores. There was a natural break through the bluffs to the wide, level stretch of beach. With the Missouri's mouth just 18 miles north, they could utilize that river's huge drainage on their trading forays. Just a few miles above the Missouri the mouth of the Illinois River gave access to the middle regions.

Chouteau's stepfather had hardly been able to contain himself, declaring enthusiastically as he paced the ground and marked trees to deliniate the site that it could become "one of the finest cities in America!"

Young Auguste agreed with him. There were springs and plenty of hardwoods and stone for building. Open area with shrubs would offer fruits and berries in the spring and room for crops. The game that abounded in the surrounding woods made him itch for ball and powder. And all this near the crossroads of the continent; it was *tres bien*.

On February 14, 1764, finally spotting the right break in the wooded bluffs, the 14-year-old gave a glad shout and signaled to the 30 workmen in his charge. The boat turned toward shore and scraped bottom on the strip of land at the foot of the bluffs. As the men began unloading crates and bales of supplies from the barge, he scrambled again to the bluff top LaClede had chosen.

At his feet the Mississippi rolled ponderously, irresistibly south. The Missouri poured in out of sight to the north -- or would, when the ice let go. To the west, one tree-topped ridge followed another to infinity, an infinity filled with brown furs they could turn to gold -- untouched, untapped, waiting.

His stepfather was a man with vision to match his ambition and the skill to carry out his plans. Young Chouteau wanted very much to prove himself to the only father he'd ever known. He could scarcely remember his natural father, a tavern keeper who'd deserted his mother when Auguste was only four. He had stronger impressions of the three hard years before his mother had met LaClede; only 20 years old, she'd needed all her grit and determination to provide for herself and her young son.

Then she'd met LaClede -- well born, educated, intelligent -- and decided to cast her lot with his, whether church and state approved or not. They could not marry because she was not legally free, but they pledged themselves to each other and Auguste had more of a father than Rene Chouteau had ever been.

Under LaClede's wing, acting as his clerk, the open-faced Auguste discovered the world of account books and ledgers. He was comfortable with their precision and predictability, finding the work not tedious but fascinating. He had learned rapidly about the trading business, so rapidly that now his stepfather was trusting the teenager to supervise the building of the post while he attended to other matters downstream at Fort de Chartres.

If the young man had any doubts he could do the job, they were only momentary, the result of the naturally cautious nature his uncertain early years had bred in him. He was young, but his direct gaze bespoke intelligence and quiet competence. LaClede was depending on him. He could and would manage 30 men of various ages and see the job was done. He turned back toward the riverbank to get things started.

The next day the bluff top rang with the sound of axes. Wood chips flew and birds protested the crash of trees as the men worked to clear the site for the new settlement. Chouteau then set them to work building a large shed to store the tools and supplies of Maxent, LaClede and Co., the partnership which had been granted exclusive trading rights to Upper Louisiana.

By the time LaClede returned in early April, the willows and elms had blossomed and the river bluffs were topped with the new green of spring. Auguste and the men were settled in 12-foot dirt-floored cabins, and though La hameau made only a tiny nick on the face of the wilderness, it was a beginning.

LaClede paced the site to lay out a grid-iron pattern of three streets paralleling the Mississippi with shorter cross streets connecting the settlement to the public plaza along the waterfront. Next he chose the location of his own home. Now 35, his almost prissy, aristocratic looks belied his capability. But Chouteau knew that behind his heavy-lidded eyes and high, wide forehead lay a mind fired with drive and energy.

LaClede did not plan to live in a dirt-floored cabin. His house would be the headquarters for the trading company and it would be an impressive one. It might sit more than 700 miles up in the Louisiana wilderness, but it would be as fine as many in New Orleans.

The site chosen and marked, LaClede called the men together for a small ceremony. Their town must have a name. Practical as well as visionary, LaClede had one chosen. He named it for the patron saint of the king sitting in Versailles: St. Louis.

Perhaps at some level of consciousness he was also planting France's banner on the Mississippi's west bank, for he knew the east bank would be British in a matter of days. Because the eastern land had been ceded to the English as a result of their victory in the Seven Years War, the residents at Fort Chartres were preparing to evacuate in the face of British occupation.

LaClede hurried back downstream to the fort to remove his goods from the reach of the British. He left Auguste to build the grand company headquarters he'd designed --

his flagship beside the Mississippi. Located on Le Grande Rue (Main Street) and between La Rue de la Tour (Walnut Street) and La Rue de la Bonhomme (Market Street), its 60-foot front faced the river. The stone structure would be the centerpiece of the small settlement, obvious to every passing traveler. Six large windows would open onto a 14-foot veranda. The steeply pitched roof was to be broken on the front with three dormers for the second floor rooms. It would be heated by two large fireplaces, and have a cellar and an outside kitchen.

His confidence bolstered by his first experience in leadership, Chouteau set the stone-cutters to work. But soon he found himself busy finding homesites for other new French settlers. Uneasy at the prospect of British rule, French-speaking settlers in Cahokia and other small towns on the Mississippi's east bank had decided to chance their futures in the new hamlet of St. Louis.

Other would-be settlers were not so welcome. One day a few weeks later Chouteau heard a warning shout and looked up from his work to see scores of Indians topping the bluffs on the waterfront. Men around him dropped their tools and straightened. Women called their children close. Bodies tense, the French watched until some 150 bare-breasted warriors had climbed up from the river and gathered around Chouteau.

Auguste hadn't had much time to learn about Indians but he'd picked up some basic knowledge. These men came openly with their families, a good sign. He welcomed them and asked the purpose of their visit.

They were Missouris, they told him. They knew and liked the French. The Frenchman Bourgmond had lived among their people some 40 winters before and had become their friend and brother. Their present village was vulnerable and often under attack by the northern tribes. When they had learned new Frenchmen were in the country, they'd decided to come live with their white friends. They would erect their new village around the white chief's new lodge.

Auguste swallowed. Somehow he managed a noncommittal reply. The Missouris did not seem hostile, but there were so many of them; he was outnumbered three or four to one. Around him the French settlers already wore the look of panic. One after another they began throwing their belongings together. Within hours they were paddling back across the river to their old village.

Auguste had no quarrel with Indians -- he was in their country and he wanted their business. But the Missouris would use up his supplies. His tools would gradually disappear. LaClede expected a trading post, not an Indian camp. The future of their settlement, recently so sanguine, was suddenly in doubt. But did he dare say "no" and risk their wrath? What should he do? He decided to send for LaClede and play for time.

Remaining cool and in control, at least outwardly, Auguste smoked and talked with the chiefs and gave the women work. Offering payment in vermillion and awls, Chouteau soon had women and children digging the cellar of LaClede's headquarters. With one eye he watched the strong, brown-skinned women scoop the earth onto baskets and wooden platters and carry it away on their heads. With the other he watched the Mississippi for LaClede's boat.

How long would it take for LaClede to get his message? How long for him to get up river? How long before he said or did the wrong thing and precipitated a crisis?

It was several days before the sleepless young man could offer LaClede a hand to shore and feel the comfort of his stepfather's arm around his shoulder. He had done his job well; he gladly let the older man take charge. They called the chiefs to council.

Eventually the tribe settled in a circle with the French leaders. The chiefs, wearing all their finery in honor of the occasion, were at the front, less important warriors behind, women and children to the rear. There was silence while the long, slender pipe was dipped in homage to the sky, earth and four directions and then the hollow "thup" of men inhaling as it made the rounds of the circle.

When he was ready, the leading chief spoke, his several earrings swaying as he nodded to emphasize his words. "We are like ducks and geese who sought open water to rest and feed," he explained to the Frenchmen. They liked where they were, he said pleasantly. They intended to stay.

LaClede heard them out and remained a gracious and smiling host, but Auguste could

see his eyes were grim. They would have to develop a strategy.

The next day the polished Frenchman had his argument ready. Seated in another council, LaClede told the Missouris that ducks and geese are bad guides, without foresight. Birds of prey attack on open water, but not in the woods. Here their enemies would find and kill the warriors. Their women and children would be slaves.

Auguste watched and listened in admiration as LaClede alternately threatened the Indians and tempted them with gifts. He treated them with understanding, but he was firm. They must not disdain his advice.

And he did not hesitate to take advantage. "Go caress your children and feed them," LaClede appealed dramatically to the women over the heads of the warriors. "Embrace your old parents while you can, because if your men settle here, 600 or 700 warriors now at Fort Chartres to war on the English will discover and destroy you."

Then he turned both barrels on the warriors. "Do you want to wait and be massacred, to see your wives and children torn to pieces and their limbs thrown to the dogs and birds of prey?" Offering them trade goods if they would return to their old village, he declared that he spoke as their good father and asked them to consider his viewpoint.

21

The Missouris considered the eloquent white man's arguments. That evening they came to LaClede with their answer. "We have opened our ears wide to your talk," they said. If he would give them provisions, powder and balls, they would go back up the Missouri.

Two days later, their spacious dugout canoes laden with corn, powder, balls, knives and cloth, they were gone. Immensely relieved and feeling unaccountably older, but satisfied they had come through a dangerous situation with colors flying, Auguste turned back to his building projects.

When his mother arrived in September with his six-year-old half brother Pierre and two younger half sisters, Auguste had his stepfather's house ready to receive them. Both men got acquainted with the newest member of the family, a six-month-old baby girl born after they'd left New Orleans a year before.

Madame Chouteau had named her Victoire and she seemed an appropriate portent for the little French village. Even that December, when the settlers learned to their surprise that their town and all French territory west of the Mississippi had been ceded to Spain, there was no panic. Twice disenfranchised and facing life under yet another foreign power, they worried, but they stayed.

When the British finally moved into Fort Chartres in October 1765, some 40 French families remaining on the east bank of the Mississippi decided to put their trust in St. Louis. For a day or two the river was dotted with strange craft as the French dismantled their homes and rafted door frames, shingles and boards across the river. Chouteau put in some strenuous, noisy days helping them all find satisfactory lots and soon their few head of livestock, the grain they'd grown the year before and their farming tools began to give the raw settlement a more substantial feeling.

Axes and saws sang again as the settlers raised vertical log walls for their small square homes, skirting them with verandas to protect them from heat and rain. As soon as there was time the chinks were plastered, and before long the wilderness *menageries* could again take pride in their whitewashed walls. Lots containing courtyards, vegetable gardens, barns, root cellars and fruit trees were outlined by stone walls or stake fences. Two-wheeled charettes rattled from homes to the common fields as the clog-shod settlers planted corn, wheat, tobacco, cotton and oats.

Maria Therese Bourgeois Chouteau, who had to retain her truant husband's name to make her children legitimate, settled into LaClede's spacious headquarters and prepared to raise her family. Slaves, both black and Indian, provided the labor they needed. While they were hundreds of miles from New Orleans, St. Louis was never far removed from its culture. LaClede's 200-book library lined the walls of Auguste's home, and LaClede saw that he was exposed to Rousseau, Descartes and Bacon's *Essays*, along with history, grammar and finance.

Having established the town that would see the hope-filled launchings and the grateful dockings of Missouri River travelers for most of the next century, LaClede and Auguste Chouteau were free to concentrate on collecting furs from the Indians, and to wonder what Spanish rule would mean to the hamlet growing beside the mounds.

A Battle Won; A Battle Lost

At first Spanish rule seemed to mean nothing. Even New Orleans did not see a Spanish governor until 1766, and royal barges bearing persons of authority did not make their way up to the little French settlement for another year.

The Spaniards established a tiny fort at the mouth of the Missouri, but it made little mark on the people's lives.

Monsieurs LaClede and Chouteau -- now addressed as "Don" -- would prove to be civilian diplomats of the highest order. They knew who held the power and how to curry it, so in 1769 they joined other citizens of St. Louis in an oath of allegiance to Spain. And when LaClede finished a fine new house he was building for his family, he offered his old headquarters for the Spanish governor's use.

In the next several years the French merchants made friends with the Osage Indians and other tribes, and built their trade to satisfying proportions. Auguste, and later his young half brother Pierre, lived for weeks with the tribes learning their languages and customs.

23

But it was an uncertain life. LaClede suffered business reverses and his health disintegrated. He died on the Mississippi during a trip to New Orleans in May 1778, bankrupt and in despair at his disgrace.

Auguste had not even a grave at which to mourn the man who had made such a difference in his life. He attended the mass Father Bernard said for LaClede's soul, consoled his mother, and took his place at the head of the family. For a while, at least, he was too distracted to worry about the war between the British and their colonies to the east, or about how he would get along with the new Spanish governor who was expected any day.

ASA BATTLES

The new Spanish governor of the province of Western Illinois, Captain Fernando de Leyba, was a bit distracted himself. He'd arrived on the tenth of June, worn from a 93-day journey from New Orleans, and in the next month he'd received seven Indian tribes and was expecting another dozen.

Receiving a tribe, he discovered to his consternation, meant that the Indians paid him tribute by asking for theirs. They landed enmasse with wives, children, bag and baggage to be feted and fed by their "new father." The visits were an annual ritual which they loved.

The Missouris had brought the whole tribe and stayed two weeks, "eating us out of house and home," Leyba complained to his superior, Gov. Gen. Bernardo de Galvez, in New Orleans. He distributed at least 50 bread rations a day -- from a town so chronically short of that staple that it bore the disdainful nickname Paincourt. Some days 200 rations went into hungry Indian mouths. He was only too aware that the king's New Orleans representatives expected him to limit his giveaways of bread to 1,072 rations a year and it looked as if he would go over that in the next month.

He also found a shortage of gift items for the tribes. The chiefs expected medals and each one required a flag. The government warehouse was empty of these and the other trade goods they needed. What could he do? Charged with maintaining friendly relations with the Indians, he ordered the reluctant merchants to provide what he needed and guaranteed the Spanish government would pay the bills.

Of course he was also expected to secure the district from invasion, stimulate the fur trade, improve the indifferent agricultural practices and increase the population -- all without spending any money. Oh, yes. And he should support the American cause.

In July, when the American Gen. George Rogers Clark struck at Kaskaskia, across the Mississippi, and took it from the British, Leyba hastened to send him congratulations "on his happy arrival." By late summer Clark was on his doorstep, without "a shirt to cover his nakedness," asking for supplies. Leyba welcomed him with a black powder salute, scheduled two festive dances in his honor and

invited him to be a guest in his home. They sat over dinner in the government house with Leyba's charming wife presiding and his two curly haired little daughters by his side.

Leyba liked Clark immediately. Both personally and professionally, he was sympathetic to his cause. The man was without resources to maintain his fight against the British. What could he do? Again Leyba ordered the merchants to sell the American commander what he needed on credit and personally guaranteed the bills would be paid.

The Spanish governor was well aware the British were recruiting Indians to fight against American settlements. Realizing St. Louis sat in a strategic position to cut the Mississippi River supply line for forces fighting in the interior, Leyba looked to his community's defenses.

There were none. The small fort which the Spanish had built at the mouth of the Missouri, was only a pile of rubble and positioned so badly it couldn't protect the mouth of that river, let alone St. Louis. To garrison the fort he had six men and a corporal.

What fences and walls there were around the town, which now boasted a population of nearly 700, were to keep livestock out of the vegetable gardens, not wild Indians out of its 120 homes. His force at St. Louis consisted of 15 men and a drummer boy, with 13 more men at St. Genevieve, a settlement 60 miles down river.

Something had to be done. By mid-November he had submitted his plan to Governor General Galvez in New Orleans. If he could have 200 men and money to build two new forts, he could guarantee the safety of the pueblo and the district.

The governor's reply reached him just after New Year's celebrations in 1779. Galvez was scandalized at his plans. He could never authorize "such extraordinary outlays from the royal treasury."

Leyba was allowed funds for salaries of the current troops and would receive no more. Of course he was still expected to prevent the British from entering the Missouri country, and he must not allow them to win over any Indians.

The war news filtering into St. Louis was even darker and colder than the winter weather. The British had a General Hamilton who was encouraging the Indians in most savage attacks against the settlers. St. Louis was said to be high on his list.

Leyba again took quill in hand to plead with Galvez. "This Almilton is a depraved man," he wrote. The settlement is totally defenseless. What can I do?

Do the best you can, Galvez replied in March. Ignoring his earlier instructions to assist the Americans, he wrote, "I hope your energy and zeal will not spare measures to avoid all conflict by remaining neutral to both parties." But since even he could not ignore the fact it was a little late to profess neutrality, he added that in case attack should come Leyba should "act in such a manner as to preserve the honor of our arms."

Luckily in the meantime Leyba's "*cher amy*" Clark took Vincennes on the Wabash River and captured the depraved Hamilton. The threat was removed, at least for the time being.

Not temperamentally suited to prolonged bouts of anxiety, the citizenry relaxed into everyday living. The farmers made cheerful, half-hearted attempts to produce enough to eat, and the smithies, coopers, baker and shoemakers plied their trades. Truth was, though, most of them preferred to be out hunting, trapping, or trading with the Indians for skins. They seeded crops in the common fields with optimism and best wishes, then left them to their own devices. Harvests were truly manna from heaven.

The populace, mostly Canadian Catholic, delighted in their new church and Father Bernard's services, but they celebrated the sabbath in their own way. Sundays after mass were given over to dancing, horse racing and gambling, the atmosphere enlivened with Gallic songs more earthy than holy.

The new administrator was besieged by merchants wanting licenses to trade with the Indians. There simply wasn't enough trade to go around, so he divided the trade into smaller areas, satisfying no one. The pitch of complaints in the taverns rose to new heights.

When the escalating war in the colonies threatened to cut off the supply of trade goods entirely, he asked certain traders to get goods from the British, then rewarded them for their service. Around town, mugs slammed on table tops and expletives flew.

Leyba's troops were equally dissentious. He grew used to staring at red and blue waistcoats across his desk while one officer complained that another had received a boon which should have come his way. Unable to get the men to work together, he formed separate companies to spread command and satisfy their egos.

With so small a regular force, he knew the defense of the community rested largely on the civilian militia. He had 176 names on his list, untrained except for an occasional merry Sunday afternoon practice -- untried, their loyalty untested. More than one-fourth of the townspeople were slaves -- black now, since the Spanish had outlawed Indian slavery eight years before, but slaves still. How would they react if the town were attacked?

Leyba tried to boost interest in the militia by forming a cavalry unit. It attracted another four dozen, but most of the boys had no horses, which made training them problematic. He could see that even the regular troops were poorly trained and undisciplined, but there were longstanding orders not "to waste the king's powder by too much practice."

Even in his bedroom he had little peace. His wife, exiled with two little girls not only to the crudity of the wilderness but into a foreign culture where scarcely anyone spoke her language, longed only for the time they could leave and return to Spain. She knew her husband was now personally responsible for at least 10,000 pesos of credit that the town's merchants had extended to Clark. Fearing other expenditures he'd authorized might not be approved, and painfully aware of his growing unpopularity, she saw their whole future threatened. Increasingly convinced they were trapped by debt and would never be able to return to their homeland, she fell ill in the fall of 1779.

In five days she was dead.

Leyba, consumed with grief himself and trying to comfort his daughters, began to crack under the pressure. When the carpenter appeared at his door to collect his bill for making Senora Leyba's coffin, there was a scene and Leyba threw him out of the house. By the middle of October he himself was ill.

But when Auguste Chouteau returned

from business in New Orleans on February 9, 1780, Leyba discovered he had even bigger problems. Spain and Britain had broken diplomatic relations seven months before, Chouteau told him. St. Louis was no longer even nominally neutral.

Leyba realized attack could be imminent, and a month later a trader came to town with frightening words. A new British general named Haldimand, with a force of hundreds of Indians, intended to destroy the town. It was clear by now he was on his own. He drew up a plan and called a town meeting.

Facing the testy crowd of men who gathered in his home, he told them what he knew. The danger was real. There would be no outside help. If they and their families were to be preserved from "the furor of the barbarians" they would have to work together and depend on themselves.

Then he laid out his plan: they would build four stone towers to protect the perimeter on each side and he would bring down the cannon from the dilapidated fort to arm them. Trenches would be dug between the towers with the earth thrown up on the outside as breastworks. He and his men would direct the soldiers and the civilian militia.

But to do this would take money and he had only his personal funds. He would put up 400 piastres. Would they help? He searched their faces for a reply.

It was not long in coming. Propelled by images of slaughtered families and bloody scalping knives, the citizens pledged themselves to 400 days work and -- even harder -- their cash resources. They gave all they could and more. Auguste and Pierre Chouteau, still feeling the effects of LaClede's death, gave as much as they could spare. The other citizens followed suit, the poorest going without food, Leyba noticed, so the work could be started.

Grateful for their sacrifice, Leyba put men to work immediately. But on April 6, before they had laid the first stone, came more news of the British force. Haldimand was said to be on his way with at least 1,000 Indians. Leyba sent for the cannon.

Spurred on by fear, the men worked feverishly to dig the foundation for the west tower. It would sit at the crest of a hill (present Walnut and 4th Street) and lift a gun platform 30 feet in the air. On April 17 the priest blessed the first stone and the walls began to rise.

But the time it took grated on them all.

While work began on the foundation for the north tower and men began to trench the meadow on the north and south ends of town, Leyba sent out reconnaissance parties to find Haldimand's position. He was fighting recurring illness now, as well as time. On May 5 he was too ill to write his report to New Orleans. He had to dictate it to a Frenchman, there being no other Spaniard about who was literate enough to write for him.

Again he pleaded for financial help. The west tower was not finished, the north only a hole in the ground and they were out of funds. "These good people have exhausted themselves and done the impossible," he told Galvez. They "are depriving themselves of necessities and food," to pay for the defenses. The pueblo needed help.

Three days later he was awakened by a midnight messenger: 300 English leading 900 Indians were within 80 leagues of town. What little color the sick man had drained from his face. The towers were not yet finished. Nothing was ready.

At first light he sent for the cannons, garrison and militia of St. Genevieve. After a long five days the 60 men arrived to the cheers of the settlers.

While the villagers fed and housed the reinforcements, Leyba sent messengers out to round up the hunters. He ordered those in town to stay there. Totaling the lists again and again, he figured he could count on 150 more men. It would be a mix of boatmen and farmers, tradesmen and hunters but at least they were all good shots. A pitiful number against 1,200, but there was no point in thinking about that. He installed the cannons on the unfinished top floor of the west tower.

Desperate to divert the enemy, an American colonel stationed across the Mississippi suggested an expedition to intercept them before they hit town. Grasping at straws, Leyba agreed to provide 100 men and waited for boats to transport them north. But the boats didn't appear, and on May 23 a reconnaissance party returned to report the huge force was 20 leagues away.

However, the French community had waited and worked and feared for weeks now. When Sunday, May 25, dawned clear and bright they could endure the tension no longer. It was spring and the Feast of Corpus Christi. The flowers were blooming and the strawberries ripe. To Leyba's distress, they scattered over the village common which stretched several miles along the town's western border.

Nothing happened. They picked their bouquets, popped sweet strawberries in their mouths and had a wonderful day.

The next day a few braver souls decided to venture out to the fields and try to get some maize sown. That morning, like Sunday's, was peaceful and quiet.

But about noon it happened. With a wild howl, hundreds of painted warriors charged toward the town from the west and north. One farmer, out with his wife, two daughters and a friend, was lucky enough to have a horse and cart. They ran toward it, gathering up their wounded friend as he fell. They piled in on top of each other, all bleeding now from bullet wounds, and whipped the horse for town. Another man, caught on foot, was hauled down near the ancient Indian mound and hacked to death. Another, gasping for breath, was within 300 yards of safety when he was run down and captured.

But were those inside the unfinished fortifications any safer? Leyba struggled up from his sick bed when he heard the first awesome sounds of the charge. He was pulling on his pants when the guard came running in with the news. There were hundreds, like the

reports said. There were Sioux and Winnebago, Ottawa, Sac and Fox -- hundreds -- with British officers urging them on.

Leyba tried to stand, but it was impossible. He was too weak and dizzy. He ordered a litter, rolled onto it and ordered the men to carry him to the fighting.

Downstairs, his house was filling with panic-stricken women and children told to take refuge in the village's most substantial structure. Leyba assigned a detail to guard them and urged his litter bearers to get him to the tower.

By now the troops and every man of the village were at the trenches. Leyba called a half dozen of the best hunters to follow him and the soldiers as he was helped to the top of the tower. Now he could see the attacking force spread below him. It was a horrifying sight. They came like madmen, screaming their war cries, not bothering to take cover, confident they would overrun the defenders.

To the north the attack was especially fierce. Sioux and Winnebago, scrambling up the Indian mounds, could fire down into the trenches and the foundation dug for the north tower. Leyba could see a chief, dressed in a red coat and cocked hat, urging his men on.

Their only hope was the cannons. Hurriedly the gunners rammed powder and balls into the mouths of the five pieces and touched fire to the holes. Leyba directed their fire.

The men cheered at the explosions as grass and dirt erupted around the Indians and they stopped in shock. They had expected no such opposition. Their attack wavered. But the British officers gathered them up and regrouped. It would not be so easy.

Now the men in the trenches began to hear screams from their families at the government house. Indians across the Mississippi were raining shot on the town. It rattled on the roofs of the houses and terrified the women.

Not knowing what was happening, some men stood to go to their aid. But discipline prevailed. Hard as it was, the citizens kept their posts and turned back to face the attack.

For two hours the issue remained in doubt. But the cannons were taking their toll. The Sac and Fox to the south of the line were losing their enthusiasm for battle. As the attack dwindled, some of the militia wanted to leave the trenches and carry the battle to the Indians. While he admired their bravery, Leyba knew it would be foolhardy to leave their defensive positions and risk ambush. He refused to allow it.

Frustrated at finding the little town was not the easy pickings they expected, the attackers slowly withdrew, taking their bile out on anything in their path. The defenders had to watch as bodies of the fallen were cut limb from limb, disemboweled and scattered over the field. Crops were destroyed; oxen, cows, horses, pigs and hens were slaughtered. "Your heart would have shed tears," Leyba wrote after the battle to Governor General Galvez.

They were safe for the time being, but Leyba knew another attack could occur at any time. He ordered old and young alike to help keep a round-the-clock guard while the community discovered who it had lost.

Twenty-one were dead, seven of them slaves. Another six whites and a black were wounded. Twelve citizens and 13 slaves could not be accounted for and were assumed to be prisoners. As news came in from the other side of the Mississippi the total climbed to almost 100 dead, wounded or missing.

It was a shattering blow. Scarcely any family was untouched. Madame Chouteau lost six of her slaves, but both Auguste and Pierre fought without injury.

Father Bernard and the little church served the mourners, and the cemetery gained what the town had lost. Once Leyba's scouting party returned to report the enemy had withdrawn up the Illinois River, the settlers trudged out to the fields to see what was left of their crops and to replant. Leyba, bedridden once more, wrote his melancholy report to New Orleans.

Two weeks later the people had the satisfaction of a token revenge. Leyba allowed 100 St. Louis men to march north with a force of Americans to punish the Indians. They didn't find the tribes but they burned some villages, destroyed some crops and left messages promising to do worse in the future. It wasn't much, but it was something.

Back in the government house, Leyba was sinking. He turned over command to Lieutenant Cartabona on June 20, and a week and a day later he was dead. His troops buried him before the altar of the new church, beside his wife.

But the citizens he had tried to serve did not regret his passing. Even as he lay dying, a townsman was composing a vitriolic letter to Governor General Galvez, charging Leyba with tyranny, cowardice, incompetence and corruption.

"Never has...death been so slow in coming, thunderbolts so tardy in overwhelming a sinner and wiping him out," wrote the anonymous scribe. Leyba had failed to provide for their defense, he charged, and had amassed a huge fortune by stealing goods intended for the Indians.

The truth was, Leyba's tower and cannons had saved them from the Indians and the Mississippi Valley from the British. The estate he left was less than a fifth of what they imagined. He had achieved victory in the Battle of St. Louis but he had not been able to win the affection of the volatile people he governed.

Prelude

In September a new Spanish governor arrived in the recovering pueblo. But even though the resident in the government house was Spanish, St. Louis remained Chouteau's Town to the Indians.

Those nearby cheerfully exchanged their British flags for banners of Spain, and in the next decade a growing stream of odoriferous pelts flowed into the Chouteau warehouse to be sorted, weighed, packed in 100-pound bundles and shipped to market. Chocolate, tea, hardware, silk stockings, seeds, wine, chamber pots and lace handkerchiefs moved the other direction to supply the citizens of the town.

Auguste and Pierre both married daughters of well-established French traders and began a family business dynasty that would dominate Missouri trade for decades.

In 1789 Auguste bought the house he had built for LaClede 25 years before. The old house, where women and children had huddled during the British attack, was falling to ruins, the roof rotten, the stone walls untended. Gradually he restored it, adding a second story, slave cabins, a stable and a stone wall. His house would reflect his status as the leading citizen and unofficial banker of the town.

While the southern Indian tribes leaned to the French/Spanish coalition, those in the north remained firmly under Britain's thumb. In the west, Russian traders were moving down the California coast, threatening Spain's holdings there. Still without accurate knowledge of the Rocky Mountains or the distances involved, paranoid Spaniards envisioned British forces marching up the Missouri to Santa Fe.

Deciding the best defense was a good offense, the Spaniards moved to establish posts of their own on the Upper Missouri, dreaming they might complete a protective arc of influence all the way to the Pacific.

The governor general established the Commercial Company for the Discovery of the Nations of the Upper Missouri and hired a St. Louis school teacher to carry the Spanish flag north. He was to expel British traders from the Mandan and perhaps establish a route to the Pacific.

But it was easier to draw plans in St. Louis than to erect forts on a river which already had occupants with their own interests in mind. Ponca, Omaha, Arikara and Sioux, (recent pro-British arrivals from the east who were challenging the hold of the river tribes), all imposed themselves between the Spaniards and the Mandan.

By 1795 the school teacher had failed to penetrate the hostile tribes and it was decided to find a new commander for a final try. Surprisingly, the man the governor chose to oppose the British was James MacKay, Scottish by birth and late of the Canadian fur trade. Even more strange was the man MacKay picked to serve as his lieutenant: a singular young man named John Evans.

John Evans' mind was also focused on the Upper Missouri, but he was not interested in the security of the Spanish empire or the possibilities of the fur trade. His mission was to discover what might have happened there more than 600 years before, and he believed that "God Almighty had laid" the mission on his conscience. Evans had left the narrow rocky streets of his home in Waunfowr, Wales, traveled the Atlantic and crossed the United States in order to accomplish it.

It had not been easy; many people had tried to discourage him. He'd had to earn his way to St. Louis and, once there, his ideas and actions had aroused such suspicion that the governor had thrown him in jail. He'd moldered there for nearly two years before someone convinced the governor that possibly he was neither insane nor seditious.

There were others who shared Evans' zeal, who believed the Indians he'd meet at the northern arc of the Missouri would greet him in his native tongue. These Indians (they were certain) would have light complexions and hair, would have tribal memories of an ancestor named Madoc and a long sea voyage six centuries before.

This Madoc, Evans believed, the son of the Prince of North Wales, had gone to sea in ten ships in the time of the Crusades. He'd landed on the coast of North America with 300 men, long before any Italian or Portuguese. His descendants were still there. Some said they had a Bible written in Welsh; some said they had an elaborate culture. It was well known that they had spared the life of a minister from New York state when he spoke to them in Welsh. There were many reported contacts.

The romance, grandeur and even the improbability of the idea appealed to the Celtic nature. Why shouldn't it be true? Evans spent exciting evenings in discussion in the ethereal atmosphere of an expatriate Welsh literary society in London.

True, the location of the mysterious tribe seemed to push west with the rest of the population. When the Delaware proved not to be the lost tribe, it became the Tusarora, then the Shawnee. As each tribe proved a disappointment, another took its place. Some decided they were the Padouca. By the late 1700s most, like Evans, believed they were the Mandan.

With missionary fervor high in England, it seemed important to settle the question and "open the door to go to the old Welsh who sailed with Madoc ab Owen Gwynedd in the year 1170." John Evans, 22-year-old son of a Methodist minister, was chosen to go.

Devout but intelligent, Evans did not give credence to some of the grander tales of an elaborate culture and a Welsh Bible. Instead he envisioned an unenlightened tribe whom he could bring to Christianity. Where could he pursue a higher calling? He'd find the Madocians, he promised, or death.

Fur trader James Mackay had already been to the Upper Missouri and had encountered no Welsh Indians. He was a practical man but his mind could stretch to encompass far-reaching possibilities. He was willing to believe they could be there. Intrigued by the history which might be uncovered and wanting to be part of it, he hired the sublimely inspired Evans as his assistant on an expedition motivated more by greed than by God.

The pair pushed into the Missouri in the thick heat of mid-August 1795 with 30 French boatmen and four pirogues of trade goods. Unschooled in the ways of the wilderness, Evans followed Mackay's lead, quickly absorbing from his experienced mentor the knowledge and skills he needed to survive.

Summer thunderstorms had yielded to autumn drizzles by the time they reached the Platte and their first human challenge. The Oto, who had waylaid and robbed earlier St. Louis traders, tried to bluff Mackay out of his goods. But Mackay yielded only what was necessary to keep them in control so he could move on north.

By now it was November and the yellow soil of the bluffs they skirted stood revealed behind denuded branches. Time was slipping away and they had yet to deal with the major tribes.

On November 3 there was a hail from the west bank and Evans looked up to see an entourage of Omaha escorting a chief. He knew at once it must be the man Mackay had told him about, the most feared Indian on the river.

He looked with mingled interest and awe at the good-sized, handsome warrior who motioned them to shore. The chief had all the accouterments of wealth but it was his attitude which was arresting. The Oto had been threatening, but there had been a kind of bombast to it. Blackbird was confident to the point of insolence. The white bourgeois would accompany him to his village. He anticipated no argument.

As Evans trailed along behind the chief who called himself the Prince of Nations, he reflected on the man's reputation. The traders often talked about the monster they'd created. Blackbird, Washinga Sahba to his people, knew too much about the whites to be intimidated. He'd been to St. Louis and learned some of their ways and he used some white magic to effect absolute, unquestioned authority over his people.

Other Omaha had quickly learned not to question one who could accurately predict the time and place of a person's death. A man who could call the punishment of the Great Spirit down on those who opposed him soon became unopposed. While the whites knew he effected those deaths with arsenic, secured in St. Louis under the tutoring of a trader, they could not challenge his authority. They were dependent on his good will if they wanted the Omaha trade and they had to put up with his increasingly outrageous demands for a cut of the profits.

At the moment, Blackbird professed a liking for the Spaniards. He could probably be persuaded to sever British ties, if the price were right. His people needed a trading post right here, well supplied with blankets, bright cloth, tobacco, kettles and, of course, guns with lead and powder.

Evans and Mackay walked into the earth lodge village ranged along a small creek (the present Homer on Omaha Creek), aware they had little choice. They would have to pacify Blackbird before they could continue. By then the river would probably be frozen. They would have to winter here. Bowing to the inevitable, Mackay began building a post he called Fort Charles.

But it took considerable food to sustain 30 men and they were nearly out. An Omaha party was going hunting and Mackay decided hunters with them would probably do better than if they tried their luck alone. He asked John Evans to command the party.

Evans had passed the test of the Missouri; a man could not struggle against those waters without revealing his character. Given to exaggeration and arrogance when he began his quest, Evans was maturing. The country cut one's ego down to size. Mackay had seen enough to decide he could depend on the Welshman.

Now, in the Moon When the Deer Shed Their Antlers, the young missionary would accompany the Omahas on a winter buffalo hunt. He discovered the hunt required much advance preparation. Father Buffalo was their staff of life and they did not harvest it without the permission and blessing of the Great Spirit. While a winter hunt, which yielded warm, long-haired pelts, did not hold the importance of the annual summer hunt, it still must be led by a hunter born into the proper division of the Earth People and must be performed in the prescribed manner.

Knowing they might be out for some time, the Indian women folded tipi skins onto travois, filled skin pouches with corn and dried squash and fixed pack racks for the dogs. Swathed in robes and blankets, quivers full, the hunters led the group out of the valley.

It was late November and the weather was bitter. The buffalo seemed to have disappeared from the frozen knolls and hollows. They scouted for days without finding a sizeable herd. Evans, suffering from the cold, struggled to keep his feet from freezing. By day the horses plodded across wind-swept ridges and stumbled through drifted gullies. At night he hunched by the tipi fire, surprised and gratified at the warmth of the dwelling. Sometimes he stepped outside into the crisp air and looked around him at the circle of conical tents, peaks lost in the darkness, bases aglow with warmth, the relaxed activities of those inside sketched in moving shadows. It had been more than three years since he'd left Wales. He was half a world away from the fire on his family hearth and had still farther to go to see the Mandan.

Would they be what he hoped? Would they accept him as a brother? Would he be able to bring them to Christ? Now aware of the intricate and spiritual organization of the Omaha society, he realized he would probably not be filling a vacuum but trying to supplant long-held beliefs.

Close to three weeks had passed before the runners finally brought news of a herd. They signaled the hunters by racing back and forth on the crest of a hill. Evans watched with fascination as the ritual of the hunt unfolded.

The hunters stripped to breech clout and moccasins; one used no tricks or deceptions in hunting the buffalo. They called for the boys tending their horses to bring up their buffalo ponies, which were kept fresh for the hunt.

Though the Indians were excited and joyous to find the buffalo, they remained under the control of the marshals, who used whips if necessary to keep them in line until the proper ceremonies had been observed and the leader gave the signal to move. Since disobedience could mean death if the action jeopardized the hunt, few were ever tempted to rash actions.

Split into two groups, the hunters surrounded the herd. Then they charged, screaming from all directions into the surprised animals, driving them in circles as they made their kills. Evans was amazed to see the strongest braves could send an arrow clear through a 1,500-pound beast to wound another running beside it. Arrow could fly after arrow, while he and his men hurried to reload. When they were finished the trampled snow was gory with blood and steam rose from brown hulks scattered over the snow.

Evans got a lesson in butchering as he watched the men push the huge animals on their backs and with a few quick strokes cut a one-piece hide from the body. These hides, thick with fur, would become robes and blankets. The meat, each carcass carved into 11 portions with the precision of long years of practice, would feed them all. It was a proud procession that wound into the village a few days later, pack ponies loaded with food and clothes for the rest of the winter. They had been out 25 days.

But the white men needed to do more than just survive the winter. Mackay believed there was urgent need to get up to the Mandan. The British flag already flew above one of their villages and every day they became more entrenched. The villainous Blackbird had commandeered so many of his goods -- keeping what he wanted and doling out the rest to his people for whatever price appealed to him at the moment -- that he'd have to wait for new supplies before he could proceed next summer. A whole valuable season of exploration would be lost.

Again he called on Evans. With a few chosen men he was to proceed to the Mandan and dislodge the audacious British. Then he was to head west for the chain of the Rockies and the Pacific sea.

Late in January Mackay sat writing in his fort at the Omaha village and when Evans left the tribe early in the Moon When the Geese Come Back Home, he carried a many-paged document of instructions for his journey: the vision of James Mackay distilled.

"From the time of your departure from this fort until your return...you will keep a journal of each day," Mackay wrote. He was to record distances, latitude, longitudes, winds and weather. He was to note minerals, plant life, animals, lakes, mountains, portages and water life. He was to chart his route and the course of the rivers, record the natives and their ways and take care not to come to harm at their hands.

Here the instructions became explicit: he was to make camp in valleys, setting up late and leaving early, avoid smoking fires -- indeed, avoid *all* fires if possible -- cut wood only with a knife and fire his gun only when necessary. He was to collect unknown animals, alive if possible, especially a beast said to have only one horn on its forehead.

Once across the Rockies he was to follow the 42nd parallel as closely as he could, marking his route by carving the date and "Charles IV King of Spain, The Company of the Missouri" into trees and stones.

At the seashore, being careful not to offend any Russians present, he should measure its tides and collect sea life to prove his presence. A sea otter pelt would be nice, an affidavit from any civilized person he encountered there would be better. Along the way he was to tell every nation that "their great father, Spain, who is protector of all the white and red men, has sent you to tell them that he has heard of them and their needs" and is ready to provide.

Evans did not reach the Mandan until late September, having been chased back to Fort Charles by a war party of Sioux on his first trip and having his second, begun in early June, prolonged by recalcitrant Arikara. But he was sufficiently skilled now in dealing with Indians that he eventually talked his way free of the Ree and arrived at the Mandan villages with his three or four men on September 23, 1796.

Greeted with ceremony and responding with flags and medals for the chiefs, he knew the disappointment Verendrye had tasted nearly 60 years before. They were just Indians. If any Welsh blood flowed through these veins it was certainly well disguised. They were a reduced tribe since the Frenchman's visit; the plague of smallpox had struck and now they could count only 3,000 in their five villages.

Still they greeted Evans kindly and when he presented them with flags and medals from the Great Father the Spaniard who inhabits the other side of the Great Lake and the Great Chief who inhabits this side of the Great Lake and the Chief who resides at the entrance to the Missouri, they promised to observe the most sincere attachment for them all.

In a few days he felt secure enough with the Mandan to take possession of the empty British fort, rename it for Mackay, lower the British banner and run up the flag of Spain. By the time a delegation of British traders arrived in early October, Evans had enough influence with the Mandan to send them back to Canada with a written declaration from

Mackay that British traders were not welcome in His Catholic Majesty's Dominions.

However, it was too late to head out for the Rockies. He'd have to stay with the Mandan and collect as much information as he could for the journey west.

So began another long, cold winter, but this time Evans did not have even the fellowship of his friend Mackay. At first the Canadians, holed up in their posts to the north, warmed the atmosphere by sending him conciliatory letters while they assessed the Spanish strength. One even loaned books and sent medications. Another, expressing surprise and pleasure when he learned from Evans' letters that such an educated countryman was wintering with the Mandan, was moved to send the Methodist flour, chocolate and sugar from his small store. Evans responded by helping some British who'd been robbed by the Pawnee and by sending one British factor a souvenir of the area, an intriguing round stone from the mouth of the Cannonball River.

But the books were read all too soon, letters took weeks to exchange and the only thing outside his door except frozen prairie were lodges filled with savages more anxious for his trade goods than for his God, more in need of medicine than Methodism. Brutal winter gales howled and sub-zero temperatures kept even the most restless confined inside day after dark day. With 10 or 12 people, their horses and dogs populating a lodge, Evans had ample opportunity to converse with the friendly Black Cat or Big White, to listen for a word that might have a Welsh beginning.

He heard none. He had to conclude the Mandan had no exotic origin that would satisfy the romantic dreams of his compatriots. Still, he did not despise them. In fact he decided those Indians who had seen the least of the whites were "of a softer and better character than those overexposed. Those who have frequent communications with the whites appeared to have contracted their vices without having taken any of their virtues," he noted. After all, Blackbird had not been created by the Omaha.

He questioned the Indians endlessly about the way west, discovering in himself a talent to sort through what they told him and sketch out the lay of the land. When the weather allowed, he measured the Missouri, realizing almost at once that the river could not be so broad if he were as close to its source as the Spanish thought. He learned about a great fall where the river issued from the Rockies. He placed the tributaries -- the White, the Cheyenne, the Cannonball and the Yellow Stone.

And he wrote in his journal about the curious animals -- not one with a single horn, but one with two, curled alongside its head in spirals like a trumpet, each so huge it could hold a meal for four men.

Though the Mandan liked Evans and willingly supplied him with information, he could not return the favor. He was soon out of goods to trade, yet he continued to deny them the resources of the British. There was grumbling through the tribe.

For their part, the British were not to be pushed out of "the best trade on the continent of America" so easily. When months went by and Evans remained unreinforced and unsupplied, they decided to challenge him. One day in mid-March 1797 a veteran French Canadian named Rene Jessaume arrived with goods, determined to trade whether Evans liked it or not. Jessaume had a Mandan family and had enjoyed a lucrative trade with the Mandan before; he did not intend to bow to a scrap of paper and an inexperienced missionary.

Evans had no illusions about Jessaume, whom he'd dealt with the previous fall, but he was shocked one day at the news Black Cat confided. Jessaume was bribing the Indians to kill the Welshman, urging them to enter Evans' lodge professing friendship, then kill him and obtain his goods. While Evans had envisioned the possibility of death on his mission, it had been cloaked in romantic mist of martyrdom, probably at the hands of some unenlightened savage. He'd not pictured death in a dirt hut dealt by a swarthy trader over a few pelts. Yet if Jessaume turned the tribe against him, he was lost. What would the Indians do? He studied Black Cat's face for the answer.

It was almost more than he could have hoped. Jessaume's scheme was too uncivilized even for the unenlightened Mandan chiefs. Horrified at this unthinkable breach of

hospitality, the chiefs refused the bribes. When they learned that Indians of less moral quality were being tempted, the chiefs themselves came to stand guard over the house of the Welshman. They promised to fight to the death to protect him.

Jessaume, stymied in his attempt to hire the dirty work done, took on the job himself. Talking his way into Evans' post, he waited until his back was turned, then drew a pistol and took aim.

There was a shout and an explosion, but Evans turned unharmed. His interpreter had seen Jessaume's intent and thrown himself against the gunman's arm. Jessaume, dragged from the post by the Indians, would have been killed had Evans given the word, but he did not. He let Jessaume leave the village unscathed.

However he knew that he, too, would have to leave. His position was precarious and he could accomplish nothing more. He had barely enough supplies for a trip back to St. Louis, let alone an expedition to cross the Rockies and reach Pacific waters. His mission was ended. Evans and his men bid the Mandan goodbye, promising them he'd return someday, not with a Bible but with the arms and ammunition they craved. He rode the Missouri like a veteran and reached St. Louis on July 15.

There he had the melancholy duty of disillusioning his literary friends about descendants of Prince Madoc residing on the Upper Missouri. "I have only to inform you I could not meet with such a people, and from the intercourse I have with Indians from latitude 35 to 49 I think you may with safety inform our friends that they have no existence," he wrote.

Mackay, facing the reality of hostile tribes and impossible supply lines, had already retreated to St. Louis in May. He made similar statements.

But those who will believe are difficult to discourage. Rather than give up their cherished legend, they decided Evans had simply not gone far enough. Everyone in London knew one had to travel three months from St. Louis to reach the Mandan. Evans had admitted he'd returned in only 68 days. Less "superficial research" would certainly reveal the elusive tribe.

Appreciated at least by the Spanish government, Evans was offered a position as a surveyor. He decided to accept and make his home in the West. Perhaps he had been weakened by his two years up the Missouri or perhaps the family curse of tuberculosis had caught up with him. Whatever the reason, at the age of 28 his thoughts were already on death.

"A reflection upon the shortness of life and the frowns of delusive fortune convinces me dayly of my duty to live a retired life as soon as I can," he wrote in June 1798. "For we can scarcely mount the stage of Life before we ought to prepare to leave it to make room for the next actors."

Less than a year later, wasted by liquor, the son of the Methodist minister was dead. The stage of the Missouri was clear for other actors but few would play stranger parts than John Evans.

A Fine Morning

John Evans had no chance to carve the name of Charles IV of Spain into the western landscape. The Spanish star was fading and a presumptuous commoner too powerful to ignore demanded Louisiana be returned to France. In 1800, less than 18 months after Evans' death, Charles had yielded to Napolean Bonaparte and signed a secret treaty relinquishing the center of the North American continent.

But in spite of his grandiose plans for a new French empire in North America, Napolean's name was not to replace His Catholic Majesty's. His armies destroyed on the fever-washed rock of Santo Domingo and Britain's power looming in his glass, the First Consul had to renounce his dreams for Louisiana. Monsieur T. Jefferson's man had been knocking on his door for a year, trying to buy New Orleans. Why not sell enough to make it worth both their whiles?

It was agreed, and the United States was suddenly larger by 800,000 square miles. But this news didn't filter up to St. Louis until August 1803. Auguste Chouteau, who had welcomed the rumors of a new French rule, was astonished to learn he'd be living instead under Americans.

Even before the territory was officially transferred, he noticed the influx of people from east of the Mississippi. And several times that winter he entertained a couple of would-be explorers who were camped across the water at Wood River. Not one to neglect an opportunity, he sold them supplies for their men.

The following March he stood with the rest of the citizens of St. Louis in front of the government house to listen to speeches and watch the Spanish flag lowered -- and to cheer a brief moment in the sun for the French tricolor before the Stars and Stripes were raised. Cannons boomed from the old fort, soldiers of both countries paraded and documents were signed. Once again the Chouteaus would have to learn the ins and outs of a new administration.

But the American army officers who came over to enjoy the Frenchmen's hospitality from their camp at Wood River had direct access to the highest levels of American government. Like Evans, they had a mission. Theirs was assigned by a secular power, but it was amazingly like the Welshman's. In fact, among their papers was a journal written by a Spanish trader who'd gone up the river a decade before. And tucked away in a notebook was a copy of the missionary's map.

The two men strode along the Missouri's bank with the determined gait of men accustomed to covering many miles before sunset, day after day, week in and week out. Sunset was near on this blustery May day in 1805, but they stretched their legs and their endurance to make a few more miles.

Their city boots had given way to moccasins and leather leggings, their wool army breeches to buckskin, their fair skin had bronzed and toughened under wind and sun. They'd been out exactly a year now. St. Louis was 2,000 miles and 365 days down river. Homes where they'd recently been guests served with bone and board instead of crystal and china, and they gulped things they'd never heard of with eager appetites.

The taller and sturdier of the two, William Clark, his red hair caught back in a single braid, gestured widely to his friend and co-commander as he walked. The friend, Meriwether Lewis, listened intently. His dark features were finer, his appearance more aesthetic, his manner more reserved.

Their conversation ended abruptly as a movement out on the river caught their attention. Transfixed, they watched the sail of their white pirogue shudder against a sudden gust of wind. The dugout began to turn her side to the gale. It was the safest of their two boats, or so they'd thought when they'd trusted her with their year's worth of meticulously recorded scientific data, their surveying instruments, books, medicines and the trade goods they would need to buy the peace and cooperation of the Indians.

In horror they realized Charbonneau was at the tiller. The most incompetent member of the expedition -- hired to interpret and good for nothing else except a bit of cooking -- panicked and turned into the wind. In an instant the square sail was yanked from the hand tending it and the boat lay on her side. Only the mast, bobbing on the waves, kept her from rolling over completely.

Everything they needed to succeed in their mission for President Jefferson -- plus a woman, a three-month-old baby and three nonswimmers -- hung only inches above the grasp of the Missouri. Charbonneau clamped his arms over the nearest bulwark and cried piteously to God to save him. The others hung on desperately to whatever they could reach.

By now Clark and Lewis were at the river's edge, shouting frantic orders to cut the halyards and haul in the sail. Nobody moved. The commanders grabbed their guns and fired in the air. Not even gunfire could penetrate the panic.

Driven to uncharacteristic impulsiveness, Lewis dropped his gun, threw his shot pouch aside and began stripping off his coat, ready to swim out and try to help.

But reason took control. He'd never survive the 300-yard swim in the icy current and wind-whipped waves.

It seemed an eternity before even the capable boatman Cruzatte moved to take in the sail. The boat righted sluggishly, filled to within an inch of the gunwales. Cruzatte screamed at Charbonneau to take the rudder while two men bailed with camp kettles. He and the two other men grabbed the oars to row for shore.

Charbonneau remained glued where he was, pleading at the top of his lungs for divine intervention. Cruzatte finally pulled his pistol and threatened to finish him off before the Missouri got the chance. That got his attention. He managed to take hold of the tiller and the craft wallowed toward shore. Charbonneau's wife, a Shoshoni girl not more than 17, made sure her baby son was secure. Then she stretched to catch parcels and precious papers as they began to float away on the current.

It was a subdued group that gathered with the commanders on shore. They unpacked sodden belongings, bailed out the pirogue and began to assess their losses.

But before the task was complete, the other members of the expedition arrived with their own tale of horror. They'd been seeing grizzlies for a month now, almost since they'd left their winter quarters with the Mandan. And while those Indians as well as the Hidatsa had told many tales of the great bear's fierceness, some of the hunters had still not been overly impressed. A grizzly, though larger and somewhat fiercer, was just another bear, and the hunters relished a different challenge.

Sighting one in open ground along the river, six of the best hunters, bringing up the rear in two canoes, decided to run the bear to ground. Creeping within 40 yards, four of the men fired balls into his bulk.

It was enough to get the bear's attention. He roared with a volume they'd seldom heard and charged with gaping jaws. The other two hunters fired the charges they'd reserved for just such an emergency.

The bear stumbled, his shoulder broken. But he came on. Six hunters with unloaded guns ran for the riverbank. Two scrambled into a canoe while the rest hid in the willows and reloaded. Their hurried shots hit home but only succeeded in drawing fresh charges from the infuriated animal. One, then another hunter, forced to the brink, threw his gun aside and leapt off the 20-foot bank into the current.

The grizzly followed. His raging hulk was within feet of one desperately swimming man when a hunter still on shore managed to put a shot through his brain and end the battle. When they skinned him, they found eight balls in his carcass. Seven shots had scarcely slowed him.

It was enough to give a man pause, even men who had forced the Missouri to give them passage mile after grudging mile...men who'd clawed their way up river against current and across sandbar, rowing, poling and pulling their heavy boats with no power but that of their exhausted bodies...men who'd learned a full sail was as rare as a gentle rain and that a sheltering bank could collapse and bury your boat without warning.

These were men who'd learned to live with voracious mosquitoes, debilitating heat, boils, abscesses, snakebites, dysentery, fever, rheumatism. They'd dealt successfully with threatening Indians and kept themselves fed and sheltered through a crackling cold winter.

They were a tough, disciplined, capable lot by now, these 28 men who made up the Corps of Discovery. They had buried one man, seen two sent home in disgrace and knew now they could depend on each other. Half-blood interpreter George Drouillard and Private John Colter would bring in the meat. One-eyed Private Peter Cruzatte could handle a fiddle as well as a boat. Private John Shields was inventive enough to fix nearly anything.

William Clark was proud to lead them,

delighted to have been invited to co-command by a fellow Virginian who had become his friend when he was in the army. The command was especially meaningful to him because the mission was one his idolized older brother, George Rogers Clark, had once been asked to fulfill. Brother George had fallen on hard times. Expenses he'd incurred for his country while fighting the Revolution had become his personal responsibility, and William had spent much time in the past few years trying to help him clear his debts and the family name.

And so, Lewis' invitation to join the mission and "share with me in its fatigues, its dangers and its honors," had been irresistible. He'd quickly accepted, for himself and for his black slave, York, pledging Lewis his "hand and heart."

Even now, he had no second thoughts. Day after day he began his journal with "A fine morning." It was a weather report, but it was also a reflection of his personality and state of mind. Physical misery was of small moment when every day brought the electric charge of discovery and challenge.

He and Lewis warmed and cheered the men with a gill of "ardent spirits" usually saved for celebrations. As soon as the gear was dry the next day, they pulled into the current again.

Each mile now brought a new vista, never seen by white men. There were new birds, new plants, new creatures like the bighorn sheep that clattered across impossible cliff sides as they passed, to fill the pages of their journals.

They were not just experiencing the country; they were absorbing it -- gathering either in specimens or words, its seeds, fruits, leaves, skins, feathers, sands and bones. Clark wrote and sketched continually, in the pirogue or on shore, holding down wind-whipped pages on his elkskin-covered notebooks by day, bending over fire-lit sheets in a red leather diary at night.

He had grown almost used to the passing pageant of wildlife. Hillsides were black with buffalo, elk moved in stately processions through the meadows and mule deer peered from the brush along the draws. The animals were so unafraid that they often followed him and the other hunters out of curiosity about these new interlopers. It was not even a chore to kill enough meat to satisfy 31 hungry men, a woman and a dog. Beaver, one of their favorite meats, dove from the banks as they approached, and day after day they were dappled with shadows as endless flocks of water birds passed overhead. The men no longer noticed the black and white flash of the magpie or remarked on the fleetness of the antelope. Wolves and coyotes were always there, sculking around the herds, and bald eagles commonplace.

But Clark could see the country was changing. They were gradually, oh so gradually, pulling nearer the Rocky Mountains. Since they'd left Fort Mandan they'd been heading almost directly west, along a Missouri which had dug itself ever deeper into the landscape. Even the ubiquitous cottonwood, which had greened the flood plain all the way from St. Louis, was now scarce. By the time they reached the mouth of the Mussellshell, hillsides were rougher and higher, with scraggly pines and cedars scattered over the tan, barren soil. Eroded gullies snaked into the river from every direction but any water they contributed flowed beneath a floor of sage and sand.

The dry air parched their lips and the unceasing wind, laden with grit and tasting of alkali, burned their eyes, but the sky was high and wide and the atmosphere did not sit on their chests. The waters of the Missouri, cold enough to take their breath away, were at least not quite so muddy.

On May 25 Clark, walking on shore as the captains did in turn, climbed a hill dotted with prickly pear and saw the Rockies.

Were they really there? He couldn't be sure. There was no question about a small, nearby range (The Little Rocky Mountains). But were there really snow-capped peaks on the far southwest horizon?

The next day he had no doubts. He climbed the highest prominence he could find to see snow-covered peaks shining in the southwestern sky. He was flooded with emotion, with pleasure at being "so near the head of the -- heretofore conceived -- boundless Missouri," with knowledge of "the suffering and hardships" the snowy barrier would cost them. Then his natural optimism took over. "But," he wrote in his journal that night, "as I have always held it little short of criminality to anticipate evils, I will allow it to be a good, comfortable road until I am compelled to believe otherwise."

The good and comfortable road the Missouri was currently providing required unceasing labor. They could seldom proceed without the tow rope and that meant the men spent days on end either up to their armpits in water or fighting their way along shore. Both paths were strewn with sharp-edged rocks which cut and bruised their bare feet until they "could scarcely walk or stand."

Perhaps the small river they next came on flowing in from the south looked more gentle and accommodating. For some reason it took Clark's thoughts back to Fincastle, Virginia and the 13-year-old daughter of his friends, the Hancocks. He called it the Judith, not realizing the girl he knew as Judy was actually named Julia.

The Missouri could also provide romance of a sort. They paused in their toil now to wonder at white cliffs which towered 200 and 300 feet above their heads. Sculpted by wind and water into a thousand novel forms, the cliffs seemed to the men to be pedestals and columns, pyramids on top of pyramids, statues and parapets -- the echo, or the inspiration, of all the architecture of civilization. The cliff swallows, darting from their wasp-nest homes in the crevices, only enforced the illusion by reminding them of other birds which congregated around the grand buildings back in the States.

Those buildings seemed farther away with every slippery step. On June 2 they faced a decision that could cost them the success of their mission. Out of the cliffs and into more open country, moving now through white spears of chokecherry blossoms and dainty pink cups of wild roses, they came to a fork of the river that wasn't supposed to be there.

It was not on John Evans' map nor had the Indians at Fort Mandan even mentioned it in long winter days filled with discussion and questions and sketching of maps. So far their knowledge of the country had been impeccable. They said the explorers would find a great falls on the Missouri just before it led them into the Rockies. The only sizeable tributary they'd sketched flowing in from the north had been passed days before. Where were the falls? Which was the real Missouri?

The north fork looked like the Missouri. It was deeper. It was muddy and turbid. It's waters boiled and rolled like the Missouri's and it had a mud bottom. The south fork was entirely different. It was shallower, swifter and perfectly transparent, with a smooth surface and a bottom of smooth, flat stones.

The men voted immediately for the north fork. Cruzatte, veteran of Missouri travel and respected boatman, declared the north fork "was the true and genuine Missouri and could be no other."

The captains didn't think so. The next day, after dispatching scouting parties to find out what they could, they climbed the height separating the two rivers. They stood above the expanse of June-green meadows, fenced only by brush-filled draws, and absently watched buffalo suckle their red-gold calves, and antelope nuzzle their spindly-legged young. Mountains poked into the horizon both northwest and southwest. Which stream would take them across the Rockies to the Columbia?

Relying on observation, analysis, logic, and his gut instinct for a country he was beginning to make his own, Clark, whose pen had charted the maps they lived by, chose the south fork. Lewis, with less natural genius for geography but as much or more analytical ability, agreed.

They had to be sure, but the scouting parties returned without evidence either way. The commanders decided to separate; Lewis would travel the north fork and Clark the south until they could prove to the men --

and to themselves -- that the south was the true Missouri. On June 4 the captains departed, each with a small group of men. Lewis, shouldering a pack for the first time in his life, was accompanied as usual by his Newfoundland, Scammon. Clark's personal needs would be cared for, as they had been since they both were children, by York.

His progress interrupted only briefly when three grizzlies lumbered into camp their second morning (they'd learned to save time and trauma by aiming for the brain) Clark traveled only 55 miles up the north fork before he was sure. The river remained good-sized, and while it looked less and less like the Missouri they knew, it looked more and more like the mountain river they needed to follow, the river whose waters must come from snow-blanketed peaks to the south and west. Beaming with satisfaction, Clark carved his name into a tree, marking the spot of a landmark decision.

His footsore party was back in camp at the forks the next evening, but they spent two anxious days before Lewis' group appeared and the captains could confer on their important decision.

Lewis agreed with Clark. He'd found the north fork he'd followed charming enough to christen it for a lady friend, Maria, but it could not be the one they wanted. They would take the south fork.

They dug a cache for the supplies they could do without until they returned from the Pacific. (The "superfluous baggage of every description" the men insisted on collecting also went into the hole.) Then they secured the red pirogue on an island and committed the expedition to the south fork.

Three days later, on June 13, Lewis, who had hurried ahead to find the falls and remove the men's still-active doubts, gazed on the series of cataracts that confirmed their choice. The thunderous confirmation inspired him to write pages of rapturous description and -- finding words inadequate -- end wishing for a camera obscura.

Clark, toiling up the rattlesnake-infested canyon with the white pirogue and the canoes, remained unassured for four more days. Immersed in the daily duel with the river's current, he also battled to keep his party healthy enough to proceed. Two men suffered with toothaches, two others had abscesses, one had both an abscess and a fever.

But the Indian woman worried him most. Sacajawea was writhing with pain in her abdomen and he was at a loss to cure her. He'd bled her twice, given her a dose of salts; applied a poultice of chincona bark (one of their favorite remedies) and administered laudanum. Nothing seemed to help. He'd known similar worry when he sat with Sergeant Floyd last summer, back near the Platte. He'd been able to do nothing for the man while he watched him weaken except write the final letter he requested.

Clark admired the young Indian woman. While he was unable to converse with her, she'd been a cheerful and helpful presence, finding edible roots for them and interpreting Indian sign they encountered. If Sacajawea died, what of four-month old Pomp, who responded nowadays with smiles and prattle he found increasingly endearing? What of their need to communicate with the Shoshoni to buy horses for crossing the mountains?

His mind was partially relieved on June 14 when he unfolded a letter from Lewis headed "from the Great Falls of the Missouri." The next morning he was hearing their roar, and with Lewis' return on the 16th, he was freed of his responsibilities as medical officer and returned his thoughts to their route. They would have to portage around the falls five, possibly ten miles. Five cascades and intervening rapids followed one another for miles upstream. He left the next morning to stake the route while Lewis supervised building crude wagon frames to carry the dugouts and supplies not even *their* men could tote over such a distance.

As Clark worked upstream, the tantalizing roar he'd been hearing for two days grew increasingly louder. Then his steps quickened as a cloud of mist caught the sun ahead. Even after Lewis's description, Clark was unprepared for what he saw.

"I beheld those cataracts with astonishment," he wrote in his journal. "...This is one of the grandest views in nature, and by far exceeds anything I ever saw."

True to his calling he began scrambling down the cliff beside the first cataract to measure its height. Suddenly his foot slipped on the spray-wet rocks and he clung desperately with his fingers, aware of churning water far below. Then a dangling foot found purchase; he inched his way back up and descended again downstream where it was a little safer. Plastered against the rocks, drenched with spray and thrilled at the spectacle, he measured the height of the falls at 97 feet, 3/4 inches. During lunch he recorded his name, the date -- June 17, 1805 -- and the height of the falls on a willow tree. Returning to camp, he was gratified to learn Sacajawea had rallied after Lewis administered foul smelling water from a nearby spring.

Thrilling though the falls might be, they were a terrible obstacle. Because he was forced to detour around the heads of many canyons which intersected the river, the route Clark finally marked across the dry, cactus covered plain measured 18-1/4 miles. The last eight were without water. He knew the fatigues Lewis had promised were upon them.

Hardened to fighting the river, the men found the land demanded Herculean labor. For more than three weeks, one load at a time, they bent nearly parallel to the ground to pull the two dugouts and their gear out of the river bed, uphill across the fissured ground and back down to the water. They had found one cottonwood tree large enough to supply wheels for their makeshift wagons, but those wheels soon shook to pieces, as did the tongues and axles they'd hewn. They made more out of willow and kept going.

Prickly pear awaiting every unguarded step stabbed through the soles of their moccasins. They double-soled them with rawhide but the thorns penetrated even that. Other areas, trod by thousands of buffalo when the clay-like soil was wet, had dried to such a maze of rock-hard ridges that it tripped them and bruised their feet like frozen ground. After a few days their feet were so painful they felt faint when they first stood.

With Lewis ahead on the river, struggling to assemble his personally designed portable leather boat, it fell to Clark to get the gear across. He watched his men "haul with all their strength wate and art, maney times every man catching the grass and knobes and stones with their hands to give them more force in drawing on the Canoes and Loads..." Close to heat prostration, they stripped naked to find relief. At every halt the men dropped to the ground and were instantly asleep.

They searched the western sky for the dark clouds that meant rain, but when it came it brought more punishment. Hail beat on them unmercifully and the ground became an impassable quagmire.

On June 29, Clark, unable to reach the end of the portage across the wet prairie, set out on foot up the Missouri with York, Charbonneau, the weakened but improved Sacajawea and Pomp. Temporarily separated from York, and wary of the wind and hail that might sweep from a black cloud which was moving in from in the west, Clark hurried the Frenchman's family into a ravine just above the falls. They huddled under a rock shelf, awed by the violence of the storm but seemingly secure from the cloudburst.

Suddenly they realized they were not safe at all. A torrent of brown water poured into the ravine, taking rocks, brush and all before it. The water rose around them almost before they could stand. Clark, grabbing his gun and pouch in one hand, used the other to push Sacajawea and her babe before him up the bank. Charbonneau, characteristically frozen in panic, made feeble attempts to help. Water swirled past Clark's waist as he boosted the woman to safety. It was 15 feet deep by the time he reached the top of the draw and met York frantically searching.

They were safe, if drenched, but Clark had lost an elaborate fusee, tomahawk and other gear; Sacajawea had lost Pomp's cradle board and clothes. Clark fortified her and the others with a drink and hurried back to camp, where they met the bruised and bloody men who'd been caught naked on the prairie by hail stones large enough to kill.

At last, on July 16, they were back on the river. Lewis' skin boat had proved a cruel failure -- there was no pitch to seal its seams -- and they'd had to take time to carve out two more canoes. The days were flowing as swiftly as the clear current. Summer was half gone and they were not yet across the Rockies.

Anxious to make contact with the Shoshoni and afraid the large party might frighten them off, Clark pushed ahead with York and two of the men. He felt an affinity for native

people. He respected their culture, and on previous encounters had taken pains to accommodate himself to their customs, remaining patient through their ceremonies and doing all he could to treat them fairly.

They had been seeing Indian sign for days -- small abandoned camps, lodge poles still standing, trees peeled of their bark -- and now Clark came on an Indian trail across the cliffs. They couldn't be far from the three forks where the Shoshoni might be. If the Corps didn't get horses and a guide from them, or at least some knowledge of the country on west, they might have come all this way for nothing.

For three days Clark drove himself up and along the painfully rocky trail. Mosquitoes bloated their faces with bites and prickly pear swelled their feet with festering sores. Gnats, the third of their "trio of pests" attacked their eyes with a viciousness impossible to repel. Clark, limping now on blistered soles, pulled 17 spines out of his feet by the light of the fire on July 19. York could scarcely walk and the other men weren't much better. Clark gave them a day to wait for Lewis and the canoes to catch up, but when they did he refused his friend's offer to take over the scouting. On July 23 he was off again.

Thus, on July 25, he could write: "A fine morning. We proceeded on a fiew miles to the three forks of the Missouri."

There, in a spreading valley that spoke more of plains than of mountains, near the foot of sandstone bluffs, three mountain rivers came together in the space of a mile to blend their waters for a journey of nearly 2,500 miles.

But there were no Shoshoni in evidence, and Clark could afford little time to feel sentimental about reaching this milestone. He decided almost at once that the north fork came from the west and was somewhat larger. It would be the one to ascend to cross the mountains.

He hiked another 20 miles up the valley of the north fork, amazed at the number of beaver and otter that populated the whole three forks area. The valleys were so filled with their dams and ponds that it was almost impossible to walk the river. Then, leaving two of the worn-out men behind, he walked west for 12 miles and climbed a peak to get a view of the river's course and make certain he was correct.

"I was fatigued," he admitted in his journal that night after returning to camp. He spent the night shaking with chills and fever, but he crossed another eight miles to the middle fork before he descended it to meet Lewis at three forks the next day. There, convinced he understood the lay of the rivers and the westward course they must take, Clark allowed himself to be sick.

They were, as Lewis wrote, at "an essential point in the geography of the western part of the continent." Agreeing none of the three tributaries was dominant enough to be considered the Missouri, the captains named the south fork for Albert Gallatin, secretary of the treasury, the middle for James Madison, secretary of state, and the north, on which they pinned their hopes, for the family friend who had sent them on this quest, President Thomas Jefferson.

Clark spent his thirty-fifth birthday trying to navigate the newly christened Jefferson River, which did eventually lead them to the Shoshoni, horses and a guide. On August 17 he watched Sacajawea dance with joy as she recognized the people she had been torn from five years before. After a tearful reunion with her family, she provided the essential link in communication, translating the Shoshonis' words into Hidatsa phrases which Charbonneau turned into French and another trapper to English.

But even the knowledge of the Shoshoni could not give them an easy route to the Pacific. As they left the Jefferson and struggled on through the chaos of the Bitterroot Mountains and over the Continental Divide, they also left behind forever the age-old dream of a practical water crossing of the continent. They knew now that the rocky backbone of North America would not be conquered with "an easy, half-day portage."

Clark spent his thirty-fifth year getting to the Pacific and back. Sick, often starving, unspeakably weary, they kept going until they found the Clearwater and could once more ride the water. On down the Snake to the Columbia they plunged with waters on their way to a different sea. On December 3 Clark carved his name and the date in a large pine by the ocean. "By land," he wrote. "U. States

in 1804-05." On January 8 he grinned while Sacajawea exclaimed over her first whale.

Penned in their soggy home, Fort Clatsop, for the winter, they were grateful to leave it in mid-March for the journey home. The two captains parted company temporarily to investigate two routes. While Lewis traveled north to descend the Marias, Clark headed for the Jefferson and Three Forks and then aimed his party overland to strike the Yellowstone. Perhaps this river, which curled northeast to join the Missouri not far above the Mandan villages, would prove a better route than the toilsome Missouri. He built dugout canoes and gave it a try. On July 25 he named a striking rock tower on its bank for Sacajawea's toddler Pompey, and on August 1 the party bided its time on shore while a herd of buffalo crossing the river blocked the way for more than an hour. Two days later he boated Missouri waters once more.

On September 26 the reunited corps was back in St. Louis, where houses seemed too small, beds too soft and the sky hardly there at all. He opened his journal and wrote, "A fine morning. We commenced writing."

The captains' writing and Clark's maps, flawed though they might be, reached through the mists of time and brought the Missouri into the modern world. For 133 years it had been Terra Incognita. It was no more.

That Spaniard Called Manuel

Back in the halls of commerce, Lewis and Clark managed to convince themselves they had mapped a route to the Pacific and the trade of the Orient, after all. However, their divergent return trips had proved the best route would leave the Missouri at the Great Falls and head directly for the Clearwater and thence to the sea. The portage would be 340 miles, it was true, and 200 of those miles would be through precipitous mountains which would be blocked with snow through June. But 340 land miles out of 3,555 didn't seem impossible to men who'd just traveled twice that plus a thousand more. In their judgment, the Missouri did offer a path to the western sea. But it offered so much more.

The Missouri flowed through a land of incredible sights. Awed in spite of themselves, men leaned forward over tavern tables so as not to miss a word spoken by the confident Corps of Discovery troopers. One watched strange ceremonies in a Mandan lodge, craned his neck at sculptured white cliff faces, marveled at the height of the Great Falls -- until he slogged up mountain passes with air so thin he could hardly breathe and found out what height could *really* be.

And the animals were without number -- feisty little rodents who popped from their burrows to bark at intruders, delicate looking deer-like creatures with such speed they left the Newfoundland panting in their wake, bears so monstrous they'd chase you a mile "with their lights full of balls."

And the beaver. My god, the beaver!

It was the mention of this animal which stirred the soul of the 34-year-old Spaniard everyone called Manuel. He was not immune to the lure of exotic sights, and he found Indians fascinating, but he was a trader and it was the thought of the pelts to be had up the Missouri that made his dark eyes gleam with intensity. The more he heard about the country up river the more excited he became. Perhaps this was the direction he should go -- the break he'd been seeking since he'd begun trading forays up from New Orleans a dozen years ago.

He'd been successful, certainly; made himself known since he'd settled in St. Louis in 1799. He had a store and a house and a land grant from the Spanish governor for 6,000 arpents. He'd single-handedly upset the balance of trade for the Chouteaus and other French merchants, agitating for free trade and, when that failed, using his knowledge of what it took to grease the wheels of Spanish politics to steal the Osage trade right out of Auguste's ledger books.

Never a shrinking violet, the attractive Spaniard had spent three days in a dark, damp cell in Leyba's tower (now the local jail) for insulting the governor once too often. He spent practically as much time in the courtroom as he did on the river or among his shelves of merchandise, filing lawsuits as if he were throwing pelts on a pile.

He was a complicated man, an enigma to the citizens of St. Louis. The fragile wife and child he'd brought with him seemed to be more objects of compassion than of love. He'd met Polly Chew at Vincennes on the Wabash. The young widow was slowly recovering from having seen her minister husband killed by Indians and from the struggle to survive captivity with her baby daughter until she was ransomed. Manuel had been so touched by the appearance of the vulnerable pair that he offered to care for them the rest of their lives. Polly had accepted, and her story was a favorite topic of conversation around French tables.

Lisa might not be popular with the French *coterie*, but he had made himself impossible to ignore. Not satisfied with the trade he'd built on the Mississipi, Ohio and Wabash, plus the business he'd captured from the Chouteaus, his aggressive, ambitious mind reached first toward Santa Fe. When that venture failed he turned to the Missouri.

Listening to the talk that swirled through the town after William Clark and Meriwether Lewis returned, he wondered. Could he find enough men willing to risk a trading and trapping venture up the Missouri? How many would he need? What kind of boats were best? Would the Indians let them through? Or would they be delayed and robbed of their goods, as had most of the traders in the past ten years. Could he get enough pelts from the Indians or would his own trappers be better? Would men be willing to stay up river through the winter, as they'd have to to get good pelts? How could he supply them?

He tumbled the questions around in his mind, pumped everyone he could find who'd been up river and gradually determined a plan. When the powers of St. Louis refused to consider his wild scheme, Lisa obtained financing from two partners he'd dealt with earlier in Illinois. Then he recruited Lewis and Clark's resourceful hunter George Drouillard and they put together a crew.

It was not too difficult. Although most of the populace thought such an expedition would be folly, a sufficient number were willing to chance it. Several of Lewis and Clark's men, chafed even by frontier civilization, signed on to hunt, be "fishermen of beaver," stand guard and obey all reasonable orders. Enough of the necessary workhorses, the French boatmen, joined in until there were 50 to 60 men on Lisa's payroll.

The Spaniard, experienced sailor of both ocean and river, had decided on keelboats and he outfitted two. The flat-bottomed vessels looked squat and clumsy even though their plank sides came to points at bow and stern, but they needed only a few inches of Missouri water to float over sand bars and snags. That mattered more than grace. A boxlike cabin amidships would shelter the cargo and perhaps a person or two; a large wooden sweep draped over the stern. The mast, fitted with two sails -- and a long cordelle -- bowed to the reality that the boat would more often be pulled by men that pushed by wind.

By spring 1807 Lisa was ready. On April 19 he bade *adios* to Polly and the son she had borne him, not able to tell her how many months or years it might be before they saw him again. Then he shouted for the boatmen to loose the lines that held them to the sandy flat and dip oars for the mouth of the Missouri.

Lisa's first problems were human. He'd scarcely poked into the mouth of the Missouri when one Jean Baptiste Bouche, an *engage* who'd signed on and received an advance, decided a tavern in the small settlement of St. Charles seemed warmer, safer and possessed of a much more dependable source of cheer. He drank up his advance and then some, falling in debt to the barkeep. The barkeep refused to let him go, which was fine with Bouche; he intended to stay right where he was. Lisa be damned.

When Lisa got the word about Bouche he was on his feet in an instant. Half his crew might disappear if he allowed this man to renege on his agreement. Bouche might not be worth much, but he'd made a bargain and he was going to keep it. Manuel stormed into the tavern, paid the bill (as the barkeep had known he would) and dragged the drunken Bouche back to the keelboat.

Then the Missouri took over.

Unable to make progress against the 4 MPH current of the main channel with their heavy craft, the boaters had to creep up the river's sides. The keelboats could be sailed -- if wind and river were ever on the same course -- with a big, square sail, but they would most often be pulled with a rope from the river's edge, or poled.

Using cleats nailed along each side of the deck for footing, the engages set pole, threw their shoulders against the padded pole end and walked back toward St. Louis. When they reached the stern they ran the 60 feet back to the bow and started over again...And again, and again, pushing through every boat length of progress twice and more; seeing, too often, the same stretch of shore remain stubbornly alongside or -- worse yet -- appear again after having been passed.

The trees the river had watered did their part, too. Broken limbs and trunks hurled along on the current, each one capable of battering a fatal hole. Hundreds of others, ends planted in the muddy bottom and invisible in murky water, stood ready to impale unwary craft. Whole trees with roots still clinging to the bank swept the river like scythes, disappearing under the current at one moment, springing up to take the bottom of your boat the next.

Logs, branches, bushes, vines, even buffalo carcasses, lifted by the rush of spring runoff, rode loose on the river until they met some obstacle. Then they packed in great tangles the men called *embarras*, sometimes blocking the channel, sometimes letting loose to run rampant on the current. A stationary one could cost days of labor to cut through or work around. A moving one could catch and crush them all.

It was enough to break strong men and it did. In mid-May when they reached the mouth of the Osage, 120 miles above St. Louis, Antoine Bissonette disappeared from camp. Lisa might have let him go. An unwilling worker was often more trouble than he was worth, as Bouche was proving. But if one man got away with it, others would be tempted. Lisa called Drouillard and ordered him to find Bissonette and bring him back -- alive, if possible, dead, if necessary.

Dead! There were shocked faces and exclamations across the campfire. Lisa ignored them. The safety of the whole expedition depended on discipline and he had to maintain control. If each man thought he could do as he pleased they were all lost. Later, when the dependable Drouillard brought back his prey, Lisa was not upset to see the deserter was wounded. "That's a rascal who got what he deserved," he said pointedly to the muttering boatmen. He ordered two men to canoe the bleeding man back to medical care in St. Charles and turned his attention back to the river.

He was used to river travel, but this was more than a river. It snarled and snatched and grabbed at you. It toppled trees on your head if it could. If it missed you by day it attacked when you rolled in wet blankets at night, devouring your resting place until you awoke to it tugging on your bedroll -- if you were lucky enough to wake at all under the weight of a collapsing bank.

Always pushing, Lisa paused at the Kansas River just long enough to sign on an experienced half-blood trader, but at the mouth of the Platte he made a true find. A canoe threaded through the sandbars and into view, bearing a figure Drouillard studied intently. He let out a whoop and a holler -- it was John Colter, on his way to St. Louis for the first time since he'd embarked with Lewis and Clark three years before!

On shore, backs were slapped and ribs crushed in bear hugs as the Corps of Discovery veterans caught up on each others' lives. Colter had resigned the Corps at the Mandan villages on the down river trip in 1806 to spend yet another year trapping with two partners in the Rockies. Now, a third year along mountain waters under his belt, he was homebound at last.

Or was he?

Drouillard and Potts and Wiser and Robinson urged him to turn back with them. Good company, exciting times, a chance to get rich -- what more could a man want? Lisa, realizing Colter knew the upper Missouri like no other man, offered him a generous contract. It was more than he could, or wanted, to resist. Colter turned back up the Missouri.

Lisa put him to work immediately as a hunter, for now they were past the Platte and meat was harder to come by. The hunters had to spend as much time watching for Sioux as tracking game, and the meal and tallow they'd brought for the boatmen were nearly exhausted. By July 12 Lisa was forced to cut their daily meat ration to four ounces per day -- a dangerously small amount for men battling the Missouri. When the reluctant *engage* Bouche stole part of this precious

horde Lisa was furious. But there was little he could do short of shooting the man and, however tempting that prospect, he was loathe to take quite so drastic a step.

Bigger danger lay ahead. As they pulled alongside the Arikara villages above the mouth of the Grand River (in South Dakota), working near the bank as usual, the volatile Ree were massed at the water's edge, 200 to 300 strong. Screaming a challenge, the Indians fired on the keelboats and ordered Lisa to shore.

There seemed little choice. The nervous boatmen nosed their craft into the bank and faced the crowd of painted warriors with a history of river piracy.

These cousins of the Pawnee led a sedentary, agricultural life which they enriched by trading with many tribes. Although reduced from their former strength by smallpox and harried by the Sioux, they could still be formidable. Sensing that the Indians might repect courage, Manuel complied only so far. He landed, but in a loud voice and with unmistakable signs he forbid the Ree to set foot on his boats.

Irritated, but hesitant to challenge him, the braves milled around. When women began to weave through the crowd with sacks of grain for trade, an angry brave ran from one to the next and slashed the grain sacks with his knife. As Lisa saw the harvest spill on the ground he knew the tense stand-off could last no longer.

Shouting rapid orders, he called the men to arms and swung the swivel guns to aim point blank at the crowd. That was enough for the Ree. They fell over one another looking for cover. After some confusion, the chiefs came forward bearing pipes for a smoke and peaceful talk. Lisa did not press his advantage. He talked with them and broke open bales of merchandise to give them gifts. He needed friends on the river, not enemies, and he had a sure instinct about the way to make them.

Then it was on to the Mandan, the friendly hosts of the Corps of Discovery. Did they still have good hearts toward the white men? Lisa had to be sure and he decided on a noteworthy way of finding out. He ordered the boats to anchor well out in the river so as to be out of range. Then, alone and afoot, carrying only a few trade goods, he entered the first Mandan village. Working his way among the dirt-covered lodges, the Spaniard asked to parley with the chief.

His show of courage (and the fact the bulk of his goods were well out of reach) impressed the leaders in the first two villages and they had friendly talks. But the chief of the third was not so easily satisfied. Seated near the center of the spacious, high-roofed lodge, with lesser leaders ranged behind him, he pushed Lisa's gifts aside with a disdainful sweep of his hand. He wanted gun powder.

Lisa thought quickly. He dared not comply. They could easily kill him for refusing. But would they, when his death would gain them nothing? Gambling that logic could rule primitive bile, he refused.

In the shaft of light from the smoke hole, Lisa could see the chief's face harden. He again demanded powder. Boldly, Manuel refused again; to show weakness now could be fatal.

The trader and the Mandan sat locked in a contest of wills, but Manuel's proved the stronger. The chief gave in and accepted what was offered. Lisa, both drained and exhilarated, signaled his men to pick him up and proceed up river.

Still, they were not in the clear. A few days later they encountered a veritable sea of Assiniboin waiting for them on the bank. As Lisa assessed their numbers he knew quick, decisive action was essential. He directed the keelboats straight at the crowd and ordered the men to fire their guns in the air. The swivels boomed and smoke enveloped the vessels. As the echoes rebounded from the cliffs, the Assiniboin fell back in terror. Tumbling and tripping in their haste, most ran for the hills.

Only a few chiefs held their ground and Lisa offered them the hand of friendship, sitting down for a smoke and giving them gifts. He was learning. You had to put on a strong face and gain the Indians' respect. Then, if you could furnish them with things they needed and treat them fairly, you could gain the allies you had to have to mine the fur fields of the Missouri.

But just where did the richest mines lie? Lisa huddled with Colter and Drouillard as they worked their way west now into more broken country.

Time was short. Already, here and there, a yellow leaf twirled on the cottonwoods. The Corps had seen more beaver at the Forks than anywhere. But the way was long and lay through Blackfoot country. Captain Lewis and his men had killed two of them in a scrape a year ago. Closer, and surrounded by the more amenable Crow, lay the Yellowstone River. Colter had been there last winter. The Crow knew the white man wanted beaver skins and they knew how to take them. They were willing to trap and trade.

Lisa considered. Obviously, Colter was no faint heart. If he advised caution with the Blackfoot there was good reason. Men couldn't produce as trappers if they were always busy protecting their scalps. And Clark had gone cross-country from the Forks to the Yellowstone. Why couldn't you cross the other way if you decided to? He slapped his hand on a crate; it was decided. The keelboats turned into the mouth of the Yellowstone.

Up that river, on the tree-covered point between it and the mouth of the Bighorn, Lisa set the men to building a fort. He named it Fort Raymond, and thought of the young son back in St. Louis who would have aged a year by the time they were together again.

Except for Bouche, who continued to be a laggard, the men needed no urging to raise the walls of the post. Most days now they had to break ice to get water, and the bite in the wind tasted of Arctic snows.

Lisa no sooner saw a problem than his

mind was seeking a solution. Arriving too late to conduct a fall hunt, he characteristically took what action was possible. Calling in Colter, he asked the man who knew the country best if he thought he could find the Crow and other tribes and invite them in to trade. Colter said he'd give it a try; Lisa watched him shoulder a pack, pick up his rifle and set off up the Bighorn.

While Colter trudged his lonely, icy way through an incredible circle that inscribed the Wind River Mountains, Jackson Hole, the Tetons, Pierre's Hole, and the corner of Wyoming that is now Yellowstone Park, Lisa tried to increase his options. He sent another trapper, mulatto Edward Rose, with an outfit to trade with the Crow for the skins in their own territory. And, adding another turn to the shadow dance with Santa Fe trade that had intrigued men for so many years, he sent Drouillard probing south in hopes he might make a connection. Even if nothing came of these efforts, he was content. The men were finding the tributaries of the Yellowstone and Bighorn choked with beaver and he could almost count his fortune made.

When the breeze warmed at last and the ice began to crack, he prepared to return to St. Louis. Most of the trappers, anticipating successful hunting and happy with Lisa's liberal offer for skins, agreed to stay another year (except Bouche, who had yet to bring in his first skin).

Lisa was packing up his belongings to board the boat when Rose finally returned from the Crow. Expecting several packs of skins, Lisa was astounded to find he'd brought none. The trapper, fond of Indian life and knowing he could gain great stature in their eyes by giving away his possessions, had grandly bestowed Lisa's trade goods on his hosts. He was empty handed.

Lisa exploded. But the fiery-tempered Rose would take no abuse. He threw himself on Lisa with deadly intent and tried to pin him to the floor. Lisa, a strong man but outweighed, was suddenly struggling for his life. Luckily John Potts heard the commotion and came running. He pulled Rose off Lisa and tried to hold him as Lisa made for the boat.

It was just swinging into the current when Rose broke free and ran to the swivel gun mounted in front of the post. Aiming quickly at the keelboat he touched it off with his pipe. The gun boomed and the cannister of shot sailed between the legs of an incredulous trapper to rake the cargo box of the boat. As it happened, everyone on board was out of the line of fire so the shots produced only splinters instead of blood. Rose was wrestled to the ground before he could fire again, able only to scream invectives at his departing bourgeois.

After that send-off, the trip home was anticlimactic. Lisa had time to figure the profit he and his partners would bank. But even more satisfying was the fulfillment of his vision. He had been right to tackle the Missouri. It had been worth all the struggle. This is where the future of the fur trade lay. The establishment in St. Louis would have to deal with Manuel Lisa from now on.

Gauntlet at Three Forks

But when Lisa mounted the streets of St. Louis on his return, he climbed not into the arms of society but into jail. Deserter Antoine Bissonette, punctured by Drouillard's bullet, had not survived to reach St. Charles; Drouillard and Lisa were charged with murder. The two men were held in detention and a trial date was set for September 23, 1808.

With the Honorable J. C. B. Lucas presiding and Lisa's rival, the Honorable Auguste Chouteau, as associate judge, the bourgeois and his right-hand man defended themselves against the charges. Luckily for Lisa, his opponents in business were as anxious to see the two cleared as were Lisa's wife and family. The doctrine of discipline on expeditions up river had to be established without question if fur trapping and trading were to continue. Without furs there would be no St. Louis. It took the jury 15 minutes to return a verdict of not guilty.

Lisa won a further victory when the Chouteau clan swallowed hard and joined him in a multiple partnership to finance an expedition up the Missouri the following spring. Lisa's mind was alive with the possibilities. He could take hundreds of trappers up river to join Colter, Potts and the rest. Working in groups large enough to protect themselves, they would be able to go with impunity wherever the harvest was richest -- into the Blackfoot country, down toward Santa Fe, across the Rockies into the Columbia drainage. Who could stand in their way?

Who, indeed? In a world unswayed by the optimistic dreams of an expectant fur baron, Lisa's pioneer trappers were finding out. John Colter stood naked on the bank of the Jefferson River about five miles above Three Forks, staring at the gory remains of his friend and fellow trapper, John Potts. He and John had covered many miles together. They'd been here before as members of the Corps of Discovery in 1805 and again in 1806. Each time they'd found it a haven, a place of rest between arduous travels, a land of plenty and promise. But this fall day in 1808 the Blackfoot were here and that made all the difference.

Colter, his own body reddened by Potts' bloody entrails -- thrown in his face by the taunting Indians -- stood waiting his fate. Death was certain. Potts had killed an Indian before they'd filled him full of holes. Only *how* he would die was open to question; he knew too much about Indians to welcome any of the alternatives.

Colter had hoped they might only be robbed when the Blackfoot ordered their canoes ashore. Knowing the odds were hopeless, he'd done as he was told, trusting the tribe could not know he was the white man who had fought with the Crow and Flathead against them along the Gallatin that summer. The wound he'd suffered then still pulled occasionally in his leg, but he'd also fired with deadly effect and the Blackfoot were not apt to forget or forgive that long gun. Telling himself they could not know which white face had aimed the rifle, he slipped his traps over the side into the water and stepped ashore with an air of confidence.

But when Potts saw his friend stripped naked, he decided a quick death was a better bargain. He managed to get off one telling shot before he died, his body bristling with arrows. Now Colter was alone. He stood stoically while the dead brave's relatives tried to force their way through the crowd around him, claiming the privilege of the first blow.

He wasn't a large man, but his 5-foot 10-inch frame, glaring white beneath his burnt-brown face, had a lean look of endurance equal to any Indian's. Now in his mid-30s. he had not taken a sick call in two years with the Corps and since then had sustained himself through two mountain winters, breaking

trails no white man before him had even pondered.

Now his ears were filled with the keening of the dead man's squaw and the angry demands of his male relatives. But some of the other braves wanted to prolong the amusement. This man would never beg for his life. Why not dangle a hope in front of him to make it interesting? Why not make it a contest? A contest they could not lose.

Colter felt the restraining hands loose their hold. A chief motioned him toward the prairie. Deciding he was to be used for target practice and having no other choice, he began to walk. But the old chief urged him to go faster, then faster yet.

Glancing at the crowd now a hundred yards behind him, he suddenly understood the game. The braves were stripping for a race. He was the prize. As he leapt into a run, the warriors howled wildly, brandished their spears and charged after him. He pounded ahead of the screaming braves, knowing it was useless but unable not to try, his back muscles tense against the expected lance.

He covered a mile, then two, then three, his naked feet churning over rocks and through prickly pear, his lungs clamped in pain. Sagebrush gashed his legs as he dashed by, but he could see the trees that lined the Madison. Perhaps if he made the river...

On he plunged, the hope carrying him another mile. Then he felt something give in his nose and his chest was warm with gushing blood. He'd always been fast, always beat the neighbor boys in the Virginia countryside where he grew up. But how much more could his body endure?

Did the voices pursuing him seem more distant? He dared a glance behind. Most of the runners had fallen back, but one brave was closing in. Streaming blood, Colter whirled to face him.

Surprised, the panting brave lunged, his blanket flapping from his shoulder, hands lifting his spear for the fatal jab.

At the last instant, Colter stepped aside, deflected the thrust of the spear and grabbed the shaft. It snapped between them as the brave lurched to the ground. Hesitating only a second, Colter plunged the spearhead into the Indian's chest. Then he yanked out the weapon, grabbed up the man's blanket and ran on, the adrenaline of hope giving him new strength.

Into the cottonwoods now, he thrashed through the willows and splashed into the river. Behind him the Blackfoot raised a howl of rage as they discovered their dead companion.

The mountain stream was too shallow to hide him, but there was a jumble of driftwood piled at the point of an island. He dove under the pile, found a place he could get his face above water and hoped he was hidden.

In moments the Blackfoot were at the water's edge, combing the banks and beating the willows. Then they were on his pile, prodding and poking for their prey. Watching them through the cracks, sure at any moment a sharp black eye would meet his, afraid they knew where he was and would set fire to his sanctuary, he lay in the icy current and waited out the day.

Toward evening the sounds of the searchers faded. Knowing someone might be keeping a silent watch, but realizing he could not stay where he was, he worked his numb body out from under the pile. Almost too stiff to move, but leery of leaving the icy water, he worked his way downstream a few miles. Then, shuddering with cold, he turned his face east.

There were nearly 250 miles between him and Lisa's Fort Raymond on the Bighorn. He'd traveled greater distances, but this time he was on foot, without food, with no weapon but a spear point and no cover but an Indian blanket. Yet it never occurred to him not to try.

He followed the spreading valley around the end of the range which separated the Madison and Gallatin rivers (the Madison Range) but he'd have to make his way through the volcanic peaks that hemmed the Gallatin on the east (the Gallatin Range). If he could make his way over them -- a 30-mile trek -- he'd reach the Yellowstone and could begin to breathe easier.

But the Blackfoot would know where he was headed and would be watching the pass. He'd have to find another way. He turned toward a rocky pinnacle a few miles south of the pass and began to climb. Feeling his way up the slope, he hoisted his exhausted body from rock to rock, clutching at fir branches, grasping for fingerholds, conscious always that

a rock clattering down the slope could give him away to any alert ear.

Before long his feet sank into snow and his probing fingers met ice. But he'd climbed through the spring storms of the Bitterroots with the Corps. He'd crossed the Wind River and the Tetons in the dead of winter. He kept going.

By daylight he was at the crest. He crawled under cover and fell into an exhausted sleep, grateful in the cold night air for what little warmth the sodden Indian blanket could provide.

At dusk he began his descent, working his way through the stunted evergreens, into the spires of gray-blue spruce, through the white trunks of the aspen glowing dimly in the moonlight. By dawn he was on the familiar banks of the Yellowstone. He looked longingly at her waters, thinking of the steps they could save his tortured feet -- lacerated, rock bruised and swollen with the festering points of prickly pear. But he had no way to make a canoe or even a bullboat.

The rolling hills he faced stretched to the east in an endless vista of dappled yellow. Steadfastly, he moved through them. It was warmer away from the mountains. In fact at midday the autumn sun was so bright he needed the blanket to protect his skin. But its slanting rays lit the hollows only for a few hours; dusk came early, and chill.

He was not alone. Buffalo herds, antelope families, elk and deer crossed his path. Prairie dogs dove for cover at his approach and rattlesnakes slipped away into the grass, taunting his empty stomach. His hunger was unrelenting, but he had no means for making a quick kill and no strength or energy for anything else.

He used the spearpoint to dig for breadroot and hungrily chewed the starchy roots. He watched for the autumn color of the chokecherry, and knocked what fruit the birds and animals had left into his blanket. He searched the gullies for rose hips, chewed on bark, anything to get a bit of sustenance.

But mostly he put one foot in front of the other, ignoring pain, dismissing fatigue, willing his body to do his bidding. On the eleventh day he saw the stockade of the post.

His fellow trappers could scarcely recognize the gaunt, bearded apparition, but they were not too surprised to find he still had his hair. If any man had mastered the mountain life, it was Colter.

He'd returned the year before after months out on his winter trek with stories they'd found hard to believe; tales of springs boiling out of the ground, crusted yellow earth so hollow your steps echoed, acrid fumes which seemed to rise from Hell. (They'd laughed at that part and poked fun. Who'd ever heard tell of such a place?)

But they were beginning to know this reticent man. He had the air of authority which comes to one who knows he need depend only on himself. They gathered around to examine the spearhead and hear his story.

It was not long before he had another to tell. His strength returned rapidly; the constitution that had served him so well remained undamaged. In the dead of winter, when he thought the Blackfoot were safely in their winter camp, he went back for his traps.

That he would go at all seemed incredible, even to other trappers who knew a man had to have traps to earn his living. He was either a brave man or a fool. Nothing about him seemed the fool, but no one stepped forward to keep him company.

Colter set out alone and began retracing his escape route. He was a few miles west of the pass, in camp on the Gallatin, when it happened.

As he bent over his evening fire to tend his buffalo steak he heard brush crack behind him. Then the click of guns cocking. Instantly he leapt over the fire to the cover of dark-

ness. Even as he leapt, bullets scattered his fire and coals arched through the air. Again he was running for his life from an enemy who was faceless but whom he knew without question.

This time, at least, he was better equipped, but he wondered as he made his way up the rocky mountain side and across the frigid plain, if his scalp was meant to decorate a Blackfoot lodge. Bargaining with the Lord, he vowed he'd never tempt fate by returning to Three Forks country if he got out a second time with his life. Once again the gates of the fort opened to admit the gaunt but determined form of John Colter.

The Blackfoot message was, however, unmistakable and Lisa's men decided not to challenge them further. The rest of that winter they stayed east of the Absaroka Range, trapping the Bighorn and Colter's Stinking Water. Men who had jeered and joked stood in quiet amazement (along the Shoshone River north of present Cody, Wyoming), breathed the moist warm sulphur fumes, watched the steaming water bubble and spout and admitted that Colter's Hell was not just a trapper's yarn.

But Colter could not keep his promise. By September 1809, Lisa and his new partners had fielded a large force and moved it up to Fort Raymond. They'd decided to beard the lion in his den; they'd build a post at Three Forks and trap its wealth in spite of the Blackfoot. Thirty-two men, some veterans of the field like George Drouillard, some greenhorn Americans, prepared to head west the next March. The partners asked Colter to guide them.

He agreed and one bright March day the brigade moved out along a snowbound Yellowstone. Perhaps Colter thought Lisa was right and they'd finally be able to thumb their noses at his old foes. Perhaps he wanted a chance to avenge Potts' death and his own weeks of torment. Perhaps he just needed the pay the job would bring. Or perhaps, like the Rockies, the Blackfoot were there and he could not resist the challenge.

By the end of the first day one man was snow-blind, begging his partner to shoot him to end the agony of his throbbing eyeballs. Before the end of the second day they stood gazing at the mutilated corpses of a Snake woman and her young son, lying in the ruins of their lodge, their heads split open by tomahawks. Colter recognized the handiwork of the Gros Ventre of the Prairie, one of the most feared northern tribes. The unfortunate Snake were friends of the trappers. Obviously they'd picked the wrong allies.

They moved on across the miles Colter knew so well and climbed into the pass (Bozeman Pass). One morning they awoke to darkness and a sense of suffocation. Snow pressed their tents onto their faces. Breaking out, they saw the horses had been buried up to their necks by the storm. Pressing on into the mountains, they discovered even the strongest horses floundered in the bottomless drifts. Men took the role of beasts to pack a trail. But if a horse stepped off the trail it was swallowed by the snow and had to be dug out. They made four miles that day.

Then the sun returned, and they were sorry, blazing and flashing as it did off every surface. The men squinted into glare almost like a physical blow. Gradually they realized their view was blurring, as if someone were drawing a silk veil over their eyes. With hot tears trickling from swollen lids and the light disappearing, they were forced to camp.

With sight went their ability to hunt. Colter, wrapped in frustration at his impotence and feeling vulnerable as never before, helped the men kill a horse for food. Later three dogs went into the camp pot. A day and a night passed and still they could not see.

Huddled miserably in camp one noon they heard a party of horsemen approach. Were they Colter's nemeses? Would they only be robbed or would they be slaughtered like the Snake? Hands reached for knives and pistols, determined to put up all the fight they could.

Listening with fierce concentration, they followed the horsemen's approach with sightless eyes. The horses stopped. But no battle cries broke the silence. Then the soft plop of hooves on snow faded into the distance. One trapper, able to see better than the rest, counted 30 forms moving across his view. They were not Blackfoot, but Snake. Colter had been granted yet another deliverance.

If he were tempted to abandon his mission, he did not. He guided the men on through the bony battlefield where he'd fought on the side of the Crow. Skulls and femurs, rib cages and finger bones glinted whitely from the grass. He had the satisfaction of knowing at least some of them were Blackfoot.

Coming up on Three Forks his memories were not so pleasant. But the men pestered him to tell the tale again and he did, pointing out his route of escape, showing the green young Americans the peak he'd twice conquered to save his life.

They were incredulous. How could a man have scaled that height, survived such dangers, yet return to court them again? Could one grow to face such challenges? The size of the Rockies seemed overwhelming, the weather impossible, the Blackfoot implacably vicious. What would happen to them? Fear flitted from tree to tree along the trail and chilled their bedrolls at night.

Colter honed his alert watch to a fine edge. Hoofprints, droppings, a stray dog, a herd of buffalo set to running, a plume of smoke on the horizon -- many signs could mean Indians, including the feeling in his gut.

Finally at the forks on April 3, 1810, the men were put to work cutting logs for a small stockade to sit between the mouths of the Madison and the Jefferson rivers. The thought of shelter raised their spirits and the beaver sign all around put them in an even more cheerful mood. There should be plenty of skins for everyone. Within a week, Colter was leading a party of 18 men 40 miles up the Jefferson to find their fortune.

Most of them were out tending traps when the Gros Ventre found their camp. An unlucky three were scraping skins, and they soon became trophies themselves. Colter and the others, returning to find the bodies of their companions, hurried back to the stockade to give warning.

After all the parties had gathered, Lisa's partner led the brigade on an expedition to recover the bodies of the dead and pursue the Gros Ventre. They found and buried two, but three others had disappeared, carried away by the Indians to a fate no one wanted to think about. The men took out their frustrations on an Indian the trapper had killed, carving him to match the white bodies.

Chasing the Indians proved futile. They recovered some traps and three horses but finally returned to the confines of the stockade, hoping the Indians could be lured into an attack where the trappers had the advantage. On the return trip to the tiny shelter, John Colter came to the decision he had threatened so many times. He would leave the mountains, forego the trapping life and return to civilization, where a man at least had a chance of dying in his bed instead of being hacked to death in some mountain meadow.

Though he knew a large group would be returning to St. Louis later that summer, he chose to leave the mountains in characteristic fashion -- alone. Then a young adventurer from Philadelphia and another trapper decided to take advantage of the chance to leave. The three men set out on April 22 to run the Blackfoot gauntlet.

This time he got over the mountains before they found him, and this time there was cover available. His gun and those of the other two men spoke from a thicket the Blackfoot could not penetrate without great cost -- a cost they were not willing to pay, even for Colter's hair.

After dark the trappers wriggled out of the thicket and stole away. But it was hardly a victory to celebrate. Forced to travel again through the darkness like an animal, hiding during the days, never able to relax or breathe free, Colter spent his last hours in the mountains fleeing the Blackfoot. Stopping at Fort Raymond only long enough to hollow out a canoe, he and his companions were in St. Louis in just a month.

He had been away for six years. He'd forgotten the feel of store-bought clothes, forgotten a man didn't always smell like a beaver, couldn't imagine why he used to crave bread and salt.

He was ready to give up the mountains. It was time. But he couldn't survive in the stone-walled lanes of St. Louis. He tried to collect the meager returns of his trapping years, sold the 320 acres Congress had granted each Corps of Discovery member and moved some 60 miles up the Missouri to find a place where he could trap and farm. Near Sullens Springs on Big Boeuf Creek (present Dundee), he settled in to fight stumps instead of Blackfoot and get acquainted with the lowland beaver.

But Colter and his new wife, Sally, had only a few seasons to clear land, plant crops and worry about where the next dollar would come from. In late summer of 1813, Colter realized something more than August heat was sapping his strength. By November the body which had endured every privation and test the Missouri could devise succumbed to jaundice.

He left one glass tumbler, one pot, one Dutch oven, three pewter basins, five pewter plates, a coffee pot, a spinning wheel, four chairs, two feather beds, five head of livestock, three books and a son who would know, when he was old enough, that his father was the first man who came close to matching the mountains.

Don Quixote and Friend

The compatriots Colter had left at the forks of the Missouri in 1810 tried to get on with their work, but the Blackfoot would have none of it. Before long three more men -- one of them the indestructible George Drouillard -- were dead. The main party gave up and retreated east, abandoning both Three Forks and Fort Raymond, bringing home a pathetically small harvest.

The post Lisa and his partners had built for the Sioux at Cedar Island had burned, reducing a year's catch to stinking rubble. Profits were hardly worth totalling. Worse yet, Lisa learned, a rival group of trappers for John Jacob Astor's Pacific Fur Company under Wilson Price Hunt had already headed up river. He was supposed to be aiming for the Pacific coast, but he could take the cream of the Missouri trade or incite the river tribes against later parties -- who knew in this cutthroat business?

But Andrew Henry and a handful of men had left Three Forks and crossed the Rockies to try their luck south of the divide. What had happened to them no one knew. Henry could not be abandoned. He had to have lead and powder to survive. Lisa reminded William Clark and another partner who had been up river of the trappers' desperate need. The three of them scraped together enough money for 21 voyageurs, one keelboat and a small outfit.

But two dozen men and one boat were not enough to provide safety from the Indians. If Lisa couldn't join Hunt's four-boat flotilla before they reached Sioux country, Henry's would not be the only party in peril.

The 25-year-old lawyer who stood in wonder at the base of a gigantic cottonwood in the Missouri bottom land on April 5, 1811 knew of Lisa's problems and was sympathetic; Lisa was one of the most bold and enterprising men he'd ever met. But Henry Marie Brackenridge was really just along for the ride. With a father who was a noted jurist and author back in Pennsylvania, Brackenridge fortunately was not driven to earn his daily bread. He'd attempted to practice law in two other cities before trying St. Louis. Even there, he'd been as interested in learning Spanish and writing newspaper articles about the countryside as he'd been in drawing up legal briefs.

But the countryside he was now moving into would be entirely different and he was intensely excited. The other passengers emphasized just how different. Charbonneau, the half-breed interpreter who'd helped and hindered Lewis and Clark on their journey was on the voyage. So was Sacajawea, whom Brackenridge found "a good creature, of a mild and gentle disposition." He could see she loved the whites and tried to imitate their dress and manners. The couple had been in St. Louis to spend time with their red-headed patron. Clark had offered to establish Charbonneau in business and raise young Pomp as his own son. But Sacajawea had fallen ill in St. Louis and now she and her husband were returning to the upper Missouri.

In two days on the river the frail-looking Brackenridge had been continually drenched by the spring storms. He'd felt the power of the river when the Missouri used an overhanging limb to amputate the keelboat's mast.

Now, forced to shore by the gale about 30 miles above St. Charles, he struck out eagerly to examine the country and measure the looming cottonwood. Its circumference was 36 feet. Its massive trunk of deeply fissured gray bark like those of its neighbors soared 80 to 90 feet overhead before diminishing or extending limbs.

He poked into the cave in Tavern Rocks nearby and noted the Indians had scratched crude figures of birds and beasts into the surface. He realized they held the site in some veneration; it was understandable.

Past a settlement founded, Lisa told him, by the legendary Daniel Boone, he spoke to a pioneer who'd pushed even farther. The man had brought his wife and six children to live in a new-wood log house and was clearing land. He had nothing he could spare to sell or trade. Lisa said trapper and explorer John Colter lived on a farm nearby.

Brackenridge began the trip disdainful of the drunken cavorting of the French boatmen. But watching them struggle with grappling hooks to pull the 20-ton vessel around an embarras, he was moved to admiration. Failing that effort, they leapt without a word into the icy current, took up the cordelle and pulled themselves and the dead weight by grasping at shrubs in the bank.

He was no stranger to river travel. His father, who had introduced him to daily lessons at two, had sent him down the Mississippi to learn French when he was only seven. But this river was different. No American, he thought, would endure such labors, despite Lisa's feeding these men prime rations to ensure their best efforts.

Lisa was a driven man and he drove the engages in turn. But he did not ask them to do anything he would not. His shoulder was against the pole one moment, his arm swinging the grappling hook the next, his voice always in their ears, extorting, encouraging. They all worked from dawn till after dark.

It was the trader's third trip up river and he was beginning to know it as well as any man could. He regularly picked the right channel and he was skilled at using every breath of favorable wind. On Tuesday, April 9, they sailed grandly past the mouth of the Gasconade River, and on the eleventh Brackenridge learned they'd gained two days on Hunt. He was disappointed. He didn't yet realize how slim their chances of gaining any at all.

But he did appreciate the beauty of the country they were encountering. He found his first glimpse of prairie near the Osage River a delight, "handsomely mixed" with woodlands of oak, hickory and ash. He could even admire the sandbars the reduced current revealed, stretching "clean and smooth" beside them for miles at a time, and the deer which "sported" on them.

One animal hadn't been so lucky. A tree draped with buzzards and cawing crows attracted their attention to an ox mired up to his back in sand. He'd been there for days, from the looks of his lacerated hide, a target for wolves, eagles and other opportunists. Even Lisa, pressed as he was, could not pass him by. He allowed the men time to dig out the bawling creature and when a fine breeze carried them along the next day, they considered themselves rewarded for their charity.

But heaven helps those who help themselves, and Lisa had them up again before daylight to take advantage of a violent wind. They saluted settlers, dressed in their Sunday best, who waved from the year-old settlement on the Mine River. At the response to Lisa's anxious questions they estimated they'd gained another two days on their quarry. Could men work hard enough, last long enough, to wrest another 15 days from this river? It seemed impossible. Yet, if they failed...

Part yet not a part of the elemental struggle, Brackenridge could see the river as something more than an enemy. Everywhere along the route he was struck with the area's richness and natural beauty. As the trees and shrubs responded to the warming days with delicate new greenery, he pictured settlements in their midst. He could imagine the fields now verdant with native grasses someday nodding with heavy-headed grain. Occasionally he took his gun and fought his way through shoreline rushes to ramble along the high ground, scaring up great flocks of pelicans, shooting ducks, geese and brant, or plucking their eggs off sandbars.

Passing the mouth of the Grand, Brackenridge remarked that it was a delightful site for a village, apparently unaware that the Missouri Indians had thought the same until finally driven out by enemies a dozen years before. They, and Fort Orleans above, were now only remnants of a former time.

On Sunday, April 21 they discovered a Pacific Fur Company camp they judged to be not more than 12 days old -- Hunt was less than two weeks ahead! But on Tuesday they labored for hours and found themselves only two miles above their fires of Monday. On Wednesday they had to try five times and put every back including Brackenridge's into oars, poles and the cordelle before they could conquer a rapid.

"This extraordinary river," Brackenridge wrote in his journal, "sometimes pursues a straight course for 10 or 15 miles, then suddenly turns to every point of the compass: In other places the whole volume of its waters is compressed into a channel of two or three hundred yards: again suddenly opening to the width of one, or even two miles, with islands and sand bars scattered through the space."

Sometimes gales made it futile to fight both wind and water and they were forced to lay by. Lisa paced in frustration, but Brackenridge discovered he could be distracted and entertained by the story of a fictional compatriot who also was driven to challenge the odds, Don Quixote. Lisa, "passionately fond" of the story, liked to hear Brackenridge read aloud so they could share favorite passages. The young lawyer got a chance to polish his Spanish pronunciation, the wind worried the shingles on the flimsy cabin, and time ticked away.

Still on April 25 they sighted the triangular Fort Osage (at present Sibley, Missouri) on a bluff which protruded into the river a few miles ahead. The substantial rock and log post had been built by Indian Agent William Clark three years before to provide a trading site for the Indians. The lawyer climbed the steep bluff to find surprisingly roomy two- and three-story quarters for the factor and the small force of troops. But the rooms were dark when the doors were closed, only the narrow gun slits admitting light.

About 60 small, rush-covered lodges of the Little Osage grouped nearby and Brackenridge had his first look at Indians in the West. The men were large and robust, many six feet or more in height, with broad shoulders and wide faces. But, as they trailed the boat along the bank, Brackenridge found them dirty and greasy-looking and deplored their "dirty, old buffalo robes." Perhaps the romantic savages were more romantic from a distance. While the fierce Osage were usually friendly with whites, thanks primarily to the Chouteaus, their good will required constant cultivation.

Brackenridge wakened with a start before dawn the next morning, his skin crawling. "Hideous howlings" filled the still-dark cabin where he and Lisa slept. But they came from outside, he realized with relief, from the Osage village. There, he was told, anyone who had suffered a loss -- be the loss child, parent, horse, dog -- began the day with vocal lamentations nearly capable of raising their dear departed. Brackenridge thought the chorus, swelled by the voices of a thousand dogs, well-suited to the devils he was told the tribe worshiped.

Perhaps it was the depressing start to the day, but that night, nine miles past this farthest outpost, he found himself dwelling on where he was and why. The man who was propelling them into the dusk had reason. So had the others. But why was he risking his life on this river in such a voyage?

Was just wanting, needing to see what he had never seen before good reason? His conscience told him it was not. He should be using his time to better effect. Sighing, he allowed himself for the first time to admit he might never see his country or his friends again. His bones might find their final resting place in "some dreary spot far from my home and the haunts of civilized man." And yet, not so far. He took comfort in his belief that wherever he might lie buried he would someday be surrounded by homes of Americans. And he fantasized that his grave would be marked and respected as the resting place of one of those who came first into this wilderness.

Lisa, noticing the gloomy mood, started a song and soon the splash of the oars kept time with the melody as the men stroked into the darkness.

The next morning, April 27, traders rafting down river gave them electrifying news. Hunt was only five days ahead. With shouts and songs of celebration, the men forgot their qualms and poured renewed energy into their efforts. For a few days the wind joined them in their battle with the current. Even the river cooperated by providing long, straight reaches they could sail. They gobbled 27, 30 miles a day as they left the woods behind and began to wind through the open prairie.

Perhaps because they now could find the energy to do so, the engages began to complain. Cold, wet, gathered around the smoky campfire -- never long enough to dry their sodden clothes -- the Canadians voiced bitter thoughts. There was scarcely time to eat or sleep; never time to enjoy a pipe. They had never been worked so long or so hard. They

could not bear this inhuman pace. Lisa would drive them to their deaths.

Brackenridge, warming his stiff hands over the flames, listened. Less and less the outsider, he had begun to think of the boatmen as "our men" and to take Lisa's goals as his own. He spoke up for the Spanish bourgeois and tried to cheer the men, assuring them the worst was past, the weather would warm, they had a leader who could carry them through. He could not say his speech was a major factor, but the next morning, May 5, they trooped aboard for another day's work.

Their complaints were not empty however. One man came down with pleurisy and several were running fevers. Coughs echoed through the camp at night. They moved from the *L'isle a'beau soleil* to the *L'oeil effroi* but they were wearing out.

May 11 brought a landmark with another French name. They had reached the Platte River. While it's mouth was virtually hidden in a maze of sandbars, it was as if they were crossing the equator. The Platte was the dividing line. Now they would pole the Upper Missouri, where grass would be shorter, vistas wider and the Indians uncowed. While Lisa allowed the men the ritual liquor rations and hijinks, Brackenridge climbed to a bluff to look north.

He would find no towering cottonwoods here. It was, indeed, a new country. Still the beauty moved him. One unusually quiet afternoon the keelboat floated under a "sky cloudless, the river as smooth as a mirror. Words cannot convey what I feel," the young lawyer wrote in his diary. "It is only the lover of nature who could understand me."

On May 24 he saw his first buffalo. While he had seen (and smelled) many dead ones in the river, he found the huge bull suddenly eyeing them from a bluff top "a striking and terrific object," a fitting introduction to the species. For a long moment his eyes followed the beast as it galloped away.

He thought the buffalo's habitat equally impressive. "The beauty of the scenery, this evening, exceeds any thing I ever beheld. The sky as clear as in a Chinese painting, the country delightful." While he found the silence of the vast plains melancholy, he wrote, "One never feels his understanding so vigorous or thinks so clearly. Were it safe, with what delight would I roam over these lovely meads!"

But it was not safe. They knew now that the Sioux and all the river tribes but the Mandan were openly hostile. Several trappers were dead at their hands. Hunt and the protection his numbers would offer was still four days ahead. With his crew near panic, Lisa knew it was time to swallow his pride. He sent Charbonneau with a letter begging Hunt to wait while his party made a final push to join forces. Word came back to the anxious men on May 26. Hunt would wait at the Ponca village.

The men breathed a sigh of relief, but Lisa did not. He confided his fears to Brackenridge. Now Hunt knew how close they were. He had nothing to gain by waiting. Instead he might buy passage from the Sioux by promising them they could have the goods Lisa carried. Lisa ordered the boatmen to push on both day and night, risking everything on treacherous black waters lit only by the moon and his knowledge of the river.

The Missouri reached for both the men in the wild dash that followed. Lisa lost his balance while swinging the grappling hook and fell into the current. For several perilous moments the boat drifted downstream while the men tried frantically to fish him out. Brackenridge, no longer the idle greenhorn, shoved a moment too long on his pole and went over the stern. Strangling on the muddy water, he felt himself being pulled under. Then the solid heft of the sweep met his hand. He grabbed on and pulled himself up, reaching gratefully for the hands that hoisted him back on deck. Dripping, breathless, he stared at the river that had almost become the grave he'd envisioned.

They reached the Ponca village but Lisa's instincts had been right. Hunt, amazed they could be so close, had hurried on the minute he received Lisa's letter.

At dawn on June 1, the meeting they had been dreading happened. A dozen Sioux warriors fired on them from the river side and ordered them ashore. Supposing a larger party lay hidden from view and expecting the worst, Lisa distributed guns to the rowers and prepared to go ashore. But he did not go alone; Brackenridge offered to accompany him. Lisa gave him an appraising glance and

quickly assented. Each checked his knife, put a pair of pistols in his belt, picked up his rifle and leapt ashore.

There, without even an interpreter, Lisa used his skill to negotiate with the small band. Pleading poverty and offering them generous presents, he promised to return and build them a trading post on his way down river.

Tensely Brackenridge watched the faces of the strong, breech-clouted braves, admiring their appearance in spite of his fear. While some of the Indians obviously wanted to take what they had in their hands, others were willing to trust the white man's words. They would wait. Lisa was free to go up river.

Hurriedly the crew set sail again and on Sunday morning, June 2, Brackenridge set out on shore. He climbed a bluff and looked ahead. Then he was running wildly back to camp shouting at the top of his lungs. Hunt's boats were only a mile or so up river.

The last mile of the 1,200 they'd pulled was pure pleasure. They'd done the impossible -- defeated both the river and the calendar -- 1,200 miles in 61 days. No one had (or ever would) equal their accomplishment. Brackenridge's triumphant shouts, swollen twenty-fold, bombarded Hunt's open-mouthed crews as they swept up to his camp.

There Brackenridge was greeted warmly by his friend, botanist John Bradbury, who had traveled up river with Hunt to pursue his studies in the company of another British scientist, countryman Thomas Nuttall.

The meeting between Lisa and the thin-faced, beak-nosed Hunt was more strained. Each believed the other had done him harm and intended more. Lisa had crossed one of Hunt's lieutenants, Robert McClellan, in earlier years and the antagonism between them remained strong. The flotilla continued north as a group, but only the threat of Indian attack kept them from each other's throats.

Three days later Brackenridge returned from a jaunt among the prairie dogs to find a furious Lisa tucking his knife into his belt. He had had words with Hunt's interpreter, Pierre Dorion. Words had led to blows and a challenge. Things would be settled now, for good, in Hunt's camp.

Brackenridge was horrified, but Lisa paid no attention to his protests. Hoping there might be some way to prevent bloodshed, the lawyer trailed in Lisa's wake over to Hunt's camp. When he saw Dorion wave a pistol in each hand he placed himself between the antagonists and appealed to Hunt to control his man. Hunt kept McClellan from joining the fracas but refused to do more.

Brackenridge found himself jockeying to stay between the combatants; the other men cleared the field. Invectives flew as the rival parties threw charges at each other. Then Hunt entered the war of words and the bourgeois were toe to toe. There was only one way to settle this. Lisa spun on his heel and headed for his boat and pistols.

Brackenridge and Bradbury couldn't believe what they were seeing. Would these men allow their anger to put all their lives in peril? Weren't there enough dangers already? They hurried after Lisa and cornered him in his cramped cabin. There, with barely room to stand, Brackenridge put all his training in persuasion to an essential use. Bradbury added his weight to the argument and Lisa began to cool down. Then the peacemakers worked on Hunt and reason began to take hold.

Assisted by the width of river water which the bourgeois placed between their parties, the tenuous peace held for the next week. But now they were near the Arikara villages and common sense told them they must present a united front. Brackenridge and Bradbury ran messages from one camp to the other, assuring Hunt that Lisa would not take advantage of his influence with the Arikara to damage the Pacific Fur Company's cause.

Finally, seated together on woven mats in the dim Arikara lodge, the white men shared the peace pipe. Lisa mollified Hunt's fears by warning the Indians that any damage done to Hunt's men would be considered damage to himself. He asked the Arikaras' cooperation in securing horses so the rival trader could head west for the Pacific coast.

Released from diplomatic duty, Brackenridge was free to wander the villages and the countryside, lost in the fascination of this different world. Though rain had reduced the settlement of 150 lodges to a quagmire and the smells sometimes drove him to the fresh air of the plains, he admitted that the ancient cities of his ancestors were probably not much different.

To his consternation the children ran from him in terror, but he was welcomed into several lodges and fed buffalo meat and corn prepared with beans and buffalo marrow. He found the people clean and attractive and puzzled over a culture which could both celebrate virginity and offer its wives and daughters to the highest bidder. He observed with an unprejudiced eye that the Indians had the same rich and poor, envious and proud, overbearing and mean-spirited people white society had, as well as many with more noble attributes.

He discovered the village was a busy place. Women spent their days in the fields or were continually at work dressing buffalo hides stretched on frames beside the lodges. Men played games with hoops and sticks when they weren't hunting or practicing their horsemanship. Couriers arrived from other tribes coming to trade, war parties departed or returned home to celebration and mourning.

"We see here an independent nation, with all the interests and anxieties of the largest; how little would its history differ from that of one of the Grecian states!" Brackenridge wrote in his journal.

He accompanied Lisa to his fort above the Mandan villages. There Lisa decided to send two small boats back to St. Louis with the year's catch. They would be manned by 12 men and captained by Brackenridge. The tenderfoot had earned his badge.

Toward the end of July the boats pushed

into a current high enough to carry them 12 M.P.H. To the dismay of passenger Bradbury, who had planned to add to his 17 trunks of specimens on the homeward journey, Brackenridge followed Lisa's orders to go day and night when possible to get the valuable furs to market. Shooting past landmarks they'd labored days to surmount on the journey up, they made St. Louis in 14 days.

As one scene replaced another on the river bank, so must the scenes have rolled through Brackenridge's mind. He remembered a giant Mandan chief with one eye which seemed to flash fire. A mere boy who skewered his sides with cords and pulled two buffalo heads for a quarter mile. A young warrior, fatally wounded by the Sioux, holding himself on his horse for the song and ceremony of the welcoming procession. And the tender grief of the mother who ran to meet him. He'd heard the reverberating bellows of the rutting buffalo, walked for miles through plains black with

their droppings, and been moved beyond expectation or reason by the rolling thunder of a stampeding herd. He'd ridden the Missouri and survived; the taste and smell of its waters would never leave him.

Aware of pending publication of material on the Missouri by Lewis and Clark and his friend Bradbury, and perhaps intimidated by their expertise, Brackenridge did not enlarge on his "hasty notes" as much as he'd first intended. However in 1814 he did publish a volume titled *Views of Louisiana* and appended the less scientific but more human journal of his epic 1811 voyage with Lisa.

Reconciled to legal life, he continued to travel and write of his experiences, authoring a book on South America and drawing up the policy which later became the Monroe Doctrine. He distinguished himself as a jurist, a member of government commissions and a congressman before a very civilized grave in Pittsburgh finally claimed him at age 85.

ASA BATTLES

As Little Harm as I Can Help

After Brackenridge went down river in 1811, Lisa met Henry, with what was left of his brigade after further persecutions by the Indians and the climate. It was still a losing battle. Lisa noticed even the Missouri tribes seemed more and more hostile.

He returned home to find his first-born son, five-year-old Raymond for whom he'd named his post on the Bighorn, had died in July. He buried his personal grief in preparing yet another expedition for the struggling, changing partnership.

But as St. Louis approached its fiftieth anniversary, it was again threatened by the forces which had tried to destroy it in 1780. Britain and America were at cross-purposes on the high seas. There was talk of war. Frontier residents knew only too well how the British could enlist the Indians in their cause.

In the summer of 1812, as British-led forces took northern forts, worried leaders in Chouteau's Town made plans to rebuild the old wall and reorganize the militia. Lisa was appointed to captain a company in the fall of 1813.

In 1814 William Clark appointed him subagent to the Missouri tribes and gave him a special mission. He was to convince the tribes to join the American cause rather than the British. With a miserly supply of trade goods, Lisa traveled up to see what he could do. He wintered at a post he'd established at the Omaha village.

Blackbird had been in his grave for six years; he'd been no more immune than the rest of the tribe when the white man's small pox had come to call. Before he died he'd made sure his bluff top grave would dominate the view, but his people, reduced to a third of their former strength, could no longer dominate the river trade.

Perhaps Lisa's wife Polly, back in St. Louis, might have found his devotion to duty extreme, but the trader warmed the Omaha hearts to the American cause by taking Mitain, comely daughter of a chief, as his wife.

In April 1815 he went alone to meet with the restless Yankton and Teton Sioux. They had ties to the British on the Upper Mississippi and Lisa knew better than most the carnage that would result if the Missouri tribes moved against the fragile defenses of the frontier settlements. Facing the wavering tribes, he tested his worth as a diplomat.

Drawing on his years of experience, offering both the carrot and the stick, he urged the Sioux to ignore the fiery speeches of the Santee Tecumseh to join the British. When the speech making was done, the Sioux danced the war dance for their new American ally.

Lisa took nearly five dozen Sioux and Omaha chiefs back to St. Louis to meet General Clark, now governor of the new Territory of Missouri, and hold a treaty council. There he learned that the major combatants had declared peace during the winter and the War of 1812 was supposed to be over.

But Missouri residents had discovered a peace treaty negotiated in a faraway place could cost lives rather than save them. While it tied the hands of the army and militia, it left the Indians free.

The Mississippi tribes, the Sac and Fox, were still loyal to the English king and not yet inclined to peace. Since March they'd rampaged through the frontier in his name. Farmers in their fields, hunters, boys tending livestock were easy prey.

The settlers built forts in each hamlet for sanctuary, but they couldn't stay in them. There were crops and chickens and livestock to tend. One fell on the White River, another at Woods Fort, two at Ewing's Mill. Four died at Cote san Dessein, four more at Loutre Island.

On the Missouri frontier there was no peace.

The old man had seen enough of violent death.

Enough. Enough.

He bent his rheumatic knees beside the battered body of the first child, whose blood and brains oozed into the dirt of the cabin floor. A glance told him there was nothing he could do.

He moved to another small body nearby. There was life, yet, but that was about all. The Fox tomahawks had done a thorough job. Fox or Shawnee or Cherokee, it didn't make a lot of difference. They could all deal death.

He moved on to a third child and was gratified to feel a stronger pulse. Perhaps this one could make it. His hands moved automatically to dress the wounds, but his mind was in a different place.

His first-born, James, had been 16 when he and Rebecca had wrapped the pitiful remains of his body in one of her precious linen sheets and buried him at Wallen Ridge. He had given his life for the rich Kentucky soil his father led them toward, but he had not yet stepped on it when the Shawnee butchered him and his young friend as they guarded their families' livestock on the trail. The Shawnee had not made his death an easy one. Boone had not been near enough to hear the screams, but he had heard them often enough afterward in his dreams.

Even a year later, when he returned to tend the wilderness grave near the Cumberland Gap in 1774, he struggled with an overwhelming melancholy. For the first time in his life he really hadn't cared whether he lived or died.

James hadn't been the first, of course. The Shawnee had gotten John Stewart, his sister Hannah's husband and his true brother in spirit, in 1770 on their first long hunt through the gap into Kentucky. The chain that stretched from John was a long and painful one.

Daniel rose stiffly from the floor and turned to Ramsey, the head of the household, who lay bleeding on the bed, a bullet in his groin. When the Fox charged the cabin, sitting on the far outskirts of Boone's Femme Osage settlement some 60 miles above the mouth of the Missouri that May morning in 1815, Ramsey had managed to grab an old trumpet and blow an alarm that cut short the attack. Afraid Ramsey's signal would bring the other settlers, the Fox had paused only to tomahawk the children, then fled.

Alerted by a boy who was hunting nearby, Boone and the other men from the surrounding farms had immediately ridden to help. Where once he would have been the first on the Indians' trail, white-haired Daniel Boone now watched the younger men ride off on the chase, his deep-set blue eyes staring beyond their retreating backs into the woods.

He could do more good here, but he was uneasy about his own family. You never knew where the Indians might strike next. His children and grandchildren knew how to handle themselves, but everybody was vulnerable. He'd had plenty of evidence of that over the years.

Working deliberately, without any show of emotion, he examined Ramsey's wound. He was no doctor, but he had seldom lived near a real doctor in his 81 years and he had learned to cope. The 100 families who'd followed him from Kentucky to settle in Missouri depended on his practical medical skills. Ramsey groaned under his touch, but the man had not let a wooden leg keep him back in civilization, and he would stand what he had to.

He made Boone think of his brother, Squire. Squire had been with him through many of the long miles as he was drawn ever west. Like grandfather, like father, like uncles, the brothers Boone had been moving west since Daniel's Quaker father and grandfather had left the green, fenced fields of Devon for Pennsylvania in 1713. South along the Shenandoah they'd gone, southwest into North Carolina and the valley of the Yadkin, then west to found Boonesborough on the Kentucky River in 1775. Sometimes alone, sometimes together, they had shared long hunts and explorations, often disappearing into the wilderness for months, even years, at a time.

They had been years of joy, especially for Daniel, who never could rest until he saw what lay over the next hill. When he had finally reached the rich, rolling clover meadows of Kentucky they had seemed God's promised land.

But these had also been years of pain. War with the Cherokee and Shawnee, egged on first by the French and then by the

British, had cost them dearly. Squire and Daniel had both suffered gunshot wounds and Squire had endured a tomahawk attack that turned his pleasant face sinister for the rest of his days.

Daniel probed for the bullet in Ramsey's groin, trying to cause as little pain as possible. Anxious as he was to get away, he couldn't leave the man like this.

There had been nothing he could do for his brother Edward. He'd left him alone only for a moment while tracking a wounded bear into woods that flamed with October color that day in 1780. He heard shots, then silence. They found Edward's body the next day, the head that looked so much like Daniel's lying by its side.

He had thought he was indurate to the pain of losing loved ones. But that was before he lost Israel at the mismanaged battle with British-Indian forces at Blue Licks two years later.

That time he had been there to share the suffering, to hear his second eldest son refuse to leave his father's side in the panic of retreat, to catch him as he fell wounded and carry the dying young man through the charging Indians toward the river.

When it was obvious he could do no more for Israel, he fled with the others. It was a week before the Kentuckians, guided by vultures circling above, could return to claim their dead. Daniel could recognize Israel only by his clothing. Even now, after 33 years, he could not speak of that day without tears.

And here he was again, 700 miles from Kentucky and embroiled in another war with Indians incited to action by the British, his family once more in peril.

Boone breathed a sigh of relief as he finally got a grip on the bullet and pulled it out. Quickly he tore strips of cloth to pack the wound. He needed to be done and on his way home.

Daniel had never enjoyed fighting. While he never shrank from either danger or combat, he preferred to avoid conflict if he could. He took no pleasure in killing Indians. Often he felt more like an Indian than a white man. He had walked their trails since he was a boy, learned their skills and gloried in their hunting grounds. He never killed an Indian unless he had to, and people who

expected him to brag about his kills were met with a level stare and silence.

The relatively peaceful years of hunting and trapping since he moved to the Missouri in 1799 had been among the happiest of his life. Not that he hadn't had a scrap or two with the Osage while out on a hunt, but only enough to add a little spice to his days. He saw himself more as an elder statesman than a soldier. He encouraged settlers, assigned them lands, and settled legal disputes in a dignified court beneath the spreading elm that local folks called his Judgment Tree.

But he had volunteered for the Missouri militia as soon as he heard the British had declared war in 1812 and he was insulted when they judged him too old to serve. His sons, Nathan and Daniel Morgan, had taken his place in the ranger units, traveling the frontier to help the settlers build sturdy log forts and prepare their defenses. Daniel did what he could, where he could, as he always had.

Ramsey taken care of, he rose and walked to the other bed to see if he could help the children's mother. Still erect in spite of his years, he seemed taller than his five foot, ten inches. He bent over the moaning woman.

She was not only wounded but in labor, much too soon.

He did what he could to ease her. His

Rebecca had borne ten, often without his presence if he was off on a long hunt. Together they had buried six; the two older boys, a baby, and three daughters since they'd come to Missouri. Life in the wilderness had ground down many a lesser woman.

He had married Rebecca when she was a slender, dark-haired 17. Her senior by only five years, he still called her "my little girl" after she had borne him four children.

The fourth, Jemima, had caused them a different kind of pain, conceived as she was during Daniel's 20-month absence in the early 1760s. But Daniel was a fair man, and he knew Rebecca had had no word from him in endless months, no reason to believe he was still alive. He never allowed himself to think less of his brother Ned or treat Jemima as anything other than his daughter. Jemima was a mother now; a grandmother. He hoped she and her family were safe.

The woman on the bed cried out and gripped his arm with hands nearly as hard and strong as a man's.

He had lost Rebecca only two years before. The old woman had been four weeks out in the woods boiling down maple sap when she was taken ill. Before he knew it she was gone. It had been months before he had stopped listening for her voice.

Rebecca had steadfastly followed him wherever he wandered for 56 years; well, almost everywhere. He smiled as he remembered. She had put her foot down about Florida even after she learned he had already put their cash down on a piece of land. But he hadn't really felt at home in the swamps anyway, so he hadn't much minded.

And it had taken a year to talk her back to Boonesborough after he'd spent four months in the captivity of the Shawnee. Having a son killed, a daughter kidnapped and a husband held prisoner for months might be enough to try the patience of any woman. And it hadn't helped when the neighbors gossiped that Daniel had enjoyed the company of a comely Shawnee squaw during his captivity.

But she had come. That's what mattered. And she'd picked up her flowered sewing basket and gone on to Missouri with him after he lost all their Kentucky land to men who looked for the letter in the law rather than the justice.

It hadn't been easy to move on and begin again with both of them in their sixties. But their last years had been good ones, settled again miles beyond everyone else on the river, establishing yet another frontier. They'd built a cabin on one son's land and lived within visiting distance of another son and Jemima. Daniel had plenty of elbow room and there were 52 grandchildren and great-grandchildren for them both to enjoy.

She'd helped him pick the spot for the cabin, near a spring that bubbled up beneath a great ledge of rock by the Femme Osage Creek. The creek was supposed to be named for a beautiful Osage woman who had drowned in it, but the whole countryside had the grace and beauty of a woman.

These past years they'd lived in comfort in a fine stone house he and Nathan had built, with oak floors to ease their feet, fine walnut mantels he'd carved himself and thick walls to keep out the heat and cold.

Mrs. Ramsey roused and asked for a drink of water. He let her have a few sips. The late afternoon sun was already slanting across the floor. Boone wondered if the woman could make it.

Daniel had had his pick of deer, buffalo, elk and bear in the early days. Turkeys by the dozens roosted in the woods and honeybees found ready homes in the deadfall of the gigantic cottonwoods. He'd hunted and trapped and sold pelts until he'd paid back every cent the men in Kentucky claimed he owed.

Of course gradually he'd been less able to shoot accurately with old Tick Licker. At first he had resorted to marking the sight with white paper, a trial for a man who remembered when he could outshoot any rifleman in Kentucky, even when they handicapped him by making him shoot with the wrong hand.

In recent years Rebecca had sometimes gone with him to help carry the heavy gun his arthritic hands found hard to hold. Or sometimes he took his little black boy, Derry, along to keep his camp. But he had not stayed home. He had never stayed home. And home had never stayed the same place for long. Civilization had always reached out and nudged him on. Civilization might mean safety, but it also meant people grating on each other and rushing to court to wave their papers.

70

Boone wrote a clear and flowing hand, and he read well enough to read for pleasure, but he never had the patience to dot his i's and cross his t's. He always felt it was what was in a man's heart that was important. If you couldn't trust him there, what good was anything he put on paper?

Many men back in Kentucky were richer for that fact.

It was dark, and Mrs. Ramsey sank in exhaustion between her pains. He sponged her brow and spoke a few words of encouragement. At least he could be sure the Indians wouldn't be attacking anywhere now; it was too late for that.

He'd thought he'd left all the lawyer troubles behind when he immigrated to Louisiana. The Spanish government had welcomed him with a public display that was almost embarrassing. He had been given his choice of land, nearly 9,000 acres all told. And they'd recognized his experience and standing with the people by appointing him administrator of his district.

But when the Missouri country came under the flag of the United States in 1804, he had lost again to those who looked for the dots. He had built his cabin on Daniel Morgan's land, not his own. He had gone off hunting instead of farming. He had trusted the wrong advice.

He and Rebecca, who had opened thousands of miles of wilderness to others who coveted land, were landless again. But their children were well provided for in Missouri. Maybe that was all that mattered. After all, it wouldn't be long until he put the cherrywood coffin he'd made to use and joined Rebecca. The knoll above the Missouri would be all they needed.

Sometimes he wished he were already there. Last year Congress had finally, after repeated petitions, granted him some land in recognition of all he had done to open the West. It was only a tenth of what the Spanish had given him, but it was better than nothing.

Then suddenly it was nothing. Creditors from Kentucky had smelled him out and circled over his grant, squawking loudly with their claims. He sold it all to be rid of them. He was glad Rebecca hadn't lived to endure that.

He was glad, too, she hadn't lived to bear her grandson's death. Jemima's boy, James, had been killed just two months ago on Loutre Island, another victim of this war with the British. Jemima, who was so special to them both, now knew what it was to lose her eldest son.

Suddenly Mrs. Ramsey arched her back and screamed. The child was coming, finally coming. Boone reached to catch the tiny, slippery body.

It was alive. Boone thanked the God he'd known since his Quaker childhood. He wrapped the baby and turned back to the mother. She was spent and white, and clammy to the touch. The bedding was soggy with her blood.

He did what he could, but without much hope. It looked like Ramsey would lose three and gain one -- if the baby survived. Wilderness families were fragile things, and it was time to think of his own. Arranging what protection he could for the Ramseys, Boone rode for home under a lightening sky.

Jemima and her husband, Flanders Calloway, were waiting for him. Calloway had loaded a canoe with as many household treasures as he had room. Too many, to Daniel's eye, but there wasn't time to argue. He would take Jemima and the grandchildren by land the four miles down the Missouri to the fort at Daniel Morgan's and hopeful safety, while his son-in-law took the canoe down the river.

It was far from the first time Daniel had raced his family to shelter from the Indians. They had "forted up" for protection from the Cherokee in 1759, 56 years ago. He wondered if Jemima was thinking of the day the Indians dragged her off into the woods when she was 13 and Boone had tracked them down and rescued her. He wasn't the man he had been then, but he guessed he could still hold his own in a scrap.

The Fox did attack the home of Boone's nephew that day and two Indians paid with their lives when Rebecca's female kin proved to be as tough as she. But the attacks cost Daniel one more loss. The manuscript containing the story of his life and adventures, patiently dictated to a grandson over the years, rode in Flanders Calloway's canoe.

As Calloway hurried to safety, the overloaded canoe struck a snag in the Missouri and sank. Calloway swam to shore, but the manuscript was lost to the Missouri's spring flood.

Boone lived for five more years. At peace with himself and with God, he spent his last years doing what he loved best -- roaming. Settlers along the river could look up to see him glide by in his canoe, white hair topped with his battered old wide-brimmed hat, stroking surely and evenly up river for another hunt. He traveled on up the Missouri and west along the Platte, staying in the Yellowstone country one winter to trap. He made plans to visit the Great Salt Lake and maybe California.

Those plans were never realized. But he watched the beginning of the migration west -- saw it move, as usual, on a trail he had marked. He shared his knowledge with those wise enough to ask, and there were more than a few who sought him out.

He spent his eighty-fifth summer on the banks of the Missouri and died peacefully in bed at his son's home just as his beloved woods were turning color. "All the religion I have," he had written his sister-in-law in a letter which could have been his epitaph, "is to love and fear God, believe in Jesus Christ, do all the good to my neighbors and myself that I can and do as litle harm as I can help, and trust in God's mercy for the rest."

Something We Crave

The war that had savaged the Missouri frontier finally ended in fact as well as on parchment. Peace released a flood of Americans seeking, like Daniel Boone's family, their piece of the wilderness.

The streets of St. Charles, on the track west, surged with crowds of those convinced the woods and prairies of the Missouri River bottoms held all they needed for a better life.

Most of them brought cattle and hogs, dogs and chickens, wagons and plows -- all the elements they needed to sustain their families.

But some men thought there were needs greater than those of the body. They brought tracts and books, hymns and rituals -- seeds of the faith they wanted to plant on the frontier.

As Timothy Flint, New England parson, Presbyterian missionary and distributor of Bibles, walked toward St. Charles on a Sunday morning in September 1816 he had a very unmissionary-like thought. He looked across a rain-freshened prairie studded with wildflowers, to cottonwoods which rose from the Missouri bottoms "like Corinthian columns" wrapped in ivy. He breathed in air soft with the scent of the tall thick grasses and watched herds of cattle and horses share their pasture with groups of deer. "Here shall be my farm," he thought, "And here I will end my days."

It was not the kind of dream an itinerant missionary should indulge, especially on a Sabbath morning. His life's work was directed to tending men's souls, to planting churches, to moving when and where he was needed.

He was 36 years old, a father of three. He'd worked in the church for 14 years. He believed in his mission. And yet he was still searching for his proper path.

He hadn't found it with a New England congregation. He had no patience with dogma, no desire to sugar-coat his messages, no ability to soothe and cajole and "get along." Pushed out of his church by parishioners who found him too interested in worldly pursuits such as science and not interested enough in bickering over details of doctrine, he'd been forced, at 34, to seek a new career.

He'd chosen missionary work on the frontier. He could preach -- he was good at that -- and hand out Bibles (not one in 50 had the Good Book) and plant the seed for churches without having to be involved in their daily affairs. And maybe sometime, somewhere -- this was only a vague dream -- he'd be able to found a Christian journal like those in the east.

In the past two years he'd moved his family steadily westward, pushing into the field at St. Louis even after he'd learned another missionary was already assigned there. Although many homes of the 2,000 people living in the town professed their faith by displaying a wooden cross over their gates, the preacher was not immediately welcome in St. Louis. It was still largely French, and Catholic, and he was a Yankee representing the Missionary Society of Connecticut and the Presbyterian church.

After a 900-mile journey by river boat, worn down by stifling heat, storms, mosquitoes, wood ticks and unaccustomed physical labor, he and his slim wife, Abigail, found "almost every heart closed against us." They walked the streets in search of a place to stay. The growing community now boasted six brick houses but no one could or would make room for them and their three children. With Micah, 13, Evaline, 11, and Ebeneezer, 8, they spent five more nights rocking on their "hot, leaky, filthy boat" tied in the Mississippi. Flint began to see why the other Presbyterian missionary had become so discouraged he'd moved on to try another field.

Sunday had brought a fellow Protestant and the beginning of acceptance. Flint found a two room log cabin to house his family and he took over management of a school.

He'd worked to enliven his preaching style to suit western tastes. His listeners would not tolerate his using notes, he discovered, and came expecting a show rather than intellectual arguments. It went against his nature, but, he wrote his favorite cousin, James, "I have broken over all early habits and have triumphed over extreme reluctance and against my own taste and feelings..." He gave them the performance they wanted.

Soon he was called on for sermons and funerals, and he often tramped the countryside as he'd done earlier along the Ohio River, spreading the word. But it didn't last. His health, which had been fragile since he was a child, could not support all he wanted to do. He could make little headway among the Catholics, and the Protestants, however few, were as given to bickering over differences in dogma as those in the east. "The more trifling (the differences) the more pertinaciously they cling to them," Flint noted in exasperation.

He cared little for which rituals a person proscribed. Religion, he thought, should "be a matter of practice and good feeling. Religion is love, love to God and to men...the religion of the heart."

Tolerant though he was of religious form, he had definite ideas of what constituted a proper life and he was constantly upset with the evil that surrounded him. A few people listened to him on Sundays, but it seemed to make no difference in their lives. They still drank and danced and dueled at the slightest provocation.

So, like the missionary before him, he'd decided to look for friendlier fields. St. Charles was closer to the Missouri river settlements he wished to travel and it looked, from a distance, like Utopia. Flint walked toward it with a light step.

He should have known better. He'd already written James that the French villages with their whitewashed log houses looked better from a distance than close up, where one became aware of the mud, the pig wallows, the horse droppings, the flies.

He'd walked overland to St. Charles, hoping to arrange housing before Abigail and the children arrived later by boat, but as in St. Louis he found it scarce and expensive. Rents as high as $20 a month were impossible on his missionary's salary and his family was forced out of one house and then another by newcomers who could pay more. Newcomers were everywhere. As many as 100 a day thronged into town, some to stay, more moving through on their way west. Flint watched wagon trains three-quarters of a mile long, trailed by herds of a hundred cattle. Horses, sheep and hogs trotted alongside pioneers whose faces shown with happy expectation.

They'd heard Boone's Lick was a paradise, the Salt River country unsurpassed. Each new name lured them on. They weren't interested in establishing schools, churches or burial grounds because they'd be off again at the first rumor of greener grass farther west.

As he watched the parade pass, Flint imagined the day the waves of emigrants would "meet the Western Ocean and sit down and weep for other worlds." He deplored the boosterism of land speculators which ignited such movements, but he could understand the appeal. He himself had come west and he knew what it was to feel "all that restless hope of finding in a new country...something we crave but have not."

One craving he was determined to fill was that for the Lord's word, but for many, that craving would have to be awakened. His first sermon in St. Charles could begin only after a horse race clattered noisily away from the dooryard of the place of worship.

Still he was getting calls for Bibles, as many as 20 a day. He worked from daybreak to ten at night, often ending his day writing letters or tracts by candlelight on a plank in a settler's cabin. He spent much time out prospecting the area farms for receptive souls, crossing and recrossing the Missouri, walking 20, 40, 60 miles alone, armed only with a Bible.

At first he was afraid of the rugged settlers, their manners as gruff as their bearded faces and unkempt clothes, their guns always ready. Their dogs, charging out to intercept a visitor, sometimes treed him until the owner appeared.

But he gradually learned to look beneath exteriors which would be so shocking in a New England parlor. He discovered a farmer might growl a welcome and then ply him with coffee from his limited stores, feed him corn bread, butter and wild meat, order him to the cabin's best bed and curtly refuse his offers of payment the next morning.

He found an honesty and morality often absent in more refined populations whose courtly manners could mask hostility and disdain. He even learned to welcome the fiercely barking dogs because their noise led him through the dark woods and fields to shelter and a cozy fire.

He visited the settlers along the Femme Osage and got acquainted with Daniel Boone and his family. The old pioneer had many exciting stories to tell and Flint was an eager listener. Often, sitting up late with him before a dying fire, the parson thought what a fascinating book his life would make.

But his mind was also occupied with more worldly concerns. Money was a constant problem. Prices on the frontier were high and he had a family of five to support. Collections from his rural parishioners often failed to cover the cost of the ferry he had to take to reach them. Of the townsmen, he said, "The people think they have done their full duty to a preacher when they've listened to what he has to say."

He and Abigail opened another school to help pay the bills. Abigail taught the young ladies of the community pattern design, painting and needlework while Timothy handled the academic subjects.

Flint's brother and his son Micah tried their luck at retailing. They opened a store in

St. Louis, but, tended by a preacher's family, it raised mostly controversy and little cash.

The family then tried the real estate business. With the pastor himself wielding ax and hammer, they built two cabins to sell. Later they bought a claim on a river island and tried to sell the timber. When that caused trouble Flint sold it and bought a farm. Whatever he tried, it seemed the wolf lurked around the family doorstep.

Flint never let himself be totally distracted from his surroundings. His mind was alive to all that was new and different. He was curious about everything, observed it intently and wrote long letters to his cousin back East.

The Indian Mounds both in St. Louis and along the river near St. Charles drew him. Convinced they were burial places, he dug into them for proof. He found pottery, mostly broken, but he treasured one drinking jug discovered whole, and thoughtfully traced a palm print on its surface made, he thought, some 1,000 years before. The mounds "filled his imagination and his heart" and he pondered the ancient people, "their joys, their sorrows, their bones all buried together."

He loved to walk the mounds at twilight, meditating as he watched the shadows move over the valley until even the tableland beyond was cast in blue. The Indians had watched the same scene and had had as many dreams, he thought. "The nothingness of the brief dream of human life" forced itself on his mind.

He'd always loved and studied nature. He'd huddled on the Atlantic shore as a boy, too thrilled with the spectacle of storm-driven surf to know whether he was wet or dry. As a college student he'd dreamed of following the track of Clark or MacKenzie across the Rockies, or floating from the headwaters of the Missouri to the ocean. Wherever he was, if he could, he walked the countryside at dawn or dusk, finding there a peace and joy in meditation that escaped him elsewhere.

His people had been part of the North Reading, Massachusetts church for 100 years and it had seemed natural for the frail, scholarly Timothy to choose that path. His best friend and cousin, James, was a preacher. His wife was the daughter of a minister. His faith was sincere and strong. But by his

second year in St. Charles, Timothy Flint was questioning his calling.

He looked for results from his labor and could see none. He felt feeble and alone, overwhelmed by evil all around him. By the spring of 1817 he was concerned that even his children's morals and spiritual life might be in danger. He decided the settlers had endured so much and witnessed such horrors that they had lost all sensitivity. In his darkest hours he imagined the very air they all breathed was fatal to religious feeling.

In August, with his unblinking honesty, he wrote the missionary society that he should no longer take money consecrated to a cause he could not achieve. He thought progress was impossible. Missouri was still "as heathen as Hindustan."

He'd changed his style of preaching, but not his message and the villagers did not take his scoldings gracefully. He deplored swearing, gambling, dueling, drinking and dancing, especially on the Sabbath.

That the French had for decades celebrated the Sabbath with lively balls and entertainments meant nothing to him. It was wrong and he told them so. Several times. Using their own language. He could not preach in French but he knew enough words to scold and he did. When the revelries continued he called the law. The revelers were punished (dancing on the Sabbath was illegal) but Flint's victory cost him dearly. He'd done a few things the citizens could criticize and they were not hesitant to voice their complaints.

In early 1818 Flint was charged with being "a speculator, avaricous, immoral and of course, not a Christian." He was guilty of unholy works. He had a worldly spirit. A minister in a store was unseemly. A preacher who worked with his hands was suspect. Dealing in real estate was unacceptable. Trying to sell them timber they'd always had free was a crime. A preacher should depend on God to provide.

When Flint learned in June that charges had been sent to the society's headquarters in Hartford, he immediately resigned. He wrote a brief explanation of his activities and allowed himself the bitter opinion that he'd been invited to St. Charles only as window-dressing; a town with a preacher made better advertising copy for speculators. The town had not expected him to take his role seriously. They didn't want to blush in Sunday services.

"I came here naked. I am naked still," he wrote. "My health is poor, but my confidence in the God whom I serve is deep and unabated. He will somehow or other spread a table for us in the wilderness..."

His health was poorer than he knew. Soon after resigning he was stricken with fever. He'd noted new settlers invariably came down with fever and he looked upon the illness as a "seasoning" or process of becoming acclimated. If the newcomer resisted fever for the first year and got it in the second, the disease was more serious, he noted. Flint fell to it in his third year.

In one day he was prostrate. In three, delirious. Abigail and his children despaired of his life.

Days went by. He lived but he did not know them. The healers came and tried emetics and blistering, but in the end they left him to die in peace.

Flint was in another world and, he thought, in God's presence. He talked, but in foreign languages. He recited long passages of poetry. He heard flutes announce the family's regular morning and evening prayers. When Abigail tended him or friends came to visit, their heads glowed with a light so bright it hurt him to look; their feet trod on air. He shook with spasms, expecting each one to be his last and willing it be so. When he finally turned back to the real world after 30 days, it was with regret.

But when, after 55 days, he was finally able to be taken outside, he was overcome with the beauty of the world. He saw the earth, the trees, the river, and the heavens as if for the first time, thrilling to colors and aspects he'd never noticed. Re-created, he could not believe life's vexations and bad feelings would ever bother him again.

The community of ill feeling toward Flint which had led to his resignation had actually peaked and begun to wane before he resigned. He probably could have remained in St. Charles. But it was too late. He accepted a position to teach and preach at Washington, Mississippi and started south with his family in April 1819.

It was the beginning of a 2-1/2 year odyssey. Fever struck the pregnant Abigail and the children at the Arkansas River and, afraid for their health in the lowlands, they decided to head back for St. Charles. On a stormy day in November, as they inched up the Mississippi, Abigail gave birth to a baby girl who died in her third day. They buried her in the river bank and moved on to spend the winter in New Madrid.

Months there, and later in Jackson, ended the same way. The people were glad to have Flint preach until he asked payment. In October 1821 the family dragged back into St. Charles. They had a new son, born in Jackson, whom Timothy would call "our Joseph," but nothing else.

Determined to make his living as a farmer, Flint leased land and started building a cabin, but fever continued to stalk them. Sick, homeless and penniless, they were taken in and nursed by the families of St. Charles while the eldest son, nearly a man now, built the cabin.

In the still-open cabin that January, Flint looked at his family and faced reality. The farm he had envisioned six years ago was beyond him. He had neither the strength nor the knowledge to build it. Shaking with ague, he took his cap in hand to write to the missionary society which had sent him west. Would the society send them money to get back to Massachusetts? He held out hope until spring, but when it was time to plant and nothing had arrived, he knew they'd have to farm to survive.

He tried, grubbing out stumps with blistered hands, toiling until he could not sleep at night for the pain in his back. They all worked -- Micah, Hubbard, Evaline, Abigail when she could bring Joseph to the field. Timothy earned a few coins preaching, when he could, but they might have starved had it not been for the charity of their neighbors.

When fall came, and with it a little money from Timothy's cousin, they prepared to go home by way of New Orleans. Flint had still not found his place, but apparently it did not lie in the West. He preached farewell sermons in St. Charles and St. Louis and committed his family again to the river.

This time the Mississippi had better things in store. They found their way to Alexandria, Louisiana where there was a small college. Flint was hired to head it and to do some preaching. For two years it seemed like Eden, with cooling breezes and pine forests to remind them of home. Then Flint was downed by another attack of fever, and in the spring of 1825, left his family to go home to die.

But instead of death at his cousin James' home he found what he was really meant to do. As the invalid regained his strength, James, the recipient of Timothy's colorful letters about the West, encouraged him to write a book of his experiences. When he returned to Abigail that fall, he left behind him the manuscript of *Recollections of the Past Ten Years*; before he reached her he had begun his first novel.

From 1827 to 1833 the Flints lived in Cincinnati where Timothy wrote and edited the *Western Monthly Review*, not the religious journal he'd first envisioned but an effort to help the western settlers he'd come to love realize their literary heritage.

In those years, books poured from his desk one after the other. The first were moralistic novels, but later works included an ambitious history of the Mississippi Valley, a book on the Indian wars and, in 1833, *A Biographical Memoir of Daniel Boone* so popular it went into 14 editions. The preacher had finally found his pulpit.

Before he died at 60 in 1840 he knew the West had supplied what he craved, even though he hadn't known what it was.

A Great Distance

While the weak and trembling Timothy Flint, gazing out on the Missouri in the late summer of 1818, gloried in the beauty of the scene, he also was struck with the river's strength. Its power made human efforts seem so feeble he thought; its everlasting roll seemed almost a cruel reminder of mankind's short span of years.

It did not occur to him that the very backwaters of the river cut that span even shorter in family after family as they played host to disease and the insects which spread it. But whether its origin was the Missouri lowlands, bad water, or a settler's wagon, disease cut into the population like the river carved into a point. The banks of the Missouri were never short of mourners.

On the damp, cloudy morning of August 17, Manuel Lisa stood above the grave of another child. This time it was his and Polly's five-year-old daughter, Mary. She'd succumbed to whooping cough the night before; the country air at the Hempstead farm had worked no miracles.

It was the second bereavement of the year for Manuel. In February Polly herself had taken ill and died. The trader had remarried only ten days before his daughter's death. His new wife, Mary Hempstead, had taken Polly's daughter to her family's farm in the hope of saving her. But it had been futile and another Lisa was laid to rest in the Catholic church yard.

Lisa's new wife was neither Catholic nor Spanish. She was of New England stock, a Presbyterian like Timothy Flint, and it was her father who'd encouraged Flint to come to Missouri. She was a widow herself, left with a three-year-old son on the death of her sea captain husband eight years before.

But 36-year-old Mary did not have a cold, unbending Puritan nature. She was warm and accepting, open to new ways and experiences. She knew she could expect her life with Manuel Lisa to be an adventure.

For one thing, she would be stepmother to nine-year-old Manuel, Polly's only surviving child, and to Rosalie, a dark-eyed two-year-old who had a different heritage. Lisa had brought his daughter by Mitain down the spring before to be raised in St. Louis and given a proper education.

The Lisa household was also home to a ten-year-old Spanish boy Lisa had rescued from the Pawnee up on the Platte. The boy had been captured by a branch of the tribe still given to human sacrifice and Lisa had bought his freedom to save his life. Felipe still woke up in the night, calling for Manuel, sure the Indians were coming to burn him.

Life with Manuel could hardly be dull. He was proudly showing off the new stone warehouse he'd built at the levy's edge and enthusiastically promoting his new mill north of town, where the saws and millstones were powered by St. Louis' first steam engine. As usual, he was at the center of happenings up the Missouri. He was organizing yet another fur company, still convinced his biggest accomplishments lay ahead.

This year he had even more reason for hope, for there would be a new presence on the river. The secretary of war, John Calhoun, had decided the army should make a show of force on the upper river and put a stop to encroaching British traders. Half a rifle regiment was already up above the Kansas River. The rest of the force would join them in the spring and push on to build forts at the Mandan villages and the mouth of the Yellowstone. It would mean security the traders had never known.

Lisa was off at the first rise in the spring of 1819 to prepare the Indians at his Omaha post for the coming troops. Already up river, he missed the news that thrilled Mary and the town on May 28. A steamboat had churned up the Missouri as far as Chariton -- 200 miles. They'd been plying the Mississippi for two years, but now a steamer had tackled the Missouri. Perhaps the days of exhausting labor on the keelboats were at an end.

The army was gambling they were. Colonel Henry Atkinson, expedition commander, "had not the least doubt of the practicability of navigating the Missouri with steam power." Four steamboats were to carry the remaining troops and supplies up the Missouri.

Any steamboat was a novelty, but one in particular fascinated the St. Louis boys. Built especially for the Missouri, the *Western Engineer* carried the scientific arm of the expedition under the command of Major Stephen H. Long. But the craft did not present a sober, scientific appearance. A huge black serpent's head reared at the bow, its open mouth spitting steam whenver the vessel was underway. The scaly monster apparently carried the boat on its back, propelling through water that splashed and foamed in its wake. It was meant to intimidate the Indians and seemed well designed for the purpose. More important, however, were its shallow draft to counter Missouri sandbars and the placement of the paddle wheel in the stern where it would be safer from snags.

The populace expected much from the *Western Engineer*. The newspapers said she would proceed to the source of the Missouri, be carried in parts over the easy five-mile portage, be reassembled, and steam triumphantly down the Columbia to the sea. William Clark must have dropped his head in his hands when he read it. Lisa's family, all the traders, knew better. But some dreams have more than nine lives.

After the *Western Engineer* puffed north on June 21 and the other three steamers loaded their troops and headed up the Missouri in early July, the town quieted. But the excitement was still to come for Mary Lisa. Manuel, who had been to his Omaha post and back while the army was just getting started, had an intriguing suggestion. She should go with him on his fall trip and they'd winter together at the Omaha post. Mary hesitated only long enough to find a friend to take along for company; then they were on board the keelboat and underway.

Mary could not help but be impressed, as nearly all voyagers were, with the beauty of the lower river, the forest of sycamores, black walnuts and cottonwoods broken at intervals with cotton fields, orchards and farms. But occasionally she caught a glimpse of one of the log stockades where the farmers had sought protection from the Sac just four years before.

However most of the settlers had stayed on their land, and villages once French were turning more and more American. Franklin, barely three years old, had more than a hundred log cabins -- many boasting two separate rooms with a covered porch between. Chariton, farther on, had 50 and some houses of stone from its quarries. There were fields of tobacco and herds of cattle and sheep. She passed landmarks she had heard about for years -- Boone's Lick's high plateau and Fort Osage's log walls.

But there were still islands white with pelicans, deer on the banks, turkeys and geese to be shot for dinner. Grapes, mulberries, raspberries and plums were everywhere and there was always honey for sweetening.

By the time they reached prairie country above the Kansas, the dry brown grasses were often in flames. Smoke settled in the river valley and made the days hazy. But the hazelnuts were ripe, the sumac red and the cottonwoods a border of gold where they arched along the banks.

On the last day of September, Lisa's men welcomed their employer and his fair-haired, creamy-skinned wife with a swivel gun salute. Mary was the first trader's wife to leave the settlements and come so far up the river.

The engineer's dragon had preceded them and lay anchored in a harbor about a mile above Lisa's post. Long's men were busy building their winter quarters, collecting rock for chimneys, seeking clay for mortar, felling timber for walls and floors. They would have to winter here, for it was far too late to push on north.

Some of the riflemen and infantry had arrived the day before and were tenting nearby, waiting for the rest of their force and a permanent campsite a few miles up the river. With their keelboats and herd of cattle grazing in the lowland, the fur trader's post did not look nearly as lonely as Mary had expected.

Long's boat was the only one powered by steam to survive the Missouri. The others had fallen on hard times -- sandbars, snags, rocks -- or choked on the river's silt-filled water. They'd had to stop at least once a day to clean the boilers, which of course had to cool before they could be cleaned. The sand had ground away at engine valves until they had to be repaired. And the machines had voracious appetites, eating 25 cords of wood in a 24-hour run. The troops had had to stop time and again to collect wood and saw it for use. To further complicate things, the pilots did not know the river and wasted hours and days threading channels that ended in a maze of rushes. With almost unlimited manpower, they had averaged about 7 1/2 miles a day. Lisa and his two dozen voyageurs had made 18 miles a day on sheer muscle power when he'd raced after Hunt eight years before.

The Indians, who might have been cowed at first sight of Long's monster, soon realized it had more bluff than bite -- spewing black smoke while it hemmed and hawed, backed and hesitated, nearly at the mercy of the current. Instead of respect they'd learned contempt, striking small parties of the soldiers at will, robbing them and leaving them to return ignobly to camp.

But Mary was with the Omaha and they were Lisa's friends. Soon after her arrival she gathered up her billowing skirts and went with Lisa to attend a council. Arriving after dark, she and the trader were shown to a tipi for the night.

Early the next morning she awoke with a

strange feeling; she felt she was being watched. Suddenly uneasy, she sat up and looked around. There was no one else in the tipi but Manuel. Then with a gasp, she saw what was wrong. All around the tipi the skins were pulled up a few inches from the ground. In that space were pair after pair of black eyes, their gaze fixed on her form, following her every motion.

Once over her start, she quickly adapted to the situation, not making a fuss but accepting the friendly curiosity for what it was. Good-naturedly, she bade privacy good-bye, imagining the way her tipi must look surrounded by Indians flat on their stomachs, shoulder to shoulder -- like spokes of a wheel -- each allowed a quick glimpse of the white squaw before giving way to the next in line.

Whenever she went out of the post with Manuel she was followed by a drove of admirers seeking to feel her light hair and touch her white skin. Her full skirts, her petticoats, her shoes and stockings, all were objects of curiosity and delight.

But there was one who watched with less enthusiasm. Mitain, ordered away from the post by Lisa, had crept back. She sat often along the wall, blanket over her face and her baby son on her back. She had known before she married him that Lisa had a white wife back home, so she didn't feel betrayed. Many Omaha men had two or more wives. But she

wanted to be near Lisa, to have him see their son. For days she sat, blanket-covered and still, while he moved about the post, waiting for a word from him. She'd mourned for weeks after giving up Rosalie, but she could not keep herself from wanting to see her husband.

Finally Lisa weakened. Worn down by the silent form, he agreed to talk to Mitain and see the baby. Needing a way out of a difficult situation, he made sure she was provided for and sent her with her family on the winter buffalo hunt. Mary, whose usual winter world consisted of skating parties and cozy hours before the fire with her needle, was now learning about her husband's. Late in October the prairies around them began to burn and for nearly three weeks the sun shone blood-red while they went about their tasks with stinging eyes.

Manuel found the Indians increasingly restless. The large camp of soldiers up the river was consuming much of the game, and as they quarried stone and cut timber for their quarters it was obvious they intended to stay. As game became scarce, inter-tribal rivalries, never long suppressed, threatened to upset the nominal peace.

Lisa called the tribes to a council to try to keep the situation from deteriorating. After feelings were soothed and agreements reached, he scheduled the customary closing feast. To his surprise, the chiefs invited Mary to be a guest of honor. Her warm and friendly personality in addition to her novelty had won their approval.

Manuel was leery. He told Mary she'd have to eat everything offered, including roast dog. Mary was revolted. She declared she could not and would not touch it. But the invitation could not be refused. She pondered a bit and got her sewing kit.

On the day of the feast she was led to her place of honor. There, in its place of honor was the dog, roasted hide and all. Steeling herself not to be sick, she put the first small bite in her mouth. Then, the test passed and attention elsewhere, she slipped the rest of her serving, bite by bite, into a pocket she'd inserted in her skirt.

The rest of the feast -- the corn, wild game, dried melon -- went down easily. Mary knew Lisa was responsible for some of the food. He'd seen the Omaha in starving years and dipped into his own pocket to feed them. Then he'd brought sacks of seeds up the river, showing the Indians how to plant pumpkins, beans, turnips and potatoes, giving them plows and iron implements, striving to keep them strong and independent.

After the ceremonies, the Indians turned to trading their furs and Mary found herself called upon to distribute the payments. Coached unobtrusively by Manuel, who was a master at knowing which goods each tribe and each chief desired, she presented the merchandise with a charm that won their affection.

The officers and scientific gentlemen at the two cantonments were also charmed to have ladies near their posts. That fall Mary and her friend attended festive dinners with the army officers, their quarters still rough and unfinished but their chivalry as correct as their attractive gray and white uniforms. While they could offer little to eat but meat, there was a variety of that. Hunting was good and they feasted on bison hump, rump roast, boiled meat, boiled tongue, spare ribs, sausages and bread.

But as the ice closed the river and snow whistled across its gray surface, the game drifted away. Temperatures dropped below zero and wolves howled hungrily in the night. The traders were well prepared, and the engineers had a hunter skilled enough to keep them supplied, but hunting parties the soldiers sent out often returned empty-handed; by Christmas the troops up at Missouri Cantonment would have given nearly anything for some of the food in the Omaha caches.

The civilian contracted to supply food had failed to deliver what he promised. They had not enough of anything and especially not enough vinegar. The flour was moldy. There were no vegetables. They were dependent on what was left of their salted pork and what the hunters brought in.

By the first of the year they were falling to scurvy. The Lisas heard that the hospital rooms were filling with pale and feeble men, their gums turned black and spongy, their teeth loosened, their skin discolored. They moved on swollen legs, with aching joints; they began to die.

The post surgeon did what he could. He knew the men needed a better diet but there

was little he could do about that. The pork was rotting now, and he had it boiled with charcoal, changing the water several times to make it palatable. He tried to keep them clean, opening the windows to the cold air and eliminating partitions.

On February 25, when the Lisas dined at the engineers' camp, they learned 19 men were dead and another hundred sick with scurvy. The surgeon estimated 60 more would die before the earth greened enough to provide a cure for the disease.

A few days later the 16-inch ice on the river began to crack. It was early for the thaw, but already too late for many of the troops. The engineers and traders were horrified at the condition of the camp, but no one had enough to share with 1,000 men. Most appalling was that, in spite of their best efforts, not one soldier in all those numbers had recovered. To get scurvy was to die. The post the war department had foreseen as being "the most desirable on the continent" was a death trap.

By March 20 the grimy ice cakes had disappeared and the air above the river bore flock after flock of ducks, wave after wave of geese and brant. But there were now 100 graves in the cemetery and the sick list contained the names of 345 men.

With the cantonment emerging from the grip of winter, the surgeon could see only one hope. He suggested shipping the men who still had some chance of recovery south to Fort Osage. There, spring came sooner and they could get fresh meat and milk from the settlements. On March 25, two keelboats loaded with 100 sick men passed Lisa's post on the way south, but 160 were left in graves at the cantonment.

In April, as the wild onions appeared and game became plentiful again, the disease diminished. The two keelboats Atkinson had dispatched from St. Louis with new supplies would arrive too late to make a difference. Congress, disillusioned by the expensive failure of the steamboats and dismayed by the mortality rate, pulled the plug on the expedition.

The ambitious plans to reach for the Yellowstone were abandoned. "The glory of planting the American flag on a point so distant..." which the secretary of war had envisioned, would have to wait for other days. The diehard dream to steamboat down the Columbia was put to rest again. Long and his scientists were ordered to explore the Platte to its sources. The rest of the 1,100 troops would stay where they were. The fort at Council Bluffs was as close to the Yellowstone as they would come.

Lisa and the others who worked the upper river were back on their own. It was time to get the winter's catch to market and time for Mary Lisa to go home. Manuel was going with her and with him, he decided, would go his son by Mitain, whom he had named Christopher after his father.

Mitain, called to the post and given the news, became hysterical. She cried that she could not bear to lose another child. With Lisa gone, the boy was all she had. She'd already risked her life to save him during a Sioux attack; her face bore the ugly scar that testified to her narrow escape. She could not survive an even deeper scar on her being.

Lisa, convinced he knew what was best for his son, was adamant. He wanted him baptized. He wanted him well-fed and educated. He was not to grow up a savage. His angry shouts and Mitain's screams attracted a crowd. Mitain's family and the other Omaha, incensed at Lisa's demand, argued angrily that the child belonged with the mother, as was their custom.

Benjamin O'Fallon, the Indian agent for the Omaha, stepped in. Moved by Mitain's grief and fearing an uprising, he forbade Lisa to take the child. Lisa already had the daughter to raise as an American. Mitain could keep the son to raise as an Omaha. Mary, understanding her husband's concern for the child, but knowing from experience a mother's need, could only hope the Missouri's Solomon had made the best decision.

Back in St. Louis in time for the strawberry parties, Mary and Manuel put their concern for Christopher in the back of their minds and concentrated on being a happily married pair. Lisa was heard to say he'd never known what joy married life could bring until he wed Mary. He liked her whole family and included her brother and father in his business dealings.

That summer Manuel began to feel ill. His eyes and skin took on the yellow caste of jaundice. Still he found the temper and the strength to thrash one Antoine Beaudoin on August 1, and be summoned into the all-too-familiar court to face charges. Before he could answer the suit, however, Mary took him out to the sulphur springs in search of help. The waters did not prove healing, the doctor could do nothing, and on August 11, Manuel made his will. He provided for all his children, Christopher and Rosalie as well as Manuel, for Mary's son from her first marriage and for his godson, the child of his brother.

Even on his deathbed he confirmed his belief in the Missouri River fur trade, convinced the stock he willed Mary would provide for her future. On the evening of August 12, 1820 he died. Mary's Presbyterian family attended the solemn high mass said for Manuel in the Catholic cathedral but took his body home for burial in their family plot.

He was 48 years old, but he had used his years to their limit. Almost single-handedly he had designed and inaugurated the Missouri River fur trade, and it would always bear the stamp of his vision. He had traveled some 25,000 miles up and down its waters and his men had mapped its drainage. He had earned the friendship of the river's tribes and bound them to the American cause at a critical time. Always a man who put action to his visions, he explained to William Clark three years before he died, "I go a great distance while some are considering whether they will start today or tomorrow."

Mary Lisa survived Manuel by 49 years, but she never remarried. Her family and friends came to call her "Aunt Manuel." Both her son and Manuel's died as young men; Lisa's only survivors were his children by Mitain.

Rosalie, educated in a convent, married a preacher and had eight children. Christopher stayed with the Omaha and was seen once, with Mitain, in 1833, stumbling along the Missouri bank. Both were bleeding from wounds.

The Breathing Corpse

The army was stalled below Council Bluffs. Colonel Atkinson had underestimated the power of the Missouri's spring floods and he and the men spent June rescuing sodden equipment and rebuilding a rectangular, palisaded post up on the bluffs.

Determined his troops would never again be defiled by the scourge of scurvy, Atkinson plowed fields and planted corn and potatoes, turnips and radishes. He ordered up beef and dairy cattle, bought hogs and built the barns to house them. The fort looked more like a country estate than a military post; the troops more like farmers than soldiers.

No longer a death trap, Fort Atkinson began to live up to its original billing as a coveted post. The footsteps of soldiers' wives and children, tradesmen and trappers sounded on the boardwalk that fronted the parade ground. Although troop strength was cut in half when Congress erased the expedition's grand goals, there were more than enough guns to make the newcomers feel secure.

But the St. Louis fur trade could not thrive on security. Men had been pushing up the Missouri for nearly 30 years without soldiers to clear the way. They would not stop now. Although Lisa was gone, there were many others ready to reach for a share of his harvest.

In 1822 William H. Ashley, miner, lieutenant governor of the newly created state of Missouri, general of the militia and hopeful fur baron, formed the Rocky Mountain Fur Company with Lisa's cohort Andrew Henry. Henry had never forgotten the teeming streams around Three Forks and he wanted another chance to harvest their promise.

The two partners, refining Lisa's methods, decided to transport a trapping brigade up the river. These would be free trappers, recruited from the streets of St. Louis. The company would be obligated only to sell them supplies and buy their catch, thereby reducing risk and expense for the partnership. Their plans carefully thought out, their men young, ambitious and well-chosen, they set off to challenge the river, the Indians and the wilds.

ASABATTLES

Huddled in damp blankets while rain pounded on the tent canvas, the man at first took the shots to be the noise of the storm. It had begun disturbing their sleep in camp on the Missouri beach an hour or so before dawn that June in 1823.

In the instant it took him to become fully awake, he realized it was Ree guns, not the storm, which were raking Ashley's sleeping hunters. Reacting immediately, Hugh Glass grabbed the rifle which was always at his side and crawled out to return fire.

Jed Smith, Tom Fitzpatrick, Jim Clyman and the rest of the 40 men also dug in for a fight. The Arikara -- who'd shared smokes, trade and women with them only hours before -- were firing from bushes and driftwood along the bank as well as from the looming walls of their stockade, pinning the trappers to the open beach.

At their back, across the swift current of the narrow channel, Ashley's two keelboats lay at anchor. Glass could hear the general's voice ordering the boatmen to weigh anchor and cross to aid the hunters. But when Glass, fighting with a reckless courage that impressed his fellow trappers, had time to glance over his shoulder again he saw the boats still sat at anchor. The boatmen refused to brave the fire pouring onto the beach from the village on the bank above.

Too busy to worry about the cowards, the hunters turned to defend themselves. Thoroughly angry now, they refused to retreat in the two skiffs Ashley had managed to send over.

Their bravado soon bowed to reality. Death or wounds silenced more and more guns. The precious horses Ashley bought (with the powder now being used against them) were screaming and falling, good only for barricades. Every moment brought light that made them clearer targets.

Now ready to retreat, the men found no boats. One was carrying wounded across the river. The other, its oarsman slumped in death, drifted uselessly downstream. There was nothing to do but swim. As Glass ran for the water a bullet thudded into his leg. He fell heavily to the sand, but managed to crawl to the water and began to swim.

He'd swum for his life before, four or five years earlier, but that time he'd choked on the salt water of Galveston Bay. That time he'd swum *toward* the shore and the Indians and away from a ship...away from Jean Lafitte and the horrors of life in his company of pirates.

It had been join or die when Lafitte had captured Glass' ship in the gulf. Not ready to die, he'd joined. For months he'd waited his chance to slip away, choosing to risk snake-infested cane jungles and cannibals on the Texas coast over Lafitte's sure response to his mutiny.

Now, in the silt-filled Missouri, he struggled against pain and the weight of his rifle to reach the side of the keelboat. He was near 40, twice the age of many of the others. Some of those swimming near him gave in to their wounds and sank. Glass made the boat.

Gathering the survivors, Ashley ordered the boats downstream. By the time they dropped anchor, he knew a dozen men were dead and three more would join them. The Ree had cost him more than a third of his force. Ten more had less serious wounds.

It was his second venture up the river; both had been hard. His partner, Major Andrew Henry, and a brigade of Rocky Mountain Fur Company trappers, bedeviled by Blackfoot, were waiting for horses and supplies at the mouth of the Yellowstone. But the boatmen refused a second try at the gauntlet of the entrenched Arikara. Stymied, Ashley sent messengers north to Henry on the Yellowstone and south to Colonel Leavenworth, who now commanded Fort Atkinson, asking for help in teaching the Ree to respect white traders. He decided to wait for their response at the mouth of the Cheyenne River.

Meanwhile the trappers buried those who'd succumbed to their wounds. Jedediah Smith, who traveled with God in his heart and a Bible in his pocket, stood over two young men and offered a prayer which moistened the eyes of many of the trappers.

Glass, an implacable foe but a tender friend, had worked to ease the pain of one particular lad from Virginia and he took time to write John Gardner's father:

"My painful duty it is to tell you of the deth of yr son," he wrote in a sensitive and graceful message. "He lived a little while after he was shot and asked me to inform you of his sad fate...I am persuaded John died in

87

peace. His body we buried with others near this camp and marked the grave with a log. His things we will send to you..."

Gardner's belongings and Glass's letter left for St. Louis on the keelboat with the wounded and those who had seen enough of life up the Missouri. But Glass stayed to help punish the Ree and see what else the West had in store.

When Henry arrived with 50 men a month later, the company's spirits rose. About August 1, Leavenworth arrived with 230 infantrymen and cannon and things looked even brighter. The fact that Joshua Pilcher and the Missouri Fur Company, who'd also lost men to recent attacks, contributed another 60 men and a howitzer was also encouraging. But when Glass and the trappers learned Pilcher had recruited several hundred Sioux to join the battle against their traditional enemies, they really began to count Arikara scalps.

The attack on August 9 started well enough. The Sioux carried the brunt of the charge, and when the Ree realized they faced a force of 1,000 or more including white soldiers, they retreated behind their log walls.

The Sioux gleefully chopped up their fallen enemies and waited to see the white man's magic destroy the town they never had been able to breach. The troops and trappers prepared for a charge. But watching the Sioux cavort with bloody body parts, the colonel lost his appetite for battle.

When the big guns finally opened up, the shells took off a curious chief's head and killed a dozen of his people. Most of the shells, however, plopped harmlessly into the dirt walls. The Arikara were safe unless somebody came after them.

Nobody did. Enlisted for temporary duty, the trappers were under Leavenworth's orders. He marched the impatient men from one position to another but would not order a charge. The Sioux, poised to take advantage of white power, found it was an empty threat. Openly contemptuous, they stripped the Ree cornfields, stole some Army mules and rode off.

The next thing Glass and the trappers knew, Leavenworth had met in council with the Ree and negotiated peace. Incredulous, they learned the Indians' only punishment was to return the goods they'd stolen. But the Ree did not do even that. When Leavenworth finally moved into the compound the next day the village was empty. There was no one left to chastise except one fragile old squaw.

As the army marched away, two furious trappers disobeyed orders and torched the village. But the billowing smoke at their backs was small comfort to the trappers who would now have to survive in country populated by a bolder, more confident enemy.

Ashley and Henry, unable to use the Missouri's road, divided their men and started two parties west. Thirteen men would hike up the Grand River and cut across country to the fort at the Yellowstone. Among those chosen to go with Henry on the journey were John Fitzgerald, Jim Bridger and Hugh Glass.

The brigade was four days up the Grand, trudging on foot through the heat of mid-August, tugging reluctant pack horses, when they discovered that the poison of the Arikara debacle was already seeping through the tribes.

Shots blasted into their camp one night and before they could move two men were dead; two more were wounded. Feeling depressed and vulnerable, they found with consternation the next morning that the arrows were not from vengeful Ree but from the usually friendly Mandan and Hidatsa. If these Indians, too, were on the prowl for white scalps, there was no safety anywhere. It was a subdued group which dug two graves on the river bank, distributed goods from two dead horses and hurried on.

Glass' companions were a motley crew. Andrew Henry had been in the mountains a dozen years now. Moses Harris, better known as "Black," needed no more than a full belly and a good yarn to be content in any kind of country. But most of the men were young and green, fresh from the farms, shops and taverns of St. Louis. Jim Bridger, still eager and earnest, could easily have been Glass' son.

Reduced to nine able-bodied men, needing food but aware that attracting a war party could be their last mistake, Henry ordered only two men to range ahead to hunt. Glass couldn't abide the restriction. He was solitary by nature, used to doing things at his own time and in his own way. Scorning the timidity of the younger men, whose courage was now sieved with the knowledge of 17 graves, he continued to leave the column when he chose. There were ripe plums to be had in the bushes crowding the draws and he intended to get some.

Late one afternoon he found them. The sweet pink juice was running down his beard when something else found him.

A she-grizzly, sunning her cubs on the beach, lifted her head, gave a rumbling growl and came for him.

There was no time and no place to retreat. Glass had time for one shot as she reared to strike. He raised the muzzle and squeezed it off with the calm of long experience.

But the monster came on. She swatted him to the ground. His shoulder was bare to the bone. With another rake of her claws he lost a chunk of thigh. Glass grabbed for his knife and plunged it into the huge weight, but it was no match for her fangs. As they grated on his bones he curled into a ball and screamed for help.

The rest of the men were quickly on the scene, but they had to dispose of a yearling cub before they could get near. By the time they reached his side, Glass' shot had taken effect. They heaved the creature aside to view her victim's mangled body.

Scarcely anything was whole. Scalp, face, chest, back, shoulder, arm, hand, thigh -- all were ripped and torn. Blood bubbled from a gash in his throat with each breath.

But, to their wonder, he still breathed.

Knowing he could not last long, sure they were tending a corpse, they did what they could. A couple of the men gave up shirts, which, torn in strips and tied in place, began to stench the flow of blood.

They had a quiet supper and bedded down for the night. Morning would be time enough to bury him.

But in the morning he still breathed.

They could not stay. Every hour in the same place invited attack. Henry ordered them to cut some branches for a litter. They would carry him while he lasted. It couldn't be long.

He lasted the first day and the second, groaning as his tortured body jounced with

their steps, crying out in pain when they stumbled under his weight. Moving in and out of consciousness, Glass had glimpses of an occasional branch, one sweaty face and then another above his head, the hat of the man who had his feet, blue sky and blazing sun.

It couldn't go on. They were creeping when they needed to run. In prolonging one life they could lose ten. When they came to a grove of trees and shrubs around a spring (near the forks of the Grand River) Henry announced his decision. They would leave Glass here to die, where he had shade and water and could lie in peace. It could only be a matter of hours.

But they were civilized men. He wanted two men to watch over him, keep off the wild animals and give him a decent burial. The company would pay a handsome bonus to the volunteers.

The trappers, relieved by the first decision, were confounded by the second. Who would risk staying, losing his own hair for one already all but dead?

The question hung heavy in the shady grove. Glass was a strange one -- hard to understand -- but they respected him. He'd always been quick to help another. Still, it was a hard thing to ask. Finally the youngest member of the party spoke up. Jim Bridger said he'd stay. He was supporting a younger sister back home. He could use the money. John Fitzgerald hesitated, coughed, and said he would, too. Before they could change their minds, Henry and the rest moved west, leaving the two to wait for the breath which rattled from the corpse to cease.

But the ragged breaths continued. Inside the blood-soaked wrappings, beyond the pain, Glass clung to life.

The sun set that evening and returned at dawn. Glass was still breathing. His keepers couldn't hide their disappointment. They gave him water, fixed some soup, shooed off the flies. In quiet voices they speculated how long it would take them to catch up with Henry. Out of sight but not out of hearing, they dug his grave.

Glass, unable to talk, slept most of the time. But the next morning he was stubbornly breathing. Even in his stupor he could sense the impatience of his watchers swelling into panic. One or the other was always out checking for sign. Cheyenne -- Sioux -- Pawnee -- Arikara -- Hidatsa -- Mandan -- it didn't matter. They were ripe plums for any war party to pick.

Glass refused to release his death grip -- refused to set them free. He hung on to see another dawn.

They paced more and began to argue. Feverish now, alternately shaking and sweating, Glass heard Fitzgerald reason with the younger man. It had been days -- not hours. They'd done their duty. Every hour here increased their peril. They couldn't stay lucky forever. The old man was taking too long to die, but death was certain. They could do nothing for him. Why should three die when two could live. They must leave him.

Bridger refused, at first. But his arguments lacked conviction. Glass was not surprised to see him, finally, nod in assent. Their decision made, the two quickly began packing up their gear. Glass grunted and followed them with his eyes, trying to force one and then the other to meet his stare. They lifted him to move his pallet within reach of the spring, but they did not meet his eyes.

Then Fitzgerald did something that astounded the wounded man. He picked up Hugh's rifle and powder horn and emptied the bullets from his pouch. As Bridger protested, Fitzgerald gathered the old man's tomahawk and knife. Then he cut the thongs that held his possibles sack with his flint and steel.

They'd have to tell Henry that Glass was dead, Fitzgerald cut off Bridger's exclamations, or they couldn't get their bonus. You didn't leave a good rifle or anything else of value with a dead man. It wasn't like he'd ever use it again.

Glass, still unbelieving, tried to lift himself from the litter. Overwhelmed by the rush of pain he sunk back, able only to lift an imploring hand. But they were gone. He listened as their steps grew fainter and died away.

Then he got angry. He'd clung to life before, almost out of habit, because he was too vital not to take whatever chance there was for life. Now he had another reason. You might leave a man, if you had to -- only realists survived in the wilderness. But you didn't leave him helpless as a newborn babe. You didn't take his gun.

A man's rifle was his second self, almost part of his arm. Awake or asleep he kept it by his side. The butt against his shoulder meant food for his empty stomach. The weight in his hand made him equal to any enemy -- except the grizzly.

He'd not let a man finish what a grizzly'd begun if he could help it. But *could* he help it? Four or five days more he sank, rallied, shook with fever, groaned with delirium. He woke to gulp a few handfuls of water from the spring, slept to dream that wolves tugged at the robe which covered him, woke to find the robe gone.

Slowly, the spark of life flared brighter. He reached above him and stripped chokecherries from the bush. Crushing the tiny, red-black fruits in his palm and moistening them with spring water, he managed to swallow some nourishment.

Recovered enough to begin feeling hunger, Glass woke to see a large rattlesnake curled nearby. His fear subsided when he noted the bulge midway down its body; it was too busy digesting a recent meal to be alert or wary.

He stretched to reach a rock with a sharp edge and brought it down on the reptile's neck with all the force he could muster. It took several blows and he had to rest before he could do more.

Instinctively he felt for his knife. It was gone, of course, but his fingers felt something hard in his shot pouch. His razor had not shaken out with the lead. He skinned the long body and soon bites of snake flesh were following the chokecherries down his damaged throat. He slept again.

With food in his body, he woke to take a firmer grip on life. Rolling to his knees, he knew at once he could not stand. But he could crawl; however slow and however far, he could crawl. He set off to find the men who'd robbed him of every chance of life.

They'd be at Fort Henry, but that lay north, across dry, rugged country. He dared not leave water. He headed down the Grand. The fur traders post called Fort Kiowa, below the Great Bend of the Missouri, would be his nearest source of help. It was 350 miles away. He thought of the man who had his rifle and lurched off down the river, pushing forward on his good arm and undamaged leg.

Most men would have known it was hopeless. After 200 yards, or 500, or a mile, knees bruised and hands bloody, they'd have resigned themselves to their fate. But Glass had hate to fuel his furnace and a mind he could focus on his next immediate need. The next step, the next drink, the next mouthful of food were his concern. To think of the enormity, the impossibility of his goal was to court disaster.

He also could draw on experience few men knew he had. He could become Pawnee again. As he crawled, his mind went back to the time he'd escaped Lafitte. He and his partner had kept out of the grasp of the cannibals on the coast, but wandering north across the plains they'd been taken by the Skidi Pawnee.

The religious Skidi did not eat their captives, at least not directly. They were sacrificed to the Morning Star before they were fed to the dogs. Colter's friend had become a human torch -- his naked, suspended body shot with hundreds of pine slivers which flared in a whoosh at the touch of a flame.

His screams had echoed in Glass' ears for weeks until the omens told the priests it was Glass' turn. Facing incineration, he'd pulled his last rabbit out of his possibles sack. He offered the chief a packet of vermillion. It was the only bit of leverage, the only thing left of the goods he'd stolen from Lafitte. It worked. The chief, delighted with a brilliant red the Indians could not find in nature, decided Glass was a sign of good fortune. He adopted the white man and Glass spent the next few years as a Pawnee, riding, hunting, warring, living as the tribes did off the fruits of the prairie.

Those years came back to him now as he crawled, grateful to make two miles a day. He remembered which bushes held edible berries, which roots could offer nourishment, which nests might provide stores of roots, or eggs or defenseless young. He knew a bone, if fresh enough, might still cradle life in its center. He cracked open those of a buffalo he came across and scraped out the marrow.

One day he crouched behind some brush and watched a pack of wolves cut a buffalo calf away from the herd and run it to ground not far from his cover. Hungrily, he waited until they'd devoured enough to appease their appetites. Then he crawled from cover, screaming, waving a branch, rearing on his knees, his tattered bandages and buckskins flapping. He bluffed the canines out of their kill. A Pawnee again, he gladly gulped whatever remained, intestines, paunch, bits of liver, replacing his blood with the buffalo's. For two or three days he tarried by the source of food, impatient to be moving on but knowing a stronger body could carry him faster.

His wounds were healing. He'd washed them often and the flesh was closing. The gash across his back tormented him because he'd not been able to clean it. It festered and attracted flies and other insects. But he could stand now, and walk. He'd joined the human race again.

The cottonwoods glowed with October color by the time he reached the Missouri. Nights were cold and food getting scarcer. He decided to detour north a few miles to the burned out Ree villages and glean their corn and melon fields.

The Sioux had had the same idea, but they were looking for corn, not coups, and the scarred, emaciated survivor inspired their admiration. They took him in, cleaned the maggots out of his torn back and escorted him down to Fort Kiowa.

The Ashley men were all gone; the

general had left for St. Louis. But Glass was an Ashley man and he was able to get an outfit on credit. He picked out a blanket capote, an ax, a knife, a blanket and a kettle. With new buckskin leggings, a cap -- and a rifle -- he was ready.

For he still had a mission. In two days he was done with recuperation and on a boat up the Missouri. The traders he rode with were headed to the Mandan villages to trade; he was bound for the Yellowstone.

The river was ruffled with cold November winds by the time the boat neared the Mandan. Glass, always pushing, asked to be put ashore just below the villages, knowing he could walk the neck of a large bend much faster than the traders could row.

He stepped ashore and into a nest of Ree. They'd moved their residence up near the Mandan, promising to forego any more white scalps, but the memory of their burning village was strong. A woman out gathering wood was the first to spot Glass and raise the alarm. As he sprang into as much of a run as he could manage, he glimpsed several braves mounting their horses to ride him down. There was no choice but to try for the questionable succor of the Mandan.

Breathless, hobbling, he quickly saw he would not make it, but he had to try. He could hear the Ree yelps closing in behind when another Indian rode at him from the side, swept him up and carried him on to the village.

His saviour was a Mandan; the tribe was again firmly on the side of the traders. Glass became an instant celebrity. Grateful as he was for their help, however, he was not interested in fame or even shelter for the winter. When he could find no boat going up river, he started alone up the north side of the Missouri.

Few men would challenge the Mandan country in winter. Beyond the villages the vegetation was scattered and poor. The only shelter from the Arctic wind was in the river bottom. But the bottom lay first on one side of the channel and then the other. There was no shelter anywhere from the sub-zero cold.

Days turned to weeks and the weeks to a month as he trudged the 300 miles to Fort Henry. The Little Missouri curled in from the

south, the bluffs and buttes stood taller. He kept on, detouring to hunt when he had to. He met no one. The only other voice he heard was the wind, the only other presence at his small fire the cold.

At last he was at the confluence and the log walls of Henry's fort stood across the river. His time had come. But as he crossed the Missouri he knew something was wrong. No smoke rose from behind the walls. No horses whinnied. The snow piled undisturbed against the gate. Unbelieving, he threw his weight against it.

The post was empty. His quarry was gone. He sagged against a doorjamb.

But he had already risen above more serious blows to both mind and body. Recovered from the shock, he looked for some sign of where Henry had taken his men. Discovering they'd headed up the Yellowstone, he followed.

It was December now. He didn't know just where they were, how far he'd have to go to find them, *if* he could find them. But he headed south up the Yellowstone.

Here in the white expanse there was even less shelter. He plunged through cold more intense than he'd ever known, using every trick and craft to keep the heat in his limbs, some fuel in his stomach, the backbone in his purpose. At night, doubts hunched just beyond the firelight. He was so tired. How many frigid miles stretched ahead?

He'd walked through December and into the New Year when he found them. One day he squinted through frost-coated eyelashes at the new post Henry had built at the mouth of the Littlehorn. The men inside, celebrating the arrival of 1824, looked up to see an apparition enter the gate. The old year had never had a more appropriate symbol, a grave never given up a colder corpse.

Knowing what they saw could not be real, they blamed the whiskey, their eyes, witchcraft. But one among them knew the blame lay elsewhere. Jim Bridger froze where he stood, his face washed first with disbelief, then guilt, then fear.

Glass stared at him. He'd come 1,200 miles, the first accomplished on his knees, to exact revenge for the wrong done him. He should be cocking his rifle. But the quaking, shamed 19-year-old in front of him invited pity, not wrath.

Bridger knew he'd done wrong. If he was a good man the memory would scar his conscience forever. If he was not...it was up to God. Glass turned on his heel and walked away.

Fitzgerald was another story, and he was not there. He'd gone east, Henry told him. He and Black Harris had packed up and pushed off for a down river post in the middle of November, just after the brigade had settled on the Little Bighorn. He'd been going down the rivers Glass had just come up.

Glass was staggered. Somehow, when he hunted, when he slept, when he cut across a bend, the man who held his rifle had floated past him. Fitzgerald probably was at Fort Atkinson by now. Hugh would have to complete another arc of the circle before he tasted revenge.

He managed to wait until the end of February. Then, hearing Henry had letters to send to Fort Atkinson, he eagerly volunteered to be one of the five-man courier party. With the Missouri route impractical, they decided to cross the country south to the Platte and follow the Platte to the fort. They were paddling bullboats near the mouth of the Laramie River when they came on a camp of Indians.

Glass took them to be his old friends, the Pawnee, and decided to stop and barter for some food. Leaving their guns under guard in one boat, the three other trappers walked into a lodge. But Glass was hardly seated on the buffalo robe when he heard a couple of words that didn't square with Pawnee as he'd known it. In sudden dread he realized. These were not Pawnee but their cousins, the Arikara -- the ones who'd lost their chief to a cannonball on the Missouri!

He dove for the door.

They ran and then swam, but two were cut down before they reached the far bank. The other three scattered. Glass, without his rifle, took cover in some rocks and lay hidden while the Ree beat the bushes up and down the stream.

After dark he crept away. There was no sign of the other men, but he was used to traveling alone. This time he was rich with knife, flint and steel. This time the meadows were dotted with new buffalo calves, fresh dropped and easy prey. The 400 miles between him and the Missouri seemed only a minor challenge.

Unarmed, he preferred the lonely tracks of the sandhills to the possibly populated Platte. He veered north for Fort Kiowa. When he reached it, his hopes were confirmed. Fitzgerald was at Fort Atkinson.

In a few days Glass was there also. After 2,000 miles -- pain filled, exhausting, starving miles -- revenge seemed finally at hand. A threatening presence even without a firearm, Glass demanded to see Fitzgerald and his gun.

But Fitzgerald was now a soldier. He'd enlisted only weeks before, but he was a soldier. The Army did not intend to offer him up for slaughter.

Glass had to be content with spitting words instead of bullets, with knowing the man was shamed in front of his superiors. Drained of the venom he'd stored for eight months, warmed by a collection the troops took up in his honor, he clasped his rifle and left the bad taste behind.

He headed down the Missouri once more, where he joined the Santa Fe trade. From Santa Fe he again entered the fur trade and the Rockies. Always independent, working as a free trapper, he became more and more the loner, placing his small fire where he could have privacy. He had survived nearly half a century doing things his own way.

Glass ranged the fur country as far north as the site of old Fort Henry and it was near there about 1833 that the Ree finally had the last word. One winter day they caught him and two fellow trappers crossing the ice of the Yellowstone. It took only moments. Yipping in triumph, the Ree rode away waving the rifle Hugh Glass would come after no more.

An Indignant Soul

When the Arikara closed the Missouri to the trappers in 1824, they succeeded only in forcing the white men to find other paths into their country. Ashley's men probed until they discovered they could cross the Rockies without the Missouri's help. That winter they stumbled across a high barren plain and up a gentle incline 280 miles southeast of Three Forks. This South Pass, they wrote the war department, could be traversed by wagons.

Wagons. Possibilities began to stir. Wagon wheels could carry troops and cannons. They could carry trade goods and pelts. But -- when the time came -- they could also carry hoes and anvils, rocking chairs and china barrels. Their occupants could better hold a country against Britain than itinerant trappers. Eyes so long focused on the upper Missouri began to swing south.

General Atkinson took another look at the situation on the upper river and decided the Indians could be controlled by an occasional show of strength. In the summer of 1825 he took troops on an expedition to convince the Ree and the other tribes to sign treaties of friendship. The Indians looked at the 500 troopers, listened to the cannons boom and signed. The Ree, as punishment, got only tobacco for their marks; the other tribes got richer presents.

By 1827 the army had abandoned Fort Atkinson. Those troops moved south to the new Cantonment Leavenworth at the mouth of the Kansas River.

But the fur trade did not abandon the Missouri. John Jacob Astor's new American Fur Company was moving in even as Ashley's men took the trail out the Platte and through South Pass. By 1828, Astor had ordered a post built at the mouth of the Yellowstone. Ambitious, capable Kenneth McKenzie was put in charge and slowly, laboriously, Fort Union took shape.

Neither had Astor and his men given up on steam power. Goods shipped by boat could undercut the opposition. Pierre Chouteau, Jr., scion of the St. Louis dynasty but now in the New Yorker's employ, ordered a steamboat built with the hazards of the Missouri in mind. He christened it the Yellow Stone and in 1831 he took it as far north as the company post at the mouth of the Teton River.

In 1832, the Yellow Stone steamed triumphantly past the Teton, and Chouteau and his passengers began to believe the "big thunder canoe" they rode might do more than terrorize the river natives -- it might actually make Fort Union.

George Catlin had been on the river nearly three months by the time he saw Fort Union in late June 1832. Above the Teton River he'd scarcely left the deck, anxious to drink in all he could of the passing wonders. Now the fort loomed above him like one of the eroded buttes he'd been sketching along the channel. His artist's eye had turned them into castles and citadels with cupolas and porticoes. Their spires, glistening in the early morning sun, throwing intriguing shadows in the evening, changed colors with the light that shed "a glory over the solitude of this wild and pictured country."

Fort Union was made by the hand of man and it had no lacy cupolas, but he couldn't help being impressed. He'd seen the flag gleaming far above the sturdy bastions while still a half hour down river. Immediately his host, Pierre Chouteau, Jr., had set the signal cannons booming.

The valley echoed back the shots, but before the air was cleared of smoke, guns from the fort answered. His head rocked with the gunfire and the yells of the frightened and excited Indians along the bank. A steamboat had made it up to the Yellowstone! It was a historic moment worth celebrating.

Catlin climbed up the north bank to see what Kenneth McKenzie had spent four years building. A rectangular stockade now reared 20 feet above the plain where Hugh Glass had trudged, frozen and starving, just nine years before. The solid line of the squared, peeled pickets posed a barrier no Indian could challenge. Stone bastions towered at opposite corners and the flag waved from a tall pole in the center of the spacious enclosed courtyard.

Facing Catlin across the yard was an imposing two-story house complete with glass windows and shutters. And here the portico was not imaginary -- an inviting porch stretched across the front. The house would have been at home on any street in St. Louis.

Ushered into the cool interior, the artist could see bourgeois McKenzie was bringing up all the comforts of civilization. He was Scottish, not French, but his hospitality would bow to no one. The table he offered his guests fairly sagged with buffalo tongue, roast and ribs, with beaver tail and venison steak.

There was no coffee, bread or butter, but iced bottles of Madeira and port helped the diners overlook that absence. Catlin enjoyed the wit of his host and the intellect of a visiting Englishman named Hamilton.

The company was stimulating, as was the thrill of his first buffalo hunt, but he had not come to Fort Union to be entertained. He'd come to accomplish the most important work of his life -- a project he'd been pursuing with single-minded determination for ten years. And he knew the time to finish this mission was running out.

Almost by chance in 1822 he'd seen a delegation of western Indians on the streets of Philadelphia. He was immediately taken with their dignified bearing and the bright beauty of their garb. Feathers, furs, shells, beads, muscular brown bodies, intricate hair styles, intriguing faces -- what more could an artist ask? He'd been searching for a subject to which he could devote his energy for a lifetime and it suddenly stood before him. But it would be so much more than a subject, he knew; it would be a cause.

The young artist had always liked and sympathized with Indians. As a frightened ten-year-old he'd held an Oneida brave in his gun sights as both stalked the same deer near his Pennsylvania home. But the Indian had turned at the critical moment and young George had looked into his face. He didn't see a wild savage that deserved extermination; he saw a human being. He lowered his rifle.

The next day George and his father found and befriended the Indian with his wife and child. He spent many fascinating days at the Indians' camp, learning to use the bow and arrows and tomahawk the brave made him. Then the Oneidas had left to return home. The brave was killed before he got ten miles. The wife and child disappeared.

George, devastated, returned to the woods and continued to practice with the tomahawk. One day as he tried to teach a friend to throw it there was an accident. The left side of George's dark, handsome face was still marred by the scar.

His conscience was burned by what was happening to the Indians. He knew that, like his Oneida brave, they were being systematically destroyed. He saw cultures vanishing before the onslaught of white civilization; vanishing before they could be recorded, before their knowledge could be shared, their values appreciated.

It was already too late for the eastern Indians. George knew they were seen as a joke -- drunken, dissolute beggars. He knew that would happen in the west, too, that it was already happening. He could not save them. But perhaps he could at least preserve their essence. He was gifted at doing portraits. He'd abandoned a law career to devote himself to art and his work had been well-received. He was a good observer and could write about what he saw. He would collect their artifacts and exhibit them to city people, perhaps spread a little understanding.

Terribly aware that even the wild tribes in the west were changing under the pressure, he began saving funds for his mission, trying to find sponsors for his work. By 1830 he'd managed to get to St. Louis and had spent the past two seasons there with William Clark as his mentor. The aging explorer, his red hair now white, but still agent and respected father to the tribes, had opened Indian doors for him. He'd set up his easel beside Clark's desk, traveled with him to see the Kansa tribe, sat in on treaty councils. He'd painted Iowa, Potawatomie, Shawnee, Kickapoo, Sac, Fox and even Pawnee clear up on the Platte.

But he'd scarcely started. He was determined, if he lived long enough, to "paint every chief of every tribe," to be the historian and biographer for "a dying nation" that had none of its own. Now, on the northern Missouri, he was at last among Indians little touched by civilization. They came in to trade with McKenzie at Fort Union, but their lives and customs were still their own. At this crossroads there were Crow from the south, Assiniboin and Plains Cree from the north and Blackfoot from the west. Catlin could hardly wait to unpack his oils.

He carried his paint pots and canvases up into one of the fort's bastions, took a seat on the cool breech of the cannon that pointed out over the prairie, and went to work.

He was conscious, as he worked in a room piled with ball and powder, that many of the warriors who lined the walls watching were lifelong enemies. They would kill on sight out on the prairie. But the fort was a truce ground. McKenzie took their weapons at the gate. He would brook no trouble.

Catlin was enthralled with the wild tribes. He found them independent and happy people, "the finest-looking, best-equipped and most beautifully costumed" of any he'd seen. The brawny Blackfoot were striking and their chiefs superbly dressed, but the Crow were without peer. Many of the men were six feet tall or more. Their black hair, shiny with bear grease, hung down their straight backs to sweep the ground behind them. The pelts they wore were white and soft as velvet.

The braves were equally fascinated with the magic the slim artist performed. Daubs of color from his pallet became images of themselves and their friends. They crowded his room until McKenzie had to ask the chiefs to guard his door, letting in only the chosen few important enough to deserve his attention. They lounged around the room, bragging about their coups, pointing to their scalp locks in proof, waiting for their turn.

He painted a Blackfoot chief, Buffalo's Back Fat, and the youngest of his wives, Crystal Stone. He sketched a Crow, Four Wolves, who had cut locks of his long hair to mourn his brother, and Eagle Ribs, who stood proudly with the scalps of eight trappers dangling from his spear.

But Catlin did more than paint. He asked

endless questions, took voluminous notes and put the information he collected in long letters to be sent back east.

He learned about the scalp dance, the way they made their bows, the unique red stone they carved into pipes, how they traveled, where they spent the winter, how they tanned their hides. He deviled the interpreters until he thought he understood their concept of medicine to be anything mysterious.

One day he watched a medicine man in action. The Cree and Blackfoot had been there for weeks, reluctantly keeping peace as McKenzie required. But when the trader returned the Cree arms as they prepared to leave, one warrior couldn't resist the opportunity to attack an enemy in the Blackfoot delegation. He returned to the stockade, sighted his prey inside talking to the bourgeois, put his rifle to a crack and fired.

The chief fell, rolling on the ground in agony. In an instant the Blackfoot grabbed their weapons and charged after the Cree. The traders, incensed at the broken truce, ran with them. Catlin vaulted up the stairs to his room in the bastion to watch the chase.

It wasn't much of a battle. The Cree, already distant, lay down a covering fire as they retreated. But the Blackfoot killed at least one and wounded more. Catlin, looking on, watched his wild tribes acting and reacting as they had for centuries.

He hurried back down when the party returned and learned the Blackfoot medicine man was on his way to help the wounded chief. The crowd of Indians and whites around the injured man was pushed back to form a ring and an aisle was opened for the conjurer's entrance. Hushed and ready, the men waited.

There was a faint tinkling. Then White Buffalo came, crouching, swaying, shaking a rattle in time to his steps, his body scarcely visible beneath a grizzly skin. The bear's head covered his own like a mask and huge claws ringed his wrists and ankles. Skins and skeletons of small animals jiggled in the fringe of his costume.

Once near his patient, he began to dance, leaping and yelling one minute, snorting and growling like a bear the next. He jumped around and over the prostrate man, imploring the help of the Great Spirit, rolling and positioning his patient. This went on for half an hour while Catlin and the others watched in silence.

But the Great Spirit refused to hear him. The chief died, and White Buffalo danced off to shed his finery and join the mourners. Catlin hurried to record the vivid experience.

White Buffalo was not the only Indian costumed strangely at Fort Union. Catlin had seen a young Assiniboin warrior, The Light, step from the steamer *Yellow Stone* in a rumpled, blue and gold army general's uniform complete with epaulets and shiny black boots. A tall red feather was stuck in the band of his high-crowned beaver; a broadsword swung at his side. He held a battered blue umbrella in one white-gloved hand and a broken fan in the other.

Even these Indians were not immune to becoming clowns for the white man. Catlin thought with despair of the apprehensive but proud and outgoing warrior he'd painted in St. Louis a year earlier -- before The Light had been feasted and feted in Washington, D.C. Now he'd come back to his people, to show the silver medal that Great White Father Jackson had given him and to tell his tribe about the wonders of the white world that filled him with delight. He took his keg of whiskey under his arm and, once his people understood who he was, became a sensation with his stories.

Soon Catlin noticed he was sharing his riches. His coattails were now new blue leggings for his pretty young wife and his lace hat band had become her garters. In a little while his brother wore the coat and The Light, though still in his linen shirt, had exchanged the painful boots for moccasins.

But he kept his keg of whiskey.

His people crowded around to hear his stories. He told of houses -- so many that he'd notched a pipestem, a war club and several long sticks to keep track of their numbers -- until he'd come to a village so large he'd have needed dozens of sticks just to show it alone. He'd seen boats with not one but many, many guns far bigger than the cannon in the fort. He'd seen paths that stretched above the rivers, soldiers without number; he'd even seen people carried into the air beneath a great round flying creature.

He had endless tales to tell. By the time

two days had passed, the keg was empty and The Light had given away everything but the medal and his blue umbrella. Catlin wondered how things would turn out for this Indian who'd sojourned through time as well as space.

But the artist could not spend all summer at Fort Union. He wanted time to study the Mandan he'd heard so much about. He and two trappers stepped into a greenwood canoe and started downstream, past bighorn sheep and through flocks of swans and pelicans. One morning George woke to find a grizzly with cubs prowling their camp and he proposed they have some sport. But the trappers paled and dragged him into the boat. You never fight Caleb, they told him, except in self-defense.

They also enlightened him on the romantic life of a free trapper, who regularly lost his horse, his gun, his beaver and even his clothes to the Blackfoot or Ree. McKenzie and the company took still more, money the trappers had yet to earn.

Taking time to explore and sketch the countryside, they were at the Mandan villages in a week. The trader of the American Fur Company made them welcome. Catlin settled himself into a dirt lodge and prepared for further studies.

Not all Indians took kindly to being painted, he'd discovered. Some found the medicine of seeing their own likeness too powerful. The trader arranged for Catlin to paint two chiefs in private, before the tribe knew what he was about; even the subjects seemed unaware of what he was doing. When he finished and showed them their portraits, they clapped their hands over their mouths in astonishment, looking at one another and the pictures again and again, then looking from the artist to his pallet and back again.

Clasping his hand, they called him Great Medicine White Man and left the lodge to tell their families what had happened to them. Soon Catlin was aware of faces peering down his smoke hole and peeping around the posts of the entry. Before long hundreds of Mandan gathered in a crush around the walls and on the roof of his lodge.

The trader appeared with the other chiefs and explained the artists' purpose. The chiefs seemed pleased and wanted their pictures done also. To quiet the excited crowd, the two portraits were carried outside for the people to see.

Some screamed. Some began to dance. Some sang. Some cried. Some drove their spears into the ground. A few fired red arrows into the sun and retreated to their lodges. Most stood, like their chiefs, with hands clapped over astonished mouths.

When Catlin stepped out he was instantly mobbed. Men wanted to shake his hand. Children crawled through the throng to touch his legs. This man made living beings, they said. Here were their chiefs in two places at once, one only partly alive, it was true, but alive. They could see the eyes move, see them smile. They expected them to speak.

But their wonder shortly turned to fear. The squaws decided the life in the picture must have come from the person. The artist could take life as well as give it. He was a danger to them all. He would take part of these men back to the white world and when the chiefs died that part would continue to live. The chiefs would never be able to rest. The women wanted him out of their village.

The panic was contagious. The chiefs who'd been in the lodge and agreed to sit for him now refused. For several days Catlin waited, afraid he would never be able to do his work.

Then the chiefs held a council to decide what to do with this dangerous man. With difficulty, Catlin got permission to speak.

I am only a man like yourselves, he assured them. I have no medicine, only a skill I've learned. You could learn to do it, too. I respect and admire your people. I will do them no harm.

He was sweating and anxious, but he had a trump card to play. He knew Indians well enough by now to know what to say. In his country, he told them, brave men never allowed their women to frighten them with foolish whims and stories. That turned the trick. The braves were again shaking his hand and offering to pose. Catlin's days were suddenly full.

He soon learned to take them in the order of their importance, and he worked again with the walls lined with observers waiting their turn. They smoked to a picture's success when it was begun and yelled and sang songs of thanks when it was finished and the sitter unharmed. Catlin shared the pipe as it made the rounds, grandstanding sometimes, pretending the smoke he blew through his nostrils helped him over difficult spots in the work.

He painted Four Bears, most loved of the chiefs, and heard about his many acts of bravery. Invited to dinner in his lodge, Catlin sat beside the fire while the husky chief, fresh from his morning steam bath and dressed for the occasion in his horned and feathered fur headdress, carved a bit of meat from the roasted buffalo ribs and cast it into the fire. With the spirits thanked, he motioned for Catlin to carve off all he wanted and urged him to try the pemmican, marrow fat and currant pudding. Meanwhile he busied himself packing an ornate pipe with red willow bark, and when Catlin had finished the two enjoyed a silent but companionable smoke. When the artist rose to leave, the kind faced Indian pressed him to accept not only the pipe but a beautiful skin the chief had painted for him, portraying the 14 enemies he had killed in combat.

Often Catlin took his sketch book to record village life. He watched boys take part in sham battles, saw dances to bring the rain or the buffalo, observed the women at work and the men at play. He filled notebook after notebook with what he learned about their culture.

There was one ceremony -- Okipa -- which he'd heard about but not witnessed. Part of it took place in the great medicine lodge, a sacred place where the holy skin of the white buffalo hung high on a pole. He knew of no white man who had ever seen it in its entirety. One sunrise after the willows were fully leafed out he was breakfasting with the traders when he was startled by terrible shrieks. The white men rushed outside to see a medicine man approaching the village. His body whitened with clay, he wore four white wolf skins and a raven headdress and carried a large pipe. Okipa, the traders told him, had begun.

The Mandan raced about excitedly as if preparing for war, but when the figure entered the village the chiefs greeted him and made him welcome. He was Lone Man, he said, the only one left alive after the great flood. He'd landed his canoe on a mountain after a dove had brought him a branch of willow. He was there to open the medicine lodge for their annual ceremony.

So began what for Catlin was an incredible four days of religious ritual and pageant celebrating the tribe's survival and initiating its young men into manhood. The first three days with their costumed characters and public dances, though frantic, bizarre and sexual by turn, were much as he'd expected. But the fourth day brought a bloody climax he could hardly endure. That afternoon the medicine men and the four dozen young men who wished to prove their courage convened in the medicine lodge. The initiates had already gone four days without food, water or sleep; now they would complete their pledge.

Catlin, ready with his sketch pad, had been warned by the traders. He had watched other religious rites, and thought he was prepared for the spectacle, but he found it surpassed his wildest imaginings.

As he watched, each participant was twice pierced through the skin and muscles of his chest or back so that skewers could be inserted under the skin. Thongs were tied to each end of the skewer and the youth was hoisted six or eight feet into the air. Skewers through his leg and arm skin were weighted with his shield, quiver and buffalo skulls and he was raised again until he hung above the heads of the crowd. There, blood streaming down his body, the initiate was spun around and around until, after ten or 15 minutes, he cried out to the Great Spirit and sank into unconsciousness. Lowered and again awake, he crawled to a buffalo skull, where he sacrificed the little finger of his left hand to the Great Spirit. His ordeal ended outside, where he was run and dragged around the Lone Man shrine until the weights were all torn away.

Catlin, watching, sketched through tears. But the Mandan shed none. They were there by choice. They put their lives in the hands of the Great Spirit. They were being judged for their courage. A man who showed his worth might one day be a chief.

At sunset it was over. Each Mandan family sacrificed a sharp tool to the current of the Missouri so that the waters should never rise to cover the earth again. The sickened Catlin retired to his lodge. There in the next week, under the light from the smoke hole, he relived the terrible scenes as he put them on canvas. Then, as much as he wanted to forget the things he'd witnessed, he faithfully recorded them in his notebook. Only then could he write, "Thank God, it is over..."

Still, as the artist rolled up his paintings and packed the robes and clothing he'd collected, he felt nothing but respect and compassion for a people who could sacrifice so much for their faith. They gathered at the river's edge to bid him goodbye, Four Bears and the other chiefs embracing him, the warriors offering their hands, the women and children calling farewell. Just as his canoe was pulling away a young brave raced up and tossed him a packet, indicating he should not open it until later.

A mile or so downstream he opened it to find an exquisitely worked pair of leggings he had tried to buy from the warrior. The young man had refused to part with them when Catlin offered a horse in payment, but now that it was too late for the artist to offer compensation, he freely made his gift.

Several minutes later, as the village disappeared from view, Catlin was startled to see a group of Mandan chasing the boat along shore. He pulled in to find them in panic because one of the women he'd painted was coughing blood and seemed about to die. Her portrait, which he carried in the boat, held too much of her, they said. He was taking her life with him -- pulling out the strings of her heart. His medicine was great, but it was too great. They must have her picture back so that she could be well again. Regretfully, but with respect for their feelings, he sorted out the painting and returned it, assuring them he wished her and all of them only the best.

Underway again, he pondered the Mandans' future. He saw that they were a small tribe, under constant pressure from the Sioux, and believed they could not long survive. He made his assessment with deep sorrow for he'd discovered that "no set of men that ever I associated with have better hearts than the Mandan...and no man in any country keeps his word and guards his honor more closely."

Catlin painted his way on down the "foaming and muddy waters" of the river, stopping to paint Hidatsa, Sioux, Sac, Iowa,

Omaha, Ponca, and Oto. The small river tribes, he could see, were already diminished.

Farther south he encountered Delaware, Shawnee and other tribes removed from the east by the government and put west of the Missouri. Then he was at the end of "this prairie where heaven sheds its purest light and lends its richest tints."

He'd had to work hurriedly, painting as many as six portraits a day, sacrificing detail for impression, slighting quality for quantity. In 87 days he'd produced dozens of portraits, tens of sketches, and thousands of words about the cultures of a half dozen plains tribes. But there was much more to do.

In 1834 he journeyed with the army to the southern plains to record the Comanche, the Kiowa, and the Wichita. In 1835 he was up the Mississippi to paint Ojibway and woodland Sioux. In 1837 he went back east, traveling against the flood tide that would doom so many of those he'd painted. He gathered his collection of 600 paintings and artifacts into a "Gallery unique" and prepared his letters and notes for publication.

He knew by then what had happened to The Light.

At first the traveled brave's audiences had been captivated and entertained. The Light didn't need the firewater to create his wild tales. He became famous for his oratory and chief of his band.

But as the stories continued (and he insisted they were not stories, but true) he began to stir envy and fear. His medicine was greater than they'd ever known, but it was lying medicine. His words could not be trusted; he was not to be believed.

Finally one brave openly challenged a tale and the exasperated storyteller whipped him with a rod, much as he'd seen white men cane their slaves. The humiliated victim of The Light's wrath pondered a way to put an end to this source of evil. Certain a rifle bullet could never harm one with so powerful a medicine, he dreamed he could use another weapon. He stole an iron pot handle from the traders, filed it to fit his gun barrel and stalked The Light to his tipi one evening. When the fire threw The Light's shadow against the tipi wall, he fired. The Light would deceive his people no more.

Looking back, remembering, Catlin was

101

struck with this waste of intelligence and promise. The brave had been struck down "for telling the truth, and nothing but the truth." The white man had sought to use him to impress his people, but the gap of understanding had been too great to cross. He recorded The Light's story and grieved.

Catlin had only begun his life's work. For the next 20 years he traveled the West and the world, to record native peoples and display his work. He exhibited his paintings and artifacts in Philadelphia, New York, London and Paris, lecturing when and where he could about the people he championed. Indians could be cruel and vengeful, he admitted, but they were more than savages.

"I love a people who are honest without laws," he wrote, "who keep the commandments without ever having read them...who never fought a battle with white men except on their own ground." The way these people were being treated, he told his audiences, was "plenty enough to claim (one's) pity and engage his whole soul's indignation."

He had some success, published books and portfolios and was honored by royalty. But he had more failures. Most people did not want to hear his message. Some of his paintings were too gruesome. His Indians rode horses too fine for them to own. His account of the Mandan's Okipa ceremony was ridiculed as too horrible to be true. Like The Light, he was not to be believed. Catlin went bankrupt and lost his collection to a creditor. It was stored away in a boiler works. When he died in 1872 at 76 he was still pleading with Congress to purchase and save his collection.

Seven years after his death, the widow of his creditor turned the "Gallery unique" over to the Smithsonian Institution where it gradually came to be appreciated as a priceless source of information on a vanished people. As the Mandan squaws prophesied, his works have made them all live beyond their graves.

Where the Saints Dwell

As George Catlin had discovered, it is easier to spread distrust than understanding. Differences can be too great to be stomached, too threatening to be tolerated. Fear, a malignant growth out of control, can engulf restraint, swallow reason.

The people who came to settle along the lower Missouri in the early 1830s did not skewer their chests, mutilate their hands or throw knives in the river to hold back the floods.

But they were strangers. And they had strange ways.

Nine-year-old Emily Partridge stood at the door of her family's home and shielded her face from the heat of the fire. Only a few yards away her father's haystack roared with flames. She stared at the tremendous blaze, almost too fascinated to be afraid.

She was not particularly surprised. Night riders had torched the stack because her father and mother were Mormons. She'd been listening for weeks as the adults talked about windows broken by rocks, bullets that came crashing into their homes at night, crops which were trampled and destroyed.

They knew the first settlers in Independence did not welcome them or their religion. The Mormons had arrived two years earlier, in 1831, to establish a New Jerusalem, a place where the followers of Joseph Smith could live in peace and prosperity. Here in Jackson County, directly south of the Missouri on the western edge of the state, beyond most other settlements, they had hoped to establish their Zion.

They'd built houses, begun farming, started a school and a newspaper. They'd marked out the square for their temple. But perhaps they'd been too successful.

Some of the early settlers had been here since 1827. Their town, often crowded with freighters preparing to take the trail to Santa Fe, was the county seat and their courthouse served more than 2,500 citizens. They grew uneasy as hundreds of Mormons poured in, bought land and settled. They were suspicious of their religious beliefs and practices, afraid of the political changes their numbers would make possible, fearful they'd cause unrest among the slaves and Indians.

The abuse was vocal at first, then it became physical. Small groups of malcontents became mobs. Emily had often heard about the mobs. The Mormons never knew where they might strike. Her parents had warned her and her sisters, Eliza, 13, and Harriet, 11, to run for home at the first sign of trouble.

Her younger sisters, Caroline, 6, and Lydia, 3, were too young to comprehend the danger. It had taken a while for the lively and mischievous Emily to be convinced. But lately she and her friends had begun to have nightmares. They would awake crying, "The mob is coming! The mob is coming!"

Often during this summer of 1833, her house was full of neighbors all night. Her father, Edward, was a bishop of the church and the colony turned to him for leadership. The men brought their guns, to be ready in case of attack. Sometimes the women and children, afraid to be left alone, came too, and crowded into the Partridge's upstairs bedrooms. It would have seemed like a party had the adults not been so tense. Emily could often hear the voices of the men at prayer and twice guns went off accidentally, making them all scream in fright.

One day in late July Emily and her sister Harriet were sent to the spring for water. Their new baby brother was just three weeks old and her mother depended on their help. As they started back toward the house with the dripping bucket, they saw a mob of men surround their home. Afraid to go closer, they watched from the distance until the mob went away. Then, the bucket forgotten, they ran home to see what had happened.

The mob had taken their father. He'd not resisted, their mother told them, he'd gone peaceably. Maybe everything would be all right.

But maybe it wouldn't. They'd been hearing death threats for weeks. Emily stood at the window, looking after her father, her wide set dark eyes brimming with tears. From the town square a few blocks away she could hear much shouting and yelling, but they dared not go see what was happening. What were they doing to him?

After a time she saw two men approaching the house. One she recognized as a friend. He was carrying a hat, coat and vest in his hand. The other looked very strange. He appeared to be dark skinned and wearing some odd garment. Emily decided he was an Indian and ran to her bedroom to hide.

She heard the men enter the house. Her mother screamed and began to cry. There was a babble of sound. She crept down the stairs until she could see what was going on. Blankets had been stretched before the fireplace and inside the cubicle some of the neighbors were working over the strange Indian.

Peering between the blankets, Emily gasped. The man she had taken to be an Indian was her father. He was plastered from head to foot with tar and feathers.

He told them, as they struggled to clean his skin before the caustic tar could burn even deeper, that the mob had demanded the Mormons cease printing their newspaper. They called it seditious, said it encouraged free blacks to settle in Missouri, a slave state. They had heard enough blasphemy about a new prophet, golden plates, a new book of the Bible, about miracle cures and speaking in tongues, about the Mormons' divine right to land and the coming of the Millennium that would destroy all unbelievers.

When their demands were refused, they'd destroyed the print shop and the house of Brother Phelps which contained it. The press had been shoved out the upstairs window, the roof torn off and the walls knocked down. The Phelps furniture and belongings were thrown into the street and trampled. They told Emily's father he was to take his 1,200 people and leave Jackson County. He'd refused, and tried to make them listen to reason, but they'd fetched the tar bucket.

Three days later, Emily's father and the other church elders, facing a mob armed with pistols, rifles, whips and clubs, promised to be out of Jackson County before the New Year. But they needed somewhere to go and a way to get there.

Bishop Partridge wrote to Joseph Smith at the church headquarters in Kirkland, Ohio for advice. It was Smith's magnetism that had brought him into the church. At first a doubter, Partridge had traveled to New York from his Ohio home to meet the prophet. Once he'd heard the story of the revelation from the prophet's own lips he was convinced.

His friends and family thought him insane. His sister ordered him out of her house. But in less than three months he'd left his comfortable home with the grape arbors where the girls played, abandoned his hat shop where Emily had loved to gather bits of bright fabric, and been ordained a bishop in Smith's church. In six months he'd been in Independence, preparing for his people's arrival.

Now it seemed they'd have to abandon all they had built and move on. The bishop appealed to the civil authorities for protection and redress, but no help was forthcoming.

The Missourians were tired of waiting. Early in November the mob struck again. A Mormon settlement a few miles from Independence on the Big Blue River was attacked. As women and children ran screaming into the woods, their houses were looted and the men of the village stoned and beaten.

The next few days were ones of chaos and confusion. The store owned by Brother Gilbert was demolished and more homes were stoned and ransacked. Emily and her family heard of attacks and threats in settlements all around Independence. The people began gathering in the square at night for the protection of the brothers' guns. As the fighting escalated and the Mormons began to defend themselves, a couple of Missourians and a Mormon were killed in a fight over the Blue River ferry.

Faced with a civil war, Lt. Gov. Lilburn Boggs, who'd refused to provide the Mormons any protection, offered them safe passage from Jackson County if they'd give up their arms and promise to leave. Believing the Missourians would also be disarmed, Partridge and the elders agreed.

But Boggs did not take the mobsters' guns. Freed of all restraint, they increased the tempo of harassment. While the men fled to the woods to save their lives, the women and children faced the threats and terror spread by the bullies. Finally, given two hours to clear out or be massacred, they loaded four wagons with what they could and headed for the Missouri.

All through November 7 they gathered at the ferry at Liberty landing. The shore was lined with hundreds of people and what chests and boxes of goods they'd managed to save. Many were separated from their family members. Tearful wives hunted for their husbands. Fathers looked desperately for their families. Terrified children wandered the throngs in search of their parents.

Some had a few belongings and had managed to put up small tents. Others had only the clothes they wore. They grouped around small fires in search of warmth. It began to rain.

The next day, while the ferry plied ever so slowly back and forth across the chill current, the men began felling small cottonwood trees to house the throngs. Eventually -- for the needs of the bishop's family were often neglected while he took care of his parishioners -- Emily found herself across the river, living in a hut with cottonwood sapling sides and a canvas roof.

Years later she remembered the cold and the wet. But she also remembered stumbling out of a deep sleep at her mother's call to witness a shower of falling stars. It was one of the grandest sights she'd ever seen. She stood, blanket-wrapped, in the crisp air and thought the heavens had been wrapped in fireworks. The brethren took it as a sign that the Lord had not forgotten them after all.

After a few weeks her father was able to secure an old log cabin. It had been used as a stable, but it became home for the Partridges and another family. They cleaned it up and hung blankets a few feet back from the fireplace of the one useable room and the 15 or 16 of them huddled inside the cubicle, trying to keep warm. Emily knew she had good reason to shiver when her father, trying to write near the fire, had to give up because the ink kept freezing in his pen.

When she'd first arrived in Missouri, Emily had thought the people there very strange. Indians and Negroes were a common sight. The settler women went barefoot in warm weather and "toated" their young ones on their hips. Children dressed in no more than a shirt, and everyone carried their bundles on their heads instead of in their hands. The youngsters said things like "I

reckon" and "a right smart chance," in a soft, slurred speech that was strange to her ear. But the citizens of Clay County made them welcome and in the spring of 1834 the brethren started a school in a small cabin.

Even though the local children who attended their school sometimes teased the Mormon students about their shabby clothes, Emily loved her hours there. The cabin sat in a papaw grove and she spent many long happy playtimes swinging on a wild grape vine that hung down from the trees or jumping rope with sections of younger vines. Some days they broke off the brittle branches of the papaws to build playhouses, but Emily found one taste of the ovular fruit enough to satisfy her sweet tooth for a long time.

Of course there was work to do, too. The Mormons, scratching to provide for themselves, scattered over the countryside and rented land or hired out as laborers. They created jobs by establishing a slaughter yard on the river bank not far from Emily's home. The men and boys killed thousands of hogs and butchered them for shipment to market. Emily and her sisters helped her mother and the other women cut up and render the lard.

For months they dreamed of returning to their Jackson County homes, but appeals to the government of Missouri and to Andrew Jackson in the White House availed them nothing. Even the prophet himself, who'd come from Ohio with a force of 200 armed men, was unable to negotiate a just settlement. His presence cheered the church pioneers. When he returned to Ohio, however, Emily's father went with him, and her mother and the girls were left to cope as best they could for several months.

But now, even the people of Clay County were getting restless. They'd offered sanctuary but they hadn't intended it to be permanent. In June 1836, as apprehensive as their neighbors in Independence, they called a meeting at the Liberty Courthouse and asked the Mormons to move on.

Once more Emily's family left their home, but this time they knew where they would go. The church had purchased land to the north, on Shoal Creek, and petitioned to establish Caldwell County. This, not Independence, would be Zion. They named their new town Far West.

The first winter the family lived on the hickory nuts, black walnuts and hazelnuts the girls gathered from the fragrant floor of the woods. In a short two years there were 4,900 Mormons in Caldwell County and 150 houses in Far West. There was also a church, a courthouse, two hotels and a school. There were Mormon settlements to the north on the Grand River in Davies County and at the mouth of the river in Dewitt.

Emily, now a tall, slim 14, had grown enough to be a real help to her father. She and her sister, Harriet, took the role older brothers would have taken had there been any. They milked the cows, helped get in the hay and sometimes carried the chains when the bishop surveyed the land.

That March the brotherhood's cup of blessings seemed to run over when the prophet brought the rest of the church to Far West. They were saddened at the troubles that had driven the church from Ohio, but it was wonderful to have Brother Joseph with them.

On July 4 they laid the cornerstone for their temple and one of their most gifted preachers declared the days of persecution were over. Any attack on their freedom or liberty would meet with immediate retaliation, he promised. "Hosannah!" the crowd cried. "Amen!" They raised the Stars and Stripes to snap against a blue sky and Emily thought only her people could know such joy.

When a thunderstorm struck a few days later and a crackling bolt of lightning shattered the flagpole, Emily regretted the charred ruins of the banner. In later years, she decided it had been an omen.

For the ugly tide of prejudice was sweeping toward them again. There was trouble between the Mormons and Missourians at Gallatin on election day. Mobs threatened the brothers at DeWitt. Homes at Adam-ondi-Ahman were burned. There was a hand-to-hand battle at the Crooked River with deaths on both sides. The Mormons, as they had promised, armed to defend themselves. One group, the Danites, went a step father and took the offensive, raiding Gentile settlements.

On October 30 Emily and the brethren learned of a devastating attack on Hauns Mill, only 15 miles down Shoal Creek. The 30 families there had been fired on by the state militia. Seventeen were dead, one an old man who'd been hacked to death. Another was a ten-year-old boy who'd hidden in the blacksmith shop through the attack. Discovered when the mob stormed the building, he was summarily executed. Fifteen others bled from wounds.

But there was even more horrifying news. The militia carried an order from the brethrens' old nemesis, Lilburn Boggs, who was now governor. The Mormons were to be exterminated! The army, with a mob following, was on its way to Far West.

Panic-stricken, the people dragged wagons, logs, boards and anything else moveable to form breastworks. They were scarcely through when 3,000 militiamen under the command of Gen. Samuel Lucas appeared the next day, placed a cannon in the middle of the road and formed a line a half-mile from town.

Under a white flag, they sent a message. Two local residents who had married Mormons would be allowed to evacuate the town with their families. Then the town would be destroyed. But the Gentiles elected to stay with their Mormon relatives and a stalemate ensued.

The next morning the emissary was back with a demand for Joseph Smith, his brothers and a number of church elders. If they surrendered, the people would be safe -- for the time being. But they must yield their arms, give up their property and leave the state.

There seemed to be no choice. While Emily watched, Brother Joseph and some of the elders stepped into a hollow square of troops. As it closed around them and began to move away, the mob sent up such an unearthly howl of triumph that she shuddered violently. Such sounds, she had always thought, could issue only from the throats of demons in the lower regions.

The next day was a horror. The men were called to the square to surrender their arms and remain under guard. The troops and the mob were free to lay waste as they chose.

A few came so close to Emily's home that she could hear their conversation. Later she was outside when several rode up and slaughtered one of her father's heifers in their dooryard. Beyond fear and filled with contempt, she watched them skin the creature, cut it up and carry the meat away.

By now Brother Joseph and the others had been court-martialed. The sentence was death, to be carried out the morning of November 1 in the Far West square in the presence of their families.

But at this point one of the Gentile officers rebelled. Gen. Alexander W. Doniphan refused to carry out the order of execution. It was cold-blooded murder, he said, and he and his troops would have no part of it. So challenged, General Lucas backed down. He agreed to hold the prisoners for a regular trial, charging them with treason, murder, burglary, arson, larceny, theft and stealing. But he demanded 56 more of the brethren as hostages. Among these was Emily's father.

Gathered into the square at gunpoint, the men were given a chance to deny their faith. Those who refused were forced to sign away their property to pay for any damages the Mormons had done in the countryside. Bishop Partridge signed the deed. Then, without blankets or extra clothes, he was herded off with the others through the cold slush of November.

Emily stood with her mother and watched him go. They themselves could go nowhere. The mob camped outside of town to make sure no one entered or left. Most of their crops and livestock had vanished with the raiders and the town was full of refugees from outlying areas. How could they all get enough to eat?

They couldn't. Emily's mother did the best she could. She had no flour so she boiled wheat to eke out the little cornmeal on hand. Sometimes she made a pie with cornmeal crust and filled it with pumpkin, hoping the pie shape might make it more palatable for the younger children. Emily knew they were luckier than many who had only parched corn to chew.

Somehow the rest of November passed, and then December. When Emily's father finally came back to them in January they learned about his experience. His group had been marched about 25 miles south to Richmond and confined in a large, cold room. With meager food and even less firewood, they'd slept on the bare stone floor. Even now that he'd been freed he was not safe. He was with them only briefly before he fled to Illinois for sanctuary.

Again Emily, her mother and her sisters were left alone. They piled what they could in a wagon and left Far West. Wherever they landed, Emily thought, it would be better than Missouri.

They crossed the state to the Mississippi River and once again waited in a tent on a frozen river bank for passage across. As they waited more brethren gathered. Wagons trailed back and forth from Far West to transport family after family.

When they were finally able to cross to Quincy, Illinois, picking their way over the ice to the ferry on the open water, Emily looked up to see throngs of people gathering to watch the crossing of the Mormons. Maybe they think we're some kind of animals, she mused, not human beings who feel sorrow, pain, cold, and hunger just like they do.

Bishop Partridge was reunited with the family in Quincy and as soon as they were able, they pitched their tent in Joseph Smith's newly founded Zion, 45 miles up the Mississippi from Quincy on a disease-infested bottom. They called this Zion Nauvoo. Smith and the other elders, after spending 4-1/2 months in the dark, dank cellar of the Liberty jail awaiting trial, had been allowed to escape and follow the brethren to Illinois.

For months the Partridges fought fever and ague while the bishop tried to build them a house. Emily watched him dose himself with quinine to control the chills so he could work a few days at a time. Realizing he would never get the house done, he finished the stable and the family moved into that. It was his last effort. He died on May 27, 1840. Emily had just survived the illness herself. She had helped bury her sister Harriet, 19, only 11 days before.

Edward Partridge's Mormon experience lasted less than ten years. His family's was to continue much longer. As Nauvoo began to build and prosper, Emily went to work in the home of Brother Joseph and Sister Emma. In 1842 the prophet announced the doctrine of plural marriage and in 1843 he married Emily and her sister Eliza. Emily was 19.

A year later a mob of Illinois citizens did what Missouri citizens had threatened. Prophet Joseph Smith lay dead in the yard of the Carthage jail and Emily was a widow. Given her choice of new husbands, she had the good sense and the spunk to ask to join the wives of the Saints' rising leader, Brother Brigham Young.

In February 1846 she was again fleeing across a frozen river. This time it was the Mississippi and Nauvoo the threatened settlement behind her.

In February 1847 Emily recrossed the Missouri. Now she was running not away from the past but toward the future. She spent a year in Winter Quarters (present Omaha, Nebraska) and then took the trail west to the Salt Lake Valley where Brother Joseph's followers, now christened the Church of Christ of the Latter-day Saints, at last built their Zion.

Emily settled into a house her husband provided, comfortable and secure for the first time in a dozen years. She had been changed by her experiences. Over the difficult years she had grown shy and withdrawn to the point of reticence. While she worked faithfully in the temple and the church's Relief Society, she was probably happiest at home, plying her needle as her father had his, turning her own designs into bedspreads and rugs.

When she wrote her autobiography in 1885, Emily had five living children and had lost two. She considered God's ways marvelous and herself blessed. "Where the Saints dwell," she wrote, "whether it is in a city or a desert, a palace or a hovel, there is my home."

ASABATTLES

To Day I am Wounded

While the southern portions of the Missouri were tarred by the brush of ignorance in the late 1830s, the upper reaches suffered under a different pall.

When George Catlin left the Mandan in 1832 he did not expect the tribe could long survive. He thought their destroyer would be one they were used to battling -- clothed in war paint, armed with tomahawk, their superior only in numbers.

But in July 1837 an enemy crept up the Missouri and caught them unaware. It attacked without a war cry and slew with merciless abandon strong men, young mothers, aged parents, babes at the breast, leaders whose medicine had always been invincible.

It was a gift from the white man.

On Wednesday, July 12, 1837 Francis Chardon, bourgeois at the American Fur Company post of Fort Clark, opened his journal and tried to think of something to write. He was not an imaginative man and the journal he kept for his employers usually recounted in laconic style the prosaic comings and goings around the small post on a bluff at the mouth of the Knife River. Some days he was content with "No news" or "Pleasant weather." Some days he came up with nothing but, "Ditto."

"Nothing stirring," he finally wrote. "No news and worst of all, nothing to eat but a little poor dried meat that I got from the steam boat on her way from this place to St. Louis."

The boat, the *St. Peters*, had tied up briefly at the Mandan post on its return trip from Fort Union. Such a visit was always a reason for celebration, as was any break in the long weeks of isolation. The stop on the upriver trip was more eagerly awaited, for it meant a chance to replenish dwindling supplies, hear from the folks back home, and catch up on what was happening in St. Louis and the rest of the world.

That visit, on June 20, had been thoroughly enjoyed by all. There'd been some fuss when a Mandan stole a blanket from a sick deckhand. Chardon, fearing it might be a source of contamination, had offered a reward for its return. But it had not been surrendered and few gave it any more thought.

This stop to load furs for the trip down river was always brief, sometimes only a matter of hours, but still it was a break in the monotony -- a chance to talk to a new face, hear a story you hadn't heard a thousand times before.

Chardon was not old in years but he was an old hand at the fur trade. He had left his Philadelphia home to come west years earlier -- long enough to be starting his second Indian family with his third Indian wife. He'd lived with the Osage on the lower Missouri and had come to the upper river nearly ten years before. He'd been at Fort Clark since the small fur post was built in 1834.

His job was to keep friendly relations with the Mandan, their neighbors the Hidatsa, and the Arikara who might happen along, so that brown pelts (more buffalo now than beaver)

would continue to weight the steamers going downstream. Like most of his underlings at the post, he had an Indian wife and family, so he could appeal to familial as well as company loyalties when there was business to be done.

Chardon was usually a cheerful man, a good storyteller around the fire at night, a welcome companion on a hunt. He liked some Indians, especially those who did as he asked. He disliked others, considering the Arikara "the meanest, dirtiest, worthless, cowardly set of Dogs on the Missouri." He was somewhat fonder of the Mandan, but treated most Indians with a certain amount of disdain.

He had no sympathy with the constant squabbles between tribes, saw no glory in their warfare. Squaws who came to the post expecting payment for performing a scalp dance were sent home empty-handed. The natives were an essential part of doing business; he accepted them as that and no more. He leaned toward flogging as punishment for troublemakers, as did most of his contemporaries. And he was honest enough to note in his journal the times he overstayed at a party in the village and received a similar punishment from his Sioux wife for his "bad behavior."

By Friday, July 14, the weather had warmed until it really felt like July. "One of the warmest days that we have had this summer," he wrote. "Weather smokey. A young Mandan died to day of the Small Pox. Several others has caught it."

Most of the young Mandan's tribe were out making meat. Buffalo had been scarce in the neighborhood that summer and the Indians were in real need of meat. Chardon thought that that circumstance might prevent a lot of illness and he sent a messenger out to warn the hunters to keep away from their village.

On Monday he noted that another case of the disease had appeared. By Thursday that week he knew the sickness had also struck up on the Little Missouri, but he was really more concerned about the tribes' lack of game. On July 25 he learned that small pox had broken out in the camp where the Mandan were making meat.

The next afternoon Catlin's friend, Chief Four Bears, appeared at the post. He and those hunting had decided they could not stay away from their village. The women needed to tend the corn crop; sure starvation was more frightening than possible disease. But Four Bears already had a fever and he was not entirely rational. The hunt had been successful; the village now had plenty of meat. But that was no longer important. Several of his people were dead of the pox. He himself was ill. What were the whites doing to them?

Four more died the next day. Their fevers were intense. Their bodies swelled. Many of them hemorrhaged from the mouth and ears, dying even before the pustules appeared.

On Friday both the Ree and the Mandan invited Chardon and the company men to attend a feast. They were dressed in their finest regalia and each tribe threw itself into frenzied dance. Chardon, in spite of himself, found he was impressed with the splendid performances. Usually their dances bored him. He'd seen so many over the years that ordinarily he wished only for them to be over. But this one seemed different and he learned why when he asked the Indians' motivation. They did not think they had long to live. Expecting to die of small pox, they'd decided "as long as they are alive, they will take it out in dancing."

By Sunday several more had met their expectation. One was Four Bears. Before he died, his strength consumed, his body a mass of eruptions, the chief summoned his resources to make a last oration.

"...Ever since I can remember, I have loved the Whites...," he said. "The Four Bears never saw a white man hungry but what he gave him to eat, drink, and a buffalo skin to sleep on in time of need. I was always ready to die for them...I have done every thing that a red skin could do for them, and how have they repaid it!

"...They have deceived me, them that I always considered as brothers has turned out to be my worst enemies. I have been in many battles and often wounded, but the wounds of my enemies I exhalt in. But to day I am wounded, and by whom, by those same white dogs that I have always considered and treated as brothers.

"I do not fear death, my friends. You know it. But to die with my face rotten, that even the wolves will shrink with horror at seeing me, and say to themselves, that is the

Four Bears, the friend of the whites --

"Listen well what I have to say, as it will be the last time you will hear me. Think of your wives, children, brothers, sisters, friends and in fact all that you hold dear, are all dead or dying, with their faces all rotten, caused by those dogs the whites. Think of all that my friends and rise all together and not leave one of them alive. The Four Bears will act his part -- "

Chardon sincerely regretted the death of Four Bears, one of the company's best friends, but he paled when he heard his message. While the dead chief's leadership could only be spiritual, it might have a powerful influence.

The Hidatsa, with a dozen or more dead, were also talking revenge for the plague. They had no doubt it had come from the steamboat; perhaps they had been infected deliberately. They thought surely the white man had medicine to cure it which he refused to share.

The first week of August was fairly quiet. Chardon had time to worry about his hay crop, which had been pounded into the ground by a violent hail storm. And he kept track (as he always did) of the daily rat kill. Sixty-one rodents had been dispensed in July; his grand total stood at 1,778.

But there were six deaths on August 7, seven on the eighth, seven more on the ninth, 12 to 15 on the tenth. By the eleventh he was writing in his journal, "I keep no account of the dead, as they die so fast that it is impossible."

The Ree, like the Mandan, tried to halt the plague. They breathed in the steam of their purifying sweat baths, then plunged into the cold current of the river. Some sought dreams that would give them medicine against its might. Some talked to the sun, others to the moon; they sacrificed their treasures.

Chardon heard threats or rumors of retaliation nearly every day. One armed Mandan, determined to take one of the whites with him, was at the gates of the fort before he was turned back. On August 15 Chardon learned the disease had spread to the Sioux.

August 16 was chilly enough that the bourgeois appreciated a fire in the hearth. Even though it was cool, those in the post were uncomfortably aware of the stench of unburied bodies. Whole families lay untended in the lodges, outside the village walls, at the base of the bluff, along the river bank, in the water.

"Where the disease will stop, I Know not," Chardon wrote on the seventeenth.

Lodge after lodge stood quiet; smoke holes were innocent of smoke. The scavenging creatures began to gather and feast. Grief-stricken fathers lurked around the post, waiting their chance for revenge. One Ree, stationed at the gate and gunning for Chardon, took his satisfaction instead by killing one of the bourgeois' men. He was killed in turn. But how many could they stop?

Chardon sprang from a dead sleep on the eighteenth and stood in his nightshirt, gun in hand, his heart pounding, certain a strange cry meant the attack he dreaded was beginning. Although it was nothing but a resident Indian having a bad dream, Chardon knew his nightmare was real. "Nothing but an occasional glass of grog Keeps me alive as I am worried almost to death by the Indians..." he wrote.

Friendly Indians warned him not to leave the post. Feeling shamed, he heeded their words.

Afraid to leave the protection of the fort to hunt, the men were driven to creeping out at night to steal fist-sized pumpkins from the Indians' fields for food. They worried Chardon almost as much as the Indians. They were threatening to leave him. And now the disease hit the post as well.

The Mandan, losing eight or ten people each day, turned to suicide. Husbands killed suffering wives and then joined them in death. Braves turned their weapons on themselves. A young Mandan mother watched her husband die. Already infected, she killed her six-and eight-year-old boys. Then she hanged herself.

A young Ree Chardon was fond of asked his mother to dig his grave and, supported by his father, went out to die. The trader tried to get him back to the village, but he refused to return. All his friends were gone and he wished to follow them. By evening he was gone, too.

Another warrior ordered his wife to dig his grave, dressed in his finery and marched to it, singing his death song. There he threw down his lance and shield and stabbed himself to death.

It had been more than a month and the deadly virus showed no signs of slowing. Chardon heard Indians intended to burn his fort. He stationed guards in the bastions and all the men went armed at all times.

On August 29 Chardon himself awoke with a high fever. The small of his back burned like fire, the back of his head throbbed relentlessly. Six of his men already tossed in delirium. The trader dosed himself with hot whiskey punch and sweated out the night. Others looked in and labeled him a dead man, but by the thirty-first he was sure he'd beaten the illness.

"Month of August I bid you farewell with all my heart," he wrote. "After running 20 hair breadths escapes, threatened every instant to be all murdered, however it is the wish of humble servant that the Month of September will be More favorable. The Number of Deaths up to the Present is very near 500 -- The Mandans are all cut off, except 23 young and Old Men."

As September began he saluted two corpses, wrapped in white skins and laid out on a raft, as they drifted by the fort. He wished them well. One of his men buried his wife.

Perhaps the sickness had spent its strength. Some who got it now survived. Most of his employees had it, and he decided to send his younger son down to Fort Pierre in the hope of saving him. He was thankful he'd taken his older boy by his Sioux wife, Sand Bar, to Philadelphia to be raised by his mother. But Andrew Jackson Chardon, only two, was in certain danger. He gave the boy a hug, handed him down into the canoe and hoped for the best.

As the weather grew windy and rainy toward the middle of the month, he learned the pestilence had also devastated Fort Union. Vigorous efforts by the traders there to keep the Indians away from the infected post had been futile. The Assiniboin and Blackfoot who frequented that fort could not comprehend the danger. The traders' wives all came down with the disease and soon their relatives and friends were falling ill. When the tribes realized what was happening they tried to run to safety, scattering in all directions and spreading the virus far and wide.

Closer to home, a visitor from the Mandan village told Chardon at least 800 were dead. He counted but 14 yet alive. Fourteen invalids in his own post were also alive, but he wondered how long they would be. There was not a stick of wood in the post for heat and he had to get in hay if the livestock were to last the winter. Chardon labored harder than he had for years, working with only two able-bodied men to haul in 64 loads of hay and boat driftwood over from a nearby sandbar.

On September 23 he wrote that one of his men had lost a second child, "a fine boy of six years old, sick eight days."

Sometime later a message came up from Fort Pierre. He turned the pages of his journal back to September 21 and added, "My youngest son died today."

By September 30 he believed that the disease had destroyed seven-eighths of the Mandan and half the Ree. Cold weather, which some had hoped would halt the pestilence, seemed to have little effect. Through the winter he heard continuing reports of its rampage through the Gros Ventre, Assiniboin, Cree and Blackfoot to the north and west. Whole villages stood with silent lodges, engulfed in the stench of death. There were 17,000 dead, it was said. Others said 150,000.

Nobody really knew. At the Mandan villages they were certain a nation had been destroyed.

On January 9, 1839, Chardon stood in the frigid air and watched the Sioux burn one of the empty Mandan villages. The dry timbers that supported the earth lodges flared across the dark night and "made a splendid sight," he wrote. "This must be an end of what was once called the Mandan Village, upwards of one hundred years it has been standing."

If Chardon was wrong about the age of those particular lodges, he was not wrong about the Mandan residency. Great-great-grandfathers of these Indians had entertained Frenchmen named Verendrye a century before. Their grandfathers had hosted Lewis and Clark, and they had given hospitality to a continuing stream of white men since.

They'd disappointed some who'd come with unfounded expectations, thrilled others -- been looked on as supermen and savages. Now, like the Indians for which their river was named, they were all but extinct.

The other tribes of the upper river survived, but they were all weakened. They'd lost not only numbers, but their leaders, their property and their faith in themselves and their gods. They would never again be mightier than the white man.

The traders did not profit by the tragedy that befell the tribes. It cost them their best customers. Chardon, continuing in the trade, spent the rest of his life on the upper Missouri. Much of the next ten years he lived west of Fort Union, trying to establish trade with the Blackfoot. He achieved some success and had one notable failure, when he was involved in the killing of a half dozen of the tribe. He worked for awhile in the new fort established where the remnants of the Mandan and Hidatsa had settled (Fort Berthoud, North Dakota).

Chardon died at Fort Pierre in 1848, so crippled with rheumatism that he could not walk, patently grateful to anyone who would sit beside his sofa and talk for awhile. His will, dictated the day before he died, provided for his current Sioux wife and the two sons she had borne him, as well as his oldest son, now nearly grown, back in the states. Other bequests included $100 for a tombstone for his mother's grave and freedom for his Negro boy, Black Hawk.

Chardon loaned his journal detailing the last days of the Mandan to compatriot Joseph N. Nicollet sometime before the scientist died in 1843. It was discovered in a trunk bearing the Frenchman's name in government archives in 1920.

The Sparrow and the Crane

Over the years, most of the travelers to the Upper Missouri had come for skins. Bundles of pelts weighted every boat downstream.

The party that came in 1843 was also interested in skins, but they were looking for more than beaver and buffalo, and they planned to use them for purposes other than tall hats and robes.

On a Wednesday morning in late June 1843, two men stood staring up at a small hole in a dead tree near Fort Union. It was ten feet in the air and they were without horse or cart. But they knew its contents might help answer a question which had been puzzling them for two days.

The older man braced himself against the trunk and the younger, lighter man scrambled up his back until he could stand on his shoulders. Wobbling on his shaky perch, he managed to squeeze his arm into the hole and felt what they were after. Ever so gently he lifted out several eggs. On the ground again, he examined his treasure and groaned with disappointment. The eggs were only those of a sparrow hawk which must have appropriated the old woodpecker's nest.

Woodpeckers were but one of the puzzles Edward Harris and John James Audubon were trying to unravel. Had they discovered another new species? Or were the red-moustached individuals they were collecting simply variations of color in the familiar golden-winged woodpecker (yellow-shafted flicker) they knew.

Audubon leaned toward a new species. Harris had the feeling he'd seen such a bird before and it couldn't be new. They had to be sure, but they'd found no answers here. They began the walk back to the fort.

They made a remarkable pair. Audubon was as angular and dramatic as a whooping crane, his beak of a nose sharpened by his 58 years, his chin jutting up to meet his toothless upper jaw. His hair and beard a tangle of curly white, he commanded attention wherever he went.

Harris, 44, was more like the new finch he'd discovered in May, just above Fort Leavenworth. Its neat black cap and bib were distinguished and businesslike, but it chose to lead a productive and private life in the brush. On May 17 Audubon had christened the bird in his honor. "I am proud to name it Fringilla Harrisii (Harris sparrow) in honor of one of the best friends I have in this world," he wrote as he recorded the new species in his journal.

Audubon had good reason to appreciate Harris' friendship. It was a young Harris who'd first expressed belief in the quality of Audubon's bird paintings when, as an un-known artist, he had sought a publisher for his *Birds of America* in 1824. While the powers-that-be in Philadelphia had cast a disinterested glance, Harris, then 25, had raved over his paintings and bought all he had to offer. When the amateur ornithologist had bid the artist goodbye, he'd pressed a hundred dollar bill into his needy hand to help finance the trip to England that resulted in his first publication.

It was not a major financial sacrifice for Harris, whose monied family had bequeathed him a large New Jersey farm, but it came at a crucial time in the artist's career. For Harris it began a pattern of moral and financial support for the sciences which he would continue all his life.

Audubon was now world-famous. His life-sized paintings of 435 birds, presented in positions more natural than any the public had seen, were a sensation. His birds fed and flew, swam and dived, squabbled among themselves and battled predators. They ate fruit from trees, huddled in the grass, and watched over their young. They were not only life-sized, they were lifelike and bird lovers were enchanted.

He'd followed his extra-sized folio of art-work with a 3,000 page, five-volume *Ornithological Biography*, detailing all the information his unquenchable curiosity and scientific observations had gleaned about each bird's life and habits. When that book, too, was well-received he had been able to ensconce his long-suffering wife, Lucy, in a 35-acre estate on the Hudson River. After 25 difficult years -- years haunted with unfulfilled expectations and unpaid bills -- he had "arrived." He was accepted in both the art world and society and his goings and comings were faithfully chronicled by the newspapers.

Through all the years he and Harris had remained friends. They shared a passion for birds and scientific observation, and Harris' steady, orderly nature had proved a quiet source of strength for Audubon's sometimes erratic temperament. "He is *infacto* one of the finest men of God's creation -- I wish he were my brother," the artist had written a few years before.

Harris, appreciating Audubon's incredible energy and enthusiasm, recognizing his genius, could overlook his sometimes vain and flamboyant posturing. They'd made one previous trip together to study the birds of Louisiana and the Gulf coast in 1837. Then Audubon had fastened on a new dream and determined to work with his sons, John Woodhouse and Victor, to produce a volume depicting North America's animals. To complete such a work, he decided, he had to visit the West so he could observe its species and obtain specimens. The first person he contacted was his friend Harris.

They'd been on the river for seven weeks, at Fort Union for 11 days. In Harris' pocket diary the green flash of parroquets had evolved into the black-on-white symmetry of the magpie; turkeys had been replaced by arctic towhees; rabbits by prairie dogs, deer by antelope and bighorn sheep. His diary had become an 11 x 16 inch folio. Even Harris' minuscule script could not crowd onto a page all the sights and sensations that packed his days.

They shot, sketched, skinned and preserved ground hogs, squirrels, rabbits, mice, wood rats, bats and 117 birds, sometimes collecting dozens of a species. Each one was painstakingly examined, measured and discussed, vignettes of feet, claws, tails and faces were recorded in portfolios and the skins were salted or immersed in barrels of rum. Back home Audubon would achieve his lifelike paintings by wiring his specimens into positions he'd observed in the field. He took all he needed and more, without qualm.

Off the boat at every stop for wood or whenever the Missouri exacted tribute, they raced to shoot specimens before the steamer's bell demanded their return. Two, three, four times a day, Harris found himself running for dear life, knowing they dare not delay the impatient captain of the fur company's steamboat. The owner, Pierre Chouteau, Jr. had extended them every courtesy, but the river was falling and the captain did not intend to get stranded. Harris would arrive at the river bank, gasping and drenched in sweat, with his pointer, Brag, panting at his side.

In addition to Harris' finch, they'd discovered a new vireo, which Audubon named for John Bell, the taxidermist he'd brought along to preserve his specimens. They were more and more sure they had a new meadowlark and, just two days before, Harris had

shot what turned out to be a new titlark (Sprague's pipit).

As Harris walked through the stubby grass toward the fort, he stopped to listen again to a high, squeaky note they'd been hearing for days. Sharp ears were as useful as keen eyes when one examined an area, and they often stood transfixed, concentrating on a new sound. They'd walked miles trying to sight this singer, but as soon as they got to what they thought was the source, the whistle would pipe from another direction.

This time they were lucky. A small bird with a streaked, brown back bobbed through the air before them, singing as it flew. The singer and the new titlark were the same.

But there were plenty of mysteries yet to solve. After tea with Fort Union proprietor Alexander Culbertson, Harris went with Audubon and Bell to collect a small hare the traders said was common near the fort. Working their way through a piece of bottom land that was a jumble of rose bushes, buffalo berries and willows, they watched until dark. But in spite of Brag's efforts to flush one out they saw not a one.

Bringing poor Brag had been a mistake. The young dog was a good hunter but a terrible traveler. He'd been in a continual fright since they'd left St. Louis. The trappers on the boat and on shore terrified him. The Indians left him nearly catatonic; when they were around he clung to his master's leg like a cocklebur. Harris fervently wished him safe at home on the farm.

Deciding it was futile to hunt any more that day, Harris whistled the pointer in and the naturalists tramped back to the fort. They had undertaken a tremendous task, he knew, but he thought they were up to the challenge.

It was a challenging country. Only the day before he'd sat with Audubon in their cramped quarters at Fort Union and listened to the horrific stories trader Francis Chardon had to tell. Chardon, who was on his way to Blackfoot country, described the terrible days at Fort Clark six years before when the Mandan had been destroyed by the pox.

Harris had seen the remains of their village on the way up river. While the small fort was still there, the village was now occupied by the Arikara; the few living Mandan had moved farther north. He and

Audubon had trudged between the lodges during a wind-whipped downpour while their Ree guide explained that the small, barren mounds of earth all around marked where bodies had fallen. The people had not had time nor strength to honor their dead with scaffold interments. A few bowlsful of earth had been all they could manage for those who'd fallen in the midst of the epidemic. Later, there had been no one to do even that.

They'd visited a medicine lodge and Harris had tried to imagine the world Catlin described in such glowing terms. All he could see were naked savages and filth.

For nearly a month they'd been trying to prove their meadowlark was new. Harris was convinced it was, although it had the same yellow breast, the same black "V" on its throat, the same white feathers bordering its tail as the eastern lark. Perhaps the yellow on its throat extended a little farther up its face. It was difficult to say. But there was no question about its song. The ripple of flute-like notes it threw out over the prairie was simply too different from the eastern bird it so closely resembled.

However, he was scientist enough to know that one did not act even on heartfelt convictions. One had to establish a specific difference. One hoped, but one did not make unsubstantiated claims.

He and the other members of Audubon's party (Audubon had brought along artist Isaac Sprague to paint backgrounds for his animals and a young neighbor, Lewis Squires, to act as all-round man) huddled over Lewis and Clark's *Journals*. The authors were both gone now. William Clark had been buried in St. Louis with sorrow and ceremony five years before. But their writings were still the bible of the western frontier. Leafing through the volume, the ornithologists found the entry they were seeking. It was dated June 22, 1805. During their laborious portage around Great Falls, the explorers had sighted a bird that looked much like the eastern lark, but its song "differs considerably."

Excited, their observation reinforced, Harris spent the next afternoon on the prairie, his glass trained to watch the meadowlarks soar into the sky for acrobatics, pause to pour out their song and soar off again. Their mates, he thought, must listen with delight from their nests in the grass.

The next day Sprague found one of those nests. He brought the half-formed grass cup and its chocolate-spotted eggs in for study. At last they were sure. They added the western meadowlark to their portfolio.

While Audubon could and would add birds to new editions of *Birds of America* he was there primarily to document animals. They longed to see a grizzly and found many places where the bears had dug into the ground for roots, but none obliged them by appearing. They wondered why they saw no rattlesnakes in a country said to abound in them. The small hare continued to be invisible.

The woodpeckers continued to frustrate. Now they shot one whose color lay between red and yellow. Harris looked at the pile of woodpeckers -- by now they had the familiar red-shafted bird, a lighter red-shafted bird with a black stripe on the cheek, a golden-winged with a red stripe on the cheek, and a golden-winged with a black stripe on its cheek. Could there possibly be four species Harris wondered? They cut down the trees where the variants and the true red birds had been shot, hoping the young would give them a clue. But the bodies of the young, starved by the death of their parents, only increased the confusion.

Harris longed for a dozen golden-wings from the East and an eastern naturalist whose opinion he valued. He pictured the lively scientific discussion their comparisons would incite. "Wouldn't we make a night of it?" he mused in his journal. Barring that, he knew they "must wait further developments before we can pretend to decide this curious question."

Harris was also interested in agricultural methods, and he welcomed the chance to ride along for the fort's hay harvest to watch the men mow a blue-stem meadow he estimated at 200 or 300 acres. Learning they usually had to go ten or 12 miles down river to find that much grass, and that they required several hundred loads to get through the winter, he had a farmer's appreciation for the labor saved.

When they had more wolves than even they needed, the hunters brought them their first bighorn and a young buck elk. However, except for one cow they'd butchered on board the steamer -- pickling its head under the fascinated gaze of Indians on board -- and a calf skin they'd preserved, they had not yet concentrated on buffalo except for food. Under the broiling sun of July 20, a skiff from the fort deposited a light, four-passenger carriage on the south side of the Missouri and the five scientific gentlemen became initiates in a buffalo hunt.

Audubon, though vigorous for his age, acknowledged his years and rode on this hunt as an observer. But Harris intended to try his luck at this most vaunted of sports. He was both thrilled and apprehensive. Just a few days before, he'd passed his gun to a fort hunter when a bison was sighted, knowing the meat was needed and uncertain of his skills. After the hunter delivered a mortal shot and the bull turned to face his foe (looking exactly like a Catlin painting, Harris thought), he and Bell had danced around his bulk, firing their pistols into his body and drawing his charge.

The wounded bull could turn only slowly and it had seemed a game without much risk. Then Harris grew careless and fled a charge straight out instead of leaping aside. The bull's huge horns were within three feet of his back when he realized his danger. Only adrenaline had given him the strength to leap aside and save his life.

The lesson was still fresh. He was confident about his marksmanship and his courage, but he was worried about his horsemanship. He never straddled a horse on the farm these days, and he'd been vastly impressed by the hunters' exhibitions of equestrian skill. He didn't think he could match their abilities, and he knew an unhorsed rider in the midst of a herd might well end up dead.

When four bulls were spotted about 20 miles up the Yellowstone a few days later, he went through all the accepted preparations, throwing off his jacket, cinching in his belt, slinging a powder horn over his right shoulder and cramming his pockets with bullets. With lead in his gun and a couple of extra bullets in his mouth, he worked his way with the others toward the herd.

Quietly each man indicated his animal. Harris' knees tightened on his buffalo pony. The roan was short but he had stout limbs and good wind. The pony was superbly

trained, he knew, to run without a hand on the reins, to keep on the right side of the prey, to follow a wounded bison wherever it ran, to evade its charges. Would he be able to stay with the horse?

The moment his first bull sprang away before him, he forgot everything but his quarry. Racing across ground so rough he would have *led* a horse across it at home, he plunged after his bull. He was distracted as young Squires, hunting beside him, hit the ground when his horse veered to avoid a charging bull. But seeing Squires was not injured he galloped on after his prey.

Closing on the beast, Harris reviewed his lessons. Raise yourself in the stirrups. Lower the gun muzzle to point just behind the shoulder. Fire.

His bull barely stumbled, wounded only in the thigh.

Drawing alongside the bison again, he urged the pony on until the ground was a blur beneath their feet. The more headlong the gallop, the truer the shot, he'd been told. He fired his other barrel, aiming the bullet for the lungs.

The bull continued to run.

Still galloping at full speed, he clamped the rifle in his left arm, poured powder from the horn into his left hand, switched the gun back to his right, stretched to dump the powder down the muzzle. He whacked the butt on the saddle to pack the powder, spit out a bullet, dropped it in after the powder and pushed in the percussion cap.

He'd watched Culbertson squeeze off eight such shots in a mile. He was lucky to manage one. Just as he accomplished the job, blood gushed from the mouth and nose of the bull and he slowed his stride.

Satisfied the animal was finished, Harris rode after poor Squires' horse. When mount and rider were reunited, the two men took off after Squires' yet unvanquished bull. The younger man managed a shot into his hind quarters, but sore from his fall, decided to give up the chase.

Harris could not bring himself to quit. On he thundered after the bison, whipping his horse to keep him close. He had almost overtaken the wounded animal when it abruptly disappeared. The pony skidded to a halt at the edge of an embankment and Harris nearly pitched headlong into the gulley. But the undaunted pony slid down in the wake of the bull.

Now they crashed through the dry gully bottom, but the wounded animal was tiring. Harris drew near enough to take aim again. He stood in the stirrups.

Just then the cornered bison wheeled and charged. The unprepared Harris went head over heels. Winded and half-stunned, he scrambled up to face the bleeding beast only 20 feet away. Luckily he'd managed to keep hold of his gun; he took deliberate aim and fired.

Both barrels snapped uselessly. The hammers were clogged with dirt.

For a long moment hunter and hunted faced each other. The bull fastened his glaring bloodshot eye on his tormentor with a ferocity that was mesmerizing. Then, to the New Jersey farmer's vast relief, the buffalo turned and continued his flight.

Harris watched him disappear, remounted his pony, which waited loyally nearby, and walked slowly more than three miles back to the other hunters. Audubon, who'd watched it all from a perch on a hillside, was relieved to see he was well and whole. Wanting a trophy, he cut the tail from his first bull and watched the hunters carve up the rest. Soon a cart with its gory load creaked away toward the fort.

Harris was ready to rest on his laurels, but Squires wanted a chance to redeem himself. As they made their way to a new campsite they spotted another herd and the chase was on. This time Harris, having learned respect, shot from too great a distance and had to run with the animal until he could put three bullets in his side. This one, too, finally turned to fight, but the hunter was ready and evaded the charge. Soon the beast's knees buckled and he fell heavily to the prairie.

The hunters, having no more carts and unable to use much meat, took only the tongues of their kill and left the rest for the wolves. This bothered Harris. He looked at the fine, fat carcasses and felt more depressed than exalted, more murderer than victor. The bull was too much like a wild steer from the farm.

Harris felt disgust for himself and all white men who came to the West and slaughtered without purpose. Audubon, too, was put off by the senseless waste. As the two discussed the larger effects of countless hunts like theirs, the painter predicted the extinction of the herds. They'd go the way of the great auk, he feared.

Still, the excitement of the hunt was intoxicating, its thrills addictive. In spite of himself, Harris was pleased at the skill he'd shown. When, after another hunt or two, the traders at the fort pronounced Bell and himself the best buffalo hunters ever to debut at Fort Union, he swelled with pride. And his conscience hardened. Later that summer, he admitted, he experienced "no more feeling at the death of a buffalo bull than at the demise a towhee bunting..."

All hunts were not that productive. Soon after their buffalo hunt they tried to lure antelope close enough to shoot. Audubon lay on his back in the grass and kicked his long legs in the air to draw a curious buck closer. When the pronghorn edged within 60 feet, the artist, still flat on his back, sent a load of buckshot in the buck's direction. Harris' gun seconded the motion but the buck bounded away unharmed.

By the first of August, Harris, who often doctored others for their ills, had to look to his own health. He'd started the expedition at 158 pounds. Now, he discovered, he weighed only 133. He'd always suffered occasional asthma attacks and his exertions, coupled with the coarse diet, were taking a toll.

He did not feel ill, but his strength evaporated in the August sun. Bitterly disappointed, he had to sit out a hunt for the cock of the plains (sage grouse). "As a sportsman the shooting of this bird is the height of my ambition, and I am now compelled to abandon forever the idea of killing one," he confided dejectedly to his journal.

Their days at Fort Union were nearing an end. A mackinaw boat to carry them down river was already under construction, but Harris tried not to think about it. He spent another afternoon attempting to bag one of the invisible hares. Failing, he rose at dawn to try again. Again, he had no luck. He consoled himself with the traders' speculation that the high water which made the bluestem so lush had decreased the hare population. When the sage grouse hunters were no more fortunate and came home without their birds, Harris struggled not to feel unworthy emotions.

On August 12 he left for one more glorious buffalo hunt, going for cows this time and learning they could charge just like the bulls. But they were quicker. He chased heedlessly after a cow he had wounded, following her straight through a bunch of racing bulls. Somehow both made it through the herd. He managed to inflict the *coups de grace*, but only after she'd routed him several times with her charges. He cut off her tail and carried it home.

Two days later they left Fort Union, and the lively, enthusiastic entries in Harris' journal ended as if a giant hand had snuffed a flame. While he continued to study the Missouri's geology, collect birds and even shot one last buffalo, his entries for the two-month trip to St. Louis are desultory and dispirited.

Audubon couldn't wait to get back to the bosom of his family at Minnie's Land. He left St. Louis within three days of their October 19 return. Harris stayed on, tantalized by the possibility of a trip the next year to Santa Fe, a region yet undocumented in ornithology.

An attack of asthma put an end to those dreams. He went south for his health and had the further misfortune to suffer the death of his pointer Brag in Florida three months later. "In him I lost one of my best friends," he wrote. "...The last and not the least devoted of my companions of the Expedition

has left me...I trust there is naught of sin in the tear which I shed in writing this short tribute to the memory of a truly devoted and disinterested friend."

Although his great adventure had been short, it had produced work of enduring value. The ornithologists came home with 302 bird and 48 animal specimens. Audubon and his son John spent the next two years duplicating in paint the contents of their many barrels and crates for the final volume of *Viviparous Quadrupeds of North America*. Each was responsible for about half the paintings.

The white-haired artist who is the cornerstone of American ornithology lived to see the first three volumes published. His prairie dogs and bison may appeal less to the modern eye than the master's birds, but they thrilled the public in their day. After his father's death in 1851, John Woodhouse Audubon brought the huge project to completion with a miniature edition of *Quadupeds* which was published in 1854.

The puzzle over the woodpeckers was a lasting one. Audubon included a "Missouri red-moustached woodpecker" in subsequent editions of his *Birds of America*. Modern ornithologists consider it a hybrid of the red-shafted and yellow-shafted flicker.

One hundred fifty years after publication, Audubon's *Birds of America* is still a staple on public library shelves. His name, somewhat ironically, designates one of the nation's largest conservationist societies as well as countless towns, streets, parks, and a mountain peak.

Harris remains in obscurity, his philanthropy known only to a few. But his name is memorialized many times every year when birders in mid-America squint through their scopes, check their bird guides, nod with satisfaction and add "Harris sparrow" to their life lists.

Cries Deep in his Soul

The Blackfoot and their allies, the Gros Ventre, whom Chardon and the other fur men were coaxing in to trade in the early 1840s, had been exchanging words instead of bullets with the white man for only a few years. Residence in their country had been a chancy business and only a few of the most daring had taken the challenge.

While small pox had diminished their power, the two tribes were still formidable nations. All of the river above Fort Union was their dominion and they raided all the tribes on their boundaries. The Crow to the south, and the Flathead, Nez Perce and Pend d'Orielle across the Rockies to the west had ample proof that their enemy had not been vanquished.

Cautiously over a decade the traders had pushed west on the Missouri, establishing a post at the Milk River, then at the Judith, then at the Marias.

To the latter post (named for Meriwether Lewis) in 1846 came two men wearing black robes and flat-brimmed black hats. It had been nearly two centuries since Father Marquette had looked up the Missouri and longed to travel its waters and minister to its native people. Finally, 173 years later, the Jesuits had come.

When Father Nicolas Point approached the Blackfoot country in the fall of 1846, it was not without misgivings. The lean, gray-haired priest had been living with Indians for four years. He'd eaten what they ate, slept where they slept, and ridden with them on buffalo hunts, sharing their lean times as well as their good fortune.

But those years had been spent on the west side of the Rockies, with the friendly Flathead and the unthreatening Coeur d'Alene. The Blackrobes had been invited guests of the Flathead. Emissaries of the tribe had traveled clear to St. Louis to plead for instruction from the white man's Bible.

Point's superior, Father Pierre Jean De Smet, had visited the Flathead in 1840 to prepare the way. When he, Point, a priest from Rome (Father Gregorio Mengarini), and the three lay brothers who accompanied them -- a blacksmith and a carpenter from Belgium and a German tinner -- arrived after their long tramp up the Platte River in 1841, they were embraced both physically and spiritually by the grateful Indians.

They found the Flathead to be good, generous, courageous people. That first year they'd established the mission of St. Mary on the Bitterroot River (30 miles north of present Missoula, Montana) and immediately begun religious instruction for the tribe.

In 1842 Father Point had been sent farther west some 130 miles to the more primitive Coeur d'Alene tribe. That had been an exhaustive struggle which undermined his health. He'd become so debilitated in both body and spirit that he'd asked for reassignment. In April 1845, afraid he was accomplishing nothing, he'd requested transfer to the Jesuit Mission of Canada where at least he could speak the language of the people.

But while he waited the long months it took for his letter to reach Jesuit authorities, for a decision to be made and that decision communicated to him in the field, his work had begun to have an impact, however small. The Sacred Heart mission which he built for the Coeur d'Alene near Lake Coeur d'Alene (Kootenai County, Idaho) could be judged a success. And the man who professed humbly, "I am nothing; I can do nothing; I am worthless," had proved that it was not so.

The Blackfoot he rode to meet now, how-ever, were a different people altogether. All Point had heard about them indicated they were a bloodthirsty, thieving nation. Whether Piegan, Blood or Blackfoot proper, their frequent attacks on the mountain tribes were a continuing threat to the missionaries' new converts. The Jesuits were convinced they'd have to be brought to peace before any lasting progress could be made.

Father De Smet needed to return to St. Louis, and since he had to travel to the Missouri to catch a boat, he'd decided it was a good opportunity to try to meet with the Blackfoot along the way and see if a truce could be achieved. He'd asked Father Point to accompany him as far as the river and remain with the Blackfoot to minister to the tribes. Point wondered as they left the reassuring sight of St. Mary's and his horse picked its way south along the continental divide, what kind of welcome they and their small escort of friendly Indians would find on the Missouri plains.

It wasn't that he wished to be any place *but* the mission field. At 16, after surviving the bombardment of his French village of Rocroy during Napoleon's final campaign, and being the oldest of a devout family, he'd begun schooling to prepare for the priesthood. When in his studies he came upon the life of St. Francis Xavier, learning how that holy man had spread Christianity from India to Japan, he knew what he wanted to do. He'd petitioned to join the Jesuit order and been accepted in 1819 at the age of 20.

Like Father Marquette before him, he had waited many years for assignment to the mission field. When he learned he was to be sent to America in 1835, he hoped at last he'd be able to work among the Indians. But he spent his first months teaching American boys in Kentucky and then was ordered to establish a college in Louisiana. Removed from control of St. Charles College in 1840, he was free to accompany Father De Smet on the mission to the Flathead. At age 42, after 20 years of looking at college walls, he would test himself as an apostle in the wilderness.

Point had been named official diarist for the mission and he fulfilled that task willingly, but he enriched his journals with a special talent. From the time he was a child he'd loved to draw, been almost compelled to re-create what he saw on paper. He never had formal training, but his widowed mother had managed to see that he had simple supplies to develop his talent. His artistic ability had lain dormant in recent years, but the vistas of the Rockies had awakened his desire to preserve this new land on paper.

He had seen hundreds of miles of mountains and plains in the past five years. He'd been the one chosen to accompany the Flathead on their semiannual hunts into Blackfoot country, so that their newly learned lessons could be reinforced, and their hard-won moral well-being protected.

He'd bedded down on snow in hungry camps where the starving dogs fought to chew on unguarded leather, ridden until he was so stiff with cold he'd nearly toppled from his mount, tried vainly to sleep through frigid nights, all the while observing every holy feast and gathering his neophytes for prayers, song, instruction and three "Hail Marys" morning and evening.

But he did not regret it. He'd discovered that "One must travel in the wilderness to learn how attentive Providence is to the needs of man." Not only had he kept the Flathead in the fold, he'd made valuable contacts with several other tribes -- especially the Blackfoot.

The first year a friendly old Piegan chief, who'd been living with the Flathead and had himself been baptized as Nicolas, was able to coax a delegation of his people into the Flathead camp. For the first time Flathead and Blackfoot had smoked together. The Blackfoot had spent the night, but the truce had been an uneasy one, and when trouble arose the next morning over a stolen horse, the priest had been able to smooth over things with a small gift.

On a hunt a year later there'd been another contact and he'd been able "to offer as a bouquet to the glorious Apostle of the Indies (St. Francis Xavier) the first baptisms of a Blackfoot on his own territory." The next day the Flathead, unusually fortunate, had surrounded 37 Blackfoot hunting on foot. Temptation to avenge old wrongs was strong, but Point reminded his charges of their duty to God to be merciful, and the Flathead offered a pipe instead of the sword. When trouble arose again, the Father had spoken for peace, and in gratitude for his intervention, the chief

of a Blackfoot band called the Little Robes had promised to bring his people for baptism.

It was a good start, and as the small party hurried through the Three Forks area and turned north for the Judith River, they were joined by the Little Robes and a band of Flathead and Nez Perce hunters. All signs seemed favorable. Then the Piegan chief Nicolas was thrown from his horse and killed. The priests' entree to the Piegan was gone when they needed him most.

The chief had scarcely been buried (with Christian rites rather than pagan to Father Point's immense satisfaction) when the Blackrobes learned the Piegan were approaching. On the morning of September 14, 1846, to the beat of drums and the sound of chants, with the Blackrobes leading the march, the two groups came together. De Smet and Point met the distinguished woman who led the bedraped horse bearing the Piegan's sacred medicine pipe and greeted the intricately costumed warriors. But the grand chief was nowhere in sight. Only after the opening speeches did he deign to appear and join in the ceremony of the calumet in the priests' lodge.

Point watched as the pipe was solemnly lit and passed from hand to hand in prescribed ritual. He knew how much the Blackfoot revered its use. The silent ceremony was scarcely complete when the Flathead made their entrance. Point thought his old friends had never looked more noble, mounted on their finest horses, facing their long time enemy in a long line, marching slowly as they chanted. With them came the Nez Perce and the Pend d'Orielle. And now Point discovered there were some Blood and Gros Ventre among the Piegan. He could hardly contain his excitement. This was a historic day.

Following an afternoon of fellowship and evening prayers, the chiefs of all the tribes gathered in the lodge of the Piegan leader. Point's heart swelled as he listened to their Flathead convert speak eloquently for his new faith and peace. The others nodded in agreement. There would be a truce. Their mission appeared to be accomplished.

The priests remained at the camp for ten days, instructing the children so they could be baptized. Father Point had discovered that in Indian country he could use his artistic talent for God's work. On first contact he used his sketches of village life and portraits of important men to earn the Indians' attention and friendship. Then his art served a higher purpose. Constrained by the language barrier and faced with explaining sacraments and religious doctrine for which the tribes had no cultural background, he'd turned to painting bright pictures to illustrate each concept.

Father Point had found the Indians could relate to concrete illustrations of sin or virtues or ceremonies. They could be made to understand what habits they must change, what they needed to do to be saved. He had worked out a daily schedule which seemed effective. In the morning -- with the help of the interpreter -- he used a pointer to explain the day's concept to the watching men. The men then explained the concept to their families. The lesson was repeated orally by the chiefs later in the day.

Point met separately with the children to teach them the prayers he had translated into Blackfoot. The young people memorized their prayers by holding a number of short twigs in their hands and sticking one in the ground for each word they could repeat. When they had mastered the words they ran to Point for examination. In the evening after supper -- the only hour the women could find time for instruction -- he worked with them.

Much as he wished for converts, Point did not allow the Indians to take the sacraments unless he felt they were ready. He baptized adults only if he judged they had demonstrated continuing efforts of good faith or if he felt death was imminent.

By September 20, the Feast of Our Lady of Sorrows, he had 96 children and two old people ready for baptism. On the twenty-fourth, the Feast of Our Lady of Mercy, he and De Smet bid goodbye to the Piegan and left for Fort Lewis. Four days later, after the fur post had witnessed its first mass, heard its first sermon and 33 more people had been baptized, De Smet left for St. Louis and Father Point was on his own.

On September 29, he conducted the lengthy baptismal rites for 22 more children. He prayed that "the bouquet of neophytes" he was offering St. Michael on his day would merit him the Saint's protection. He knew he had great need of it in the country he would now serve as an apostle.

Father Point had warm support from the residents of the post. Most were of French extraction and nearly all were Catholic. He immediately began a course of instruction so the traders and their Indian wives could be married in the church and their children legitimized. He reflected how important the contribution of the French voyageurs had been. They and their descendants had not lived holy lives, he knew, but they had respected their religion, their priests and their country and had passed their affection on to the Indians.

Still it was a strenuous winter. Temperatures reached as low as -38 degrees, often while Father Point was away from the post visiting Indian camps. He crossed and recrossed the treacherous ice of the Missouri and struggled up snow-piled ravines, wise enough now to dismount and walk to keep his feet from freezing.

The tribes' friendliness could never be taken for granted. There were times when the white interpreters at the post were afraid to accompany him. When that happened he turned to the Indians, often to a youth of 12. Several times he found himself refereeing conflicts between the tribes, struggling to maintain the truce with only his wits and his Lord as allies.

One day in autumn he promised to visit a tribe of Blackfoot he called the Fish Eaters. No white men were willing to go because they believed the tribe too hostile. Point turned to a Blackfoot who, like himself, spoke some Flathead through which they could communicate. The Blackfoot said he would go, but they had just crossed the river when he changed his mind and refused to continue. Point was forced to postpone his visit.

Late in November Panarquinima, chief of the Fish Eaters, visited the post and Point offered to accompany him back to his camp. "If you wish," the chief said shortly.

Taken aback, Point said he wanted to go only if the people wished to see him. "Get your horses," said Panarquinima.

After a silent ride of three or four hours, the priest dismounted in the Fish Eaters' camp and was ushered into the chief's lodge without ceremony. Beyond the usual center fire he found himself looking at what was almost a throne. A bed of thick furs lay opposite the door. Ranged before it were a richly ornamented pipe, an elegant perfuming pan, a war bonnet, the chief's arms and medicine bundles. When Panarquinima settled himself on the bed and leaned on his elbow rest, he had a dog on his left and a cock on the right.

Father Point, increasingly uneasy, tried to guess where he should seat himself. Unknowingly he moved between the cock and the fire. The interpreter gasped. He tugged at Father Point's robe and whispered urgently in his ear. The chief never allowed anyone to transgress on the cock's territory. Panarquinima sat as expressionless as the black and yellow bird that topped his headdress.

The Blackrobe was served a light meal. The camp would move the next day, he learned. He had no time to lose. He waited silently while the leaders of the tribe gathered to conduct the calumet ceremony. Wondering, worrying, he watched the pipe pass from mouth to mouth until it had completed the circle. Then he gathered his courage and announced that he had something to say.

He knew the ice he now trod was as full of dangers as the Missouri's. Whatever was wrong, he dared not offend them further. He thanked them for their hospitality and for their willingness to see him and hear the word of the Great Spirit. Then he reminded them of the advantages that peace with the Flathead would bring and suggested they might profit from a mission such as St. Mary's in Blackfoot country.

He finished his speech to dead silence.

Father Point had been in enough councils to know approval should have been vocal. Ordinarily the audience would respond with a chorus of "Ai, Ai." Now there was nothing. The silence dragged on.

Finally Panarquinima turned haughtily to the interpreter and demanded to know how the Blackrobe could be telling the truth. "The truth has never come from the mouth of a single white man," he challenged.

The interpreter, glancing in fright from one face to the other, agreed. "It is true that there are many white men who lie," he said diplomatically. "But the Blackrobes are not like them. No one has ever reproached them even for the smallest lie."

The chief considered his words and said noncommittally, "If this is so, it is good."

He turned to Point and looked him in the face for a long moment. Then, his voice warming slightly, he said, "Blackrobe, since you are not lying when you say that you love the redskins no less than the whites, and the Blackfoot no less than the Flathead, if you wish to come into our lands, you are welcome." This time the assembly voiced its approval. Father Point breathed a prayer of thanks that God had been able to touch the chief's heart. He prepared to work.

The next morning he had 100 children ready for baptism. As the lodges were dismantled around him, mothers brought their children for the sacrament. There, in cold so intense the holy water froze between his fingers and glistened in tiny rivulets of ice on his neophytes' black hair, he gathered the lambs into his flock. He entered each name in his registry, struggling gamely to pronounce and record the strange names until the children had to duck their heads to hide their giggles.

In March 1847 Father Point learned his request for transfer had been granted. He boarded a flatboat for the down river trip. Although he had asked to go, he could not help sighing as the boat put into the current to leave "a land in which my heart had struck such deep roots." He philosophized that all things change and pass away, but he hoped what would not pass "are the riches gained for Heaven this year." He *had* accomplished some things. There were the 625 children he had baptised among the Blackfoot;

127

their souls should be safe. The 26 adults were in more jeopardy. Still, when even Panarquinima, humbled by defeat in battle, could come to understand he needed a greater god and relinquish his sacred medicine bird to the missionary's hand, there was always hope. "The time given God is never wasted," he knew.

He thought of the cross which now stood at Fort Lewis and others he had erected at the sites of several hunts. He hoped they "will tell future travelers that this land, however desolate it may appear, was a true land of blessings...for all those who heard the voice of the Lord." He thought of the traders' wives, duly instructed in their duties as wives and mothers, their feet set on the proper path, who could now serve as examples to every native who visited the post.

Even the terrible Blackfoot had greeted him with sympathy, asked that their children be baptized, asked his blessing before setting out on a campaign. He had faith that the peace the Blackrobes had established among the tribes would be a lasting one.

On board the flatboat, able to relax from the press of duty for the first time in five years, Point allowed his artistic eye and hand free rein. He spent much of the day documenting the sights as he floated downstream.

On the Feast of the Holy Trinity, he was able to say mass on board and he thought no other evening had ever been as beautiful. He recorded the memory in his journal. "As the sun set in a light haze, it exchanged the gold of its fire for the color of rubies. Above it, and outlined sharply against a blue background, a formation of clouds tinged with purple, blue, and violet hung like drapery. A row of beautiful trees cast their shadows to the middle of the river." In front of him, the women and children sang hymns in honor of Mary. It was an experience he never forgot.

He also was unable to forget his Indian charges. While he was delighted to be in Canada and among French-speaking people again and knew he was accomplishing important work at the mission there (present Windsor, Ontario), he asked repeatedly to be sent back to his Indians in the American Rockies. He worried about their welfare and tried to alert the American government to their needs.

As the years passed, his call to the western tribes remained so strong that he believed it was God's will he go back. Again and again he pleaded for permission. Thirteen years later he wrote of his longing, referring to himself, as he often did, in the third person. "Nothing has made it possible for him to forget the Rocky Mountains; they are at the bottom of all his thoughts, their cries have gone deep into his soul. If he forgets them he has reason to fear, so it seems to him, that God may forget him."

But his health was questionable and the hierarchy of the Society of Jesus, which had never entirely understood the artistic priest, did not grant his petition. From 1859 to 1865 he worked to copy and compile his journals and drawings. In page after page of painstakingly regular script, he recorded not only his religious experiences, but information about the tribes' daily lives. His miniature paintings demonstrated the beauty of the Indians' homeland, showed their leaders in their prime, and celebrated the minutiae of their cultures.

He could not believe that his work was of much value, but he was persuaded that the history of the mission should be preserved. As he worked, he hoped his *Recollections of the Rocky Mountains* would help readers understand the Indians and realize they deserved consideration. After several years of delicate health, he died in 1868.

For many years his extensive and colorful journals, known only to a few, sat with other Jesuit documents, including the journal of Father Marquette, in the the archives of College Sainte-Marie in Montreal. Point's journals were not to see publication until 1967. Although their publication came much too late to help the people he loved, they have provided modern scholars and laymen a unique and fascinatingly detailed look into Indian life on the Upper Missouri in the 1840s.

Call Me Jane

During the winter of 1846-47, when Father Point was witnessing his faith among the Blackfoot, those faithful to another religion settled on the Missouri's banks among the Omaha and Potawatomi. They had not sought the wilderness. They'd been driven to it. And while they were usually fervent missionaries for their church, this winter they found they had a higher duty than proselytizing among the Indians. It was called survival.

"I wouldn't give or sell a thing to one of you damned Mormons!"

The words rang in Jane Richards' ears as she lay on the bed in her rocking wagon. She'd been too sick to go herself, so her mother had walked to the small house beside the field of potatoes edging the road just west of the river. But Jane's request for a few potatoes to satisfy her sick child's wish had been met with scorn, and the grandmother had been taken by the shoulders and marched from the yard. As Jane listened to her mother try to comfort the hungry, disappointed two-year-old, Jane's control collapsed and she turned on her bed and wept.

It had been weeks since Wealthy had shown any interest in food. More often than not, weak and shaking with fever, she had shared Jane's bed in the wagon. They'd both taken ill in July as the Saints dragged themselves and what was left of their belongings across Iowa. Jane, watching desperately for some sign of improvement, had been tremendously relieved to hear the little girl ask for potato soup. That she could not supply even this simple wish for her daughter brought tears Jane seldom shed for herself.

Not that she hadn't cried. It had been hard for the 23-year-old woman to be driven from the new house she and Franklin had scrimped to build in Nauvoo. Hard to start west in a wagon, with two cows, one trunk of clothes and a food supply which obviously would not last the trip. Hard to find faith for a journey with no known destination, with little Wealthy ill, and an unborn child swelling her belly. Unspeakably hard only one day down the trail to tell Franklin goodbye when the church called him for a mission to England. Unbearably hard, three weeks later, to wrap her newborn son for burial.

Through it all she had clung to the hope that Wealthy would live. If only her daughter survived, she thought, all the other hunger, suffering and loss would be unimportant. Now that they had finally crossed Iowa, ridden the ferry to the Missouri's west bank, and pulled into the camp called Cutler's Park, perhaps the worst was over.

Though she was without her husband, she was certainly not alone. The Saints had been gathering along the river for weeks, led by their efficient new president, Brigham Young.

Some remained on the east bank (present Council Bluffs, Iowa); more crossed the river to range their wagons on Omaha land and begin the business of building a community. It was already September and the Mormons knew they'd have to winter here.

They were still shocked by the violence that had driven them from Nauvoo. Killing their prophet had not been enough. The mobs hadn't been satisfied until they had dragged them from their beds and hounded them across the Mississippi, until their temple stood smoking in desecration.

This was only a temporary stop, they knew. The next time they built it would be far beyond the reach of Gentiles -- somewhere in the vast, unsettled land on west. But it had taken them all summer to reach the Missouri. They were ill with nameless fevers, exhausted from pushing wagons, carts and stock through interminable mud, debilitated by heat and air so thick it was like breathing water, and weak with hunger. It was obvious even to the most fervent believer they could go no farther this year. The Omaha and Potawatomi had granted them refuge. The new Zion they planned to found would have to wait for spring.

But already they'd changed the face of the country. Creeks that usually watered Omaha ponies were now lined with tents and wagons. Roads connected one camp with another, herds grazed in the meadows, washing was spread to dry on bushes and smoke swirled up from hundreds of cook fires. The teamster who drove the Richards' wagon pulled it into an established line of wagons and tents near that of her parents.

Both her family and Franklin's had come west to be part of the Mormon church after converting to the faith in the northeast. Educated, successful people, they'd followed the call to Missouri and Nauvoo. Franklin's brother had been shot down at Haun's Mill in Missouri. His uncle was an apostle. Franklin himself had already traveled widely to recruit new church members. She'd fallen in love with him when he roomed with her parents for a time while on such a mission.

But he was in England now, with his brother, Samuel, and would not return for two years. For weeks she'd been too weak and dizzy to walk and she wondered for the hundredth time one September night if she'd live to see him again. More than a month ago the elders had visited her wagon, annointed Wealthy and herself with sacramental oil and prayed for their recovery. But this time, unlike the miracle which had followed her baptism and rid her of consumption, the laying on of hands had not stemmed their sickness.

Nearly every wagon, tent and cabin in the community of 3,500 held victims of malarial fever that seemed to waft with the stench of the weedy mud flats. Others, skin hanging on malnourished bones, already bore the disgusting sores of black canker. Jane's two brothers sweated and shivered with fever in her parents' wagon nearby and she could hear Elizabeth Richards cry out in delirium in the next tent, calling her name. Unable to respond, she cuddled Wealthy beside her and drifted off to sleep.

When she roused again, the child was dead.

It seemed too much, this final, crushing loss. She willed herself to die and join her children. But the prayed-for release did not come.

Instead, when morning arrived and the small body had been cared for, Jane was carried to the bedside of Elizabeth. Pretty, 17-year-old Elizabeth, her lungs full of phlegm and her body swollen with Franklin's child, needed her comfort.

When Franklin had first raised the possibility of taking another wife, eight months into their marriage, Jane had been devastated. The thought of sharing her husband was repugnant to all her ideas of a virtuous life. Nothing had prepared her for such a sacrifice, and she told Franklin she did not know if she could bear it.

But Joseph Smith had said it was not only acceptable but required by God. It was required of Franklin as an elder. It was required of her as an elder's first wife. It was necessary for her salvation.

For weeks after Wealthy's birth she'd prayed to understand and struggled to accept the idea. She pressed Franklin for reassurance on her myriad doubts. Would he keep matters between the two of them confidential? Would he care for her in her old age? Would he be faithful to her then?

He promised not to marry again if it made her unhappy -- not to marry anyone she could not learn to love. Still she agonized. Perhaps she could yield herself to sharing Franklin. But could she be strong enough to accept his other children? She knew she must, for it was her duty to the Lord.

Accept the covenants of your church, she told herself. Look for the reason later. Finally she'd seen a vision of the prophet, assuring her that in time all would be explained. She told Franklin she'd try to bend to God's will and accept another woman into their home. But, she warned, if the two of them could not get along without quarreling, she would leave him.

Sweet, gentle Elizabeth, when she came with Jane's consent, caused no dissension. "I'll try and not make you miserable, Mrs. Richards," she'd said.

"Don't call me Mrs. Richards," Jane had responded, "call me Jane." She decided to ignore the gossiping neighbors -- Mormon as well as Gentile, for polygamy was a new and shocking idea to them all -- and refer to her husband's new wife as Mrs. Elizabeth Richards. They'd each taken a floor of the new house in Nauvoo and learned to share a husband.

Now he was thousands of miles away and they had only each other. Jane sponged Elizabeth's hot, dry brow and tried to comfort her. With so many others sick and in need, the heartsick Jane had little time to dwell on her own losses. There was much to do to prepare the community for winter. The air rang with the sound of axes and saws as the Saints scurried to get under cover. Those who could built with logs, others cut sod or burrowed into sides of hills.

Some faced the winter in tents and wagons but, when the camp moved down on the river bottom out of the wind, relatives provided Jane and Elizabeth with a small log cabin. It was just big enough for two beds, two log chairs and a fireplace with a clay hearth. Jane's dirt roof dripped muddy water with every rain, but she felt lucky to have it.

She also felt fortunate to have her family. Franklin's mother made her feel like a daughter and his brother Samuel's wife, Mary, was becoming a warm friend. Mary had only six months with Samuel before he was off to England, and she commiserated with Jane in her cheerful, lively way over their loneliness. Mary often spent the night at Jane's; they sewed for themselves and others, did washing and read to each other from letters they would send their absent husbands.

They knew they were not the only lonely wives. Homes which held a man or two were the exception. While only a few were away on missions, many spent weeks out with the stock, and 500 of their youngest and strongest had marched away to fight for the government which had not raised a voice to protest their treatment.

The government's request that they provide a battalion to fight the Mexicans had at first seemed a gigantic joke. Why *should* they, why *would* they give their urgently needed strength to a cause for which they cared nothing? But Brother Brigham explained it was manna from a Gentile heaven. The wages of the men would buy supplies to help them through the winter. Providing a battalion of Mormons gave them leverage with the government to stay on Indian land. They were lucky they'd been asked. Trying to believe him, they sent their young men to war.

At first, gathering grapes and plums on hillsides draped with scarlet vines, listening to stock bells signal the end of day, it seemed a pleasant, if austere, existence. They organized themselves into wards and kept the log meeting house busy with services, sessions of choir and band practice and energetic dances. The fact that the dancers were plainly dressed, devoid of rings, brooches, watches and chains, did not seem to dim their gaiety. They supplemented their brass band with violins, tambourines and even sleigh bells, glorying as they always did in the music, believing they praised God in their dance.

However the Saints knew God's laws demanded more serious attention, and every Sunday morning the temple bell rang to call them to meeting where their leaders reinforced their faith. Often in the evening they studied the Book of Mormon and the elders did not hesitate to remind each of his duty. One evening Mary, accused of the sin of pride, demonstrated humility by kneeling beside her uncle and eating from his plate. But Jane, charged by her father-in-law with some transgression, spoke up in her own defense

with such spirit and wit that the stern parent beat an uncharacteristic retreat. She would and did accept what she must, but she refused any extra servings of humble pie. Mary admired her spunk.

On December 12 the sisters-in-law happened in at their uncle's house while the Council of Twelve met with a delegation of Omaha. They watched with interest as the painted braves spoke and a French trader interpreted. The Omaha, caught on the brim between two worlds, voiced disparate needs: protection from their wild Pawnee neighbors, and help in learning to farm. The Indian spokesmen seemed sincerely troubled and the young women were intrigued by their performance, but their thoughts were on their own problems. Where would they meet their husbands again, they asked as the council adjourned, here on the Missouri or in the yet unfounded Zion? Probably here, the elder assured them. They should be content. All things should go right.

Snow didn't come until December 14, and then it melted as soon as the sun touched it. Christmas Day was bright and beautiful. Jane and Mary spent it over the washtubs. It was best to keep busy. On Sunday, December 27, the two young wives sat in the meeting house and listened to the elders' plans for spring, when a company would be sent west to find their new Zion and plant a crop of wheat. The talk turned to preparing the wagons for the journey and they all looked ahead.

But as 1847 began, the cold descended. Their washing froze before they could get the clothes on the line and their hands and feet ached even on short walks from house to house. The hems of their dresses became encased in ice that rattled against the snow-lined paths, and against the rough floors of houses never warm enough to thaw them.

Wood was scarce and at times they had to ration themselves to one fire. Proud and independent as she was, Jane occasionally found herself at Mary's tent door asking wryly, "Shall I freeze or ask you for wood?" Other times, when visitors crowded Mary's tent, Jane was grateful that she could offer her a small measure of warmth at her hearth. Smoke from Jane's inadequate chimney was often so intense, however, that tears ran uncontrollably down their cheeks as they tried to make their frigid hands ply a needle.

Her small supply of cornmeal almost gone, Jane traded everything she could spare for food. As the weeks passed, her wardrobe disappeared until she had left only a shabby calico wrapper and a dressy black silk. The calico was too worn to be decent in company and she felt incongruous in neighbors' wagons in the elegant black silk, pretending she wore it by choice, afraid they all knew she had only the silk to wear -- and had that only because no one would take it in trade.

One winter day Jane helped deliver the weakening Elizabeth of her child. She was learning to love her husband's other wife, but when she saw that the wet form pushed into her hands was a girl she reeled as if from a blow. Her Wealthy was gone, but Franklin was to have another daughter. A little girl who wasn't hers would call him Papa. She had to turn away from Elizabeth and fight to control her feelings. It was a long moment before she could reach again for the tiny, squalling infant, clean her body and dress her in the waiting clothes. She was glad Franklin was too far away to see the depth of her bitterness and pain.

Still she cared tenderly for the child and for the sinking young mother who now spent most of her time in bed. Soon Jane had to lift Elizabeth from the bed to her chair and back again. Knowing she'd never gain strength on their diet of corn bread and milk, Jane studied the contents of her nearly empty trunk. All that was left was Franklin's violin, which nobody seemed to want. When Brigham Young's nephew stopped to ask how he could help, she swallowed her pride and told him they must have food, but all she could offer was Franklin's violin. A little later she returned triumphantly to Elizabeth holding up a gallon of wine. It was disallowed by the Word of Wisdom, but it might keep the scurvy from their door.

Elizabeth, bright-cheeked with fever, smiled wanly at her excitement and said, as she had so many times before, "Jennie, the Elder never would have married me if he had known I should have been so much trouble to you."

But wine could not work magic on Elizabeth's lungs, any more than herbal teas or holy oil. As she got weaker and the terrible coughs shook her body, she began to talk of dying. Jane tried not to listen. She could not bear to think of being all alone. And in a corner of her mind she wondered if Franklin would understand how things were here.

Scarcely a household was still whole. A day seldom passed without a procession to the cemetery. Her neighbors died of dysentery, asthma, croup, pleurisy and whooping cough. Their malnourished bodies repaid them with rotting gums, swollen ankles, ulcerated calves and eventually prostration. Exposure and injuries took even those who were relatively healthy. But Franklin was not here to see. Would he believe she had done all she could for his second wife?

Elizabeth clung to life as the snow melted and the air began to warm, as the wild onions and pigweed greened the swales, as the preparation for the Pioneer Company began to change from talk to action. Then she was gone. Jane walked to the graveyard to see the girl buried. Wealthy Lovisa lay among the 600 graves here. Her tiny son lay along the trail in Iowa. Now, she thought, I am left.

In April she heard from Franklin for the first time since he'd left her nine months before. But the joy that mounted as her shaking hands opened the envelope was short-lived. Samuel had smallpox, Franklin wrote. He was doing his best to nurse him. Small pox! Would Franklin be taken, too? The letter had been written months before. Was he already dead? She'd kept her sanity through the months by forbidding herself to think of where her husband was and what he was doing. Now she built a wall between herself and further pain by deciding her next letter would be news of his death.

Numbly she listened to the excited speculation about the progress of the Pioneer Company; watched other companies organize and take the road to join them. Trying to care, she joined in celebration of the news that they had found a valley along a great salt lake and planted their seed in Zion.

But when the remainder of the Saints moved west the next summer, Franklin was at her side. He'd not only survived, he'd brought a company of converts with him from England. In another year Jane cuddled a new son, and with quiet joy watched her husband irrigate the rows of peas in their garden.

If his time with her was limited, if he spent ten of the first 15 years of their marriage away on missions, if she supported the family by braiding straw hats and taking in boarders, if she had to share his time and modest income with three more wives and listen to a number of children call him Papa, she never complained. She had been hardened in the crucible of Winter Quarters. She did not believe in telling her troubles or dwelling on them, she said, because her mission was to give comfort to her poor and afflicted brethren.

"Polygamy was not such a trial as I feared," she told an interviewer 34 years later. "My face may be wrinkled and careworn but polygamy has been the least of my troubles. I would have left Franklin or the church if I had reason, but I never had a reason yet."

Small Ankle's Daughter

While white civilization crept above the equator of the Missouri, and its women and children faced the challenges of a different life, those who resided on the upper river lived as their grandfathers and great-grandfathers had. They, too, sometimes suffered cold, hunger and loss, sometimes knew times of joy and plenty. They, too, cherished their families and tried to please their gods.

For Waheenee, young daughter of the Hidatsa chief Small Ankle, the winter the whites counted as 1846 was bleak. Though her tribe had know terrible losses in the smallpox epidemic nine years before, they were only stories to her, accounts of times before she was born.

She did not even remember the long march her grandfather, Missouri River, had led from the fatal Knife River villages north to their new home at Like-a-Fishhook Point when she was four. She'd been too young to realize they and their neighbors, the Mandan, were trying to leave behind both the sorrow and the Sioux. She had only faint memories of how they'd camped in tipis that first year when it was more important for the women to get a corn crop planted than to spend their strength building lodges. The men were busy keeping watch for the Sioux who'd been making their lives so hazardous and bringing home enough meat to last the people through the winter.

The next year the women had had time to erect the spacious earth lodges on the bluff tops where they spent the warm months each year. The winter camps, in less substantial lodges, were made at the water's edge where the trees gave both shelter and fuel.

In those days, Waheenee had little knowledge of the cares of the world. Her memories were of warmth and love, of her father's voice singing her to sleep by the firelight, of the affection of her natural mother as well as her mother's three sisters, who were also wives to her father and mothers to her. Their children were her brothers and sisters, she knew, and she particularly enjoyed playing with Cold Medicine, two years younger than she.

She still cherished the doll her grandmother, Turtle, had made for her from a long, green-striped squash. She took care to keep it carefully wrapped in a piece of skin, especially when the cold winter winds blew and the only cozy place was the small, peak-roofed twin lodge where the youngest and oldest spent much of the winter months. Waheenee, named for the brown bird which often sat on the buffalo's back, was not strong and her mother took special pains to keep her warm.

One Buffalo, this year's winter leader, had thought he'd chosen the site of the winter camp well. It was near a holy place where the young men fasted and spoke to the gods. But snow had hit before the lodges were even well-covered with earth, and with it came their recurring curse, the smallpox. Almost before she knew what was happening, Waheenee had lost her brother, one of her aunts and her mother.

A winter lodge had never seemed more dark and cold. Waheenee often wept with loneliness for her mother. Old Grandmother Turtle, trying to comfort her, made her a new doll of soft deerskin and stuffed it with antelope hair. It had two white bone beads for eyes, until she bit one off. Then Turtle managed to get a blue glass bead from the trader and Waheenee decided eyes of two colors was much the better.

Gradually her pain subsided. She took interest again in her father's fur hunting cap. It had ears like the jack rabbit and she knew he valued both the warmth of the buffalo fur and the spirit of the jack rabbit it represented. When he came in from a snowy hunt he hung it by the fire to dry, and when it was warmed she asked for it. Sometimes she sat in it, enjoying the feel of the fur on her ankles. Sometimes she marched around the lodge with it on her head and her dolly on her back, making Grandmother Turtle laugh.

By the time they heard the high, muted trumpets of the geese calling and she rushed outside to watch great flocks fly north along the river, they were all more than ready to move back to their more spacious permanent lodges. The women of the Goose Society called for the spring dance and prayed that the gods would give them good weather for the corn planting. One Buffalo sent the crier around the village to warn the people to pack their travois, and with much laughter and celebration they were off.

Led by the older chiefs and medicine men, the warriors and their families followed. Nearly all were on foot, for few Hidatsa were rich enough to have horses. Most of the women carried belongings in slings across their backs, and the poles of the travois, mounted on dogs, marked their path, for they were heavy with tent skins, pots, bedding and sacks of food.

It promised to be an early spring and

almost as soon as they were settled again in their summer lodge, Waheenee heard her father speak of a war party. Seated with her grandfather, Big Cloud, and two of their friends around their lodge fire he smoked a shiny, black pipe and had a long conversation. Then he stood and walked to his medicine bundle, hanging near his bed. Waheenee saw his lips move in prayer. He opened the bag and reverently unrolled a bear skin which had been painted red. Followed by the other braves, he carried it out of the lodge.

The next morning when Waheenee went outside, she saw the bear skin again. It was tied to a high post beside their lodge door. She gazed at it in wonder, almost afraid to go in and out of the house with a holy thing so near.

The next days were busy ones, for many young men were attracted to Small Ankle's notice. Waheenee's mothers, Red Blossom and Strikes-Many Woman, kept a pot of meat boiling all the time to feed the many visitors. When they had time, they opened the cache pits and worked sunflower meal into balls for traveling.

One night she woke to the sound of men's voices and peeped between the skins of her grandmother's bed. In the moonlight that came through the smoke hole she could see the curved backs of many men and the dark, narrow rectangles of their filled quivers. A flint scraped against steel and a glowing pipe lit each face briefly. Her grandfather's voice raised a prayer for safety and success while they struck the camp of their enemy to steal horses; then they filed from the lodge. Waheenee heard the whinny of her father's war pony and then silence. She snuggled down against the warmth of her grandmother, feeling both excited and afraid.

They'd gone to raid the Sioux, Grandmother Turtle told her the next morning. But Waheenee didn't have much time to worry about her father because the ice broke on the Missouri the next day and the air was filled with the anger of its letting go. Huge blocks crashed against each other in the current, grinding and splitting as they started south.

The young men armed themselves with poles and lined the river bank, shouting excitedly over the din. Then a dark shape whirled among the ice cakes, and with a yell

they leapt from block to block to reach it. Balancing precariously, riding when they could, vaulting to a new perch when they had to, they poled a buffalo carcass to shore.

Kept in the Missouri's ice box since last fall, it was fine and fat, for the animal had tried to cross the river before the ice would hold it. Now it and many others who'd met similar fates were released by the thaw to feed the Hidatsa with meat much richer and more tender than the gaunt-ribbed spring herds could offer.

Even the old men were astonished at the warmth of the weather so early in the season. The sun fell on the land like a benediction and the bushes were already leafing out. Waheenee followed Turtle to the family corn field and watched her plant sunflower seed around the border.

Then the north wind claimed the country for his own again and they woke to a blinding blizzard. Wind shrieked down the smoke hole, blowing ashes from the fire in their faces and making cooking all but impossible. Red Blossom threw a robe over her head and started out the entrance for a neighboring lodge. But she could not see her fingers in front of her face, let alone the lodge only a few yards away, and she was afraid to go. Luckily they had firewood. And they could gather snow at the doorway for water. But even with an extra calfskin belted around her, Waheenee shivered continuously, her teeth chattering in the cold.

Only after they ate did Red Blossom voice the fear weighing on them all. Where were Small Ankle and his party? If they had reached the shelter of the river bottom, they should be all right, Red Blossom said. If they were caught on the plains they would die.

Turtle remonstrated immediately, glancing at the children. "Big Cloud's prayers are strong," she said, "and Small Ankle is a good plainsman." They would find shelter. Shamed, Red Blossom offered a hopeful story. She'd known a Mandan who'd survived a three-day blizzard by wrapping his robe tightly around him and burrowing under the snow.

Darkness came and the wind continued to scream. Turtle tried to parch some corn for supper, but had to give up when it was only half done. A handful of the corn and a lump of dried chokecherries made Waheenee's supper.

She crept into bed, shaking in spite of the heavy robes. Where in the bitter, snow-blown night was her father?

The next morning the smoke hole shone clear and bright blue. She joined the other children as they climbed the shining drifts that tailed the east side of every lodge and hillock. But there was no word from her father.

It was afternoon the next day before she heard the hoofs on the fringe of the door skin tinkle and he was home. He led his exhausted war pony to the corral on the right side of the lodge and sank down on his bed by the fire.

Waheenee's mothers said nothing. Red Blossom put some dried meat to boil and Turtle went out to gather green cottonwood bark to feed the pony. Small Ankle hung his fur cap to dry and wrung out his fur-lined winter moccasins. Then he began to eat. Only in the evening, when his friends came to smoke and talk, did they hear the story.

They'd been caught on the prairie about a day north of the river and soaked by rain that turned to snow. Knowing the only shelter was in the riverbottom to the south, they'd kept the west wind on their right as they'd pushed through the deepening snow. When the ponies had been unable to go farther, they'd dismounted and broken the path themselves, while their robes froze stiff in the wind and the cloths wrapped around their heads became hard with ice.

By the time they'd reached the river, most of them were too numb to function. But Small Ankle had used his flint and steel to start a fire with the dry inner bark of a dead tree. They'd nursed it along until it was big enough to thaw and partially dry their frozen clothes. They'd toasted a little dry meat and started home when the weather cleared the next morning.

Several found they'd frozen the right side of their faces. One teenager lost his right foot and part of his right hand. "Perhaps the gods were angry with us," Small Ankle said regretfully.

Some of the elders thought he'd been foolish to take a party out so early, but another party out at the same time had had two men frozen to death, so there was not much said. Small Ankle thanked the spirit of

the jack rabbit -- and his warm fur cap and mittens -- that he had not suffered more.

Now that he was safely back, Waheenee's days began as they should, with the sounds of her father blowing the coals of the fire into flame. As the thin pillar of smoke began to rise she'd hear him call, "Up little daughter. Up sons! Get up wives! The sun is up. To the river for your bath! Hurry!" As she crawled from bed she could hear his light steps on the roof as he checked the countryside for enemies and made sure the horses he'd left outside were safe.

After washing, Waheenee loved to watch Red Blossom prepare herself for the day, brushing her black hair with a piece of trimmed porcupine tail and braiding it in two thick plaits, painting her cheeks and rubbing vermillion into the part in her hair. Her own hair was cut short, an operation she hated because Turtle's old knife pulled. She and the other small children each had a little tuft on each side of their center part above their forehead that looked like the ears of an owl. This was to remind the owl to make them strong and healthy, as he had promised long ago, Turtle explained. But since the owl had once been a bad bird, it also reminded them to behave if they didn't want him to come and get them.

Breakfast, eaten from wooden bowls with mussel shell spoons, was sometimes meat and broth and sometimes a mess of squash and beans cooked with corn. Afterward, her mothers busied themselves sweeping the lodge and carrying out the horse droppings, but Turtle was always anxious to get out to the fields.

Turtle was a small woman, bent now with age, but she was an energetic farmer. She and Small Ankle's wives had marked out one of the largest fields in the open river bottom near the village. While most of the other women now used hoes of iron, she clung to her fire-hardened digging stick and her bone-bladed hoe. "I am an Indian," she would tell the children. "I use the ways my fathers used."

Most of the heaviest work -- clearing willows and grubbing out roots and brush -- had been done the year before. Turtle kept working to add new ground, being careful not to impinge on any other's chosen plot. It did not do to squabble about anything as sacred as the family field.

Waheenee was too little to be of much help, but it amazed her to see how the old woman could start a small clear spot and work around it day after day until it was a respectable bit of land. Cushioning her digging stick with her robe, she pried up the soil and broke the clods with a sharp blow. Clearing away the grass and roots, she dropped a half-dozen kernels of corn into each hill.

The girl reveled in the soft spring sun, the sweet, light air, the calls of the birds. Often she laughed at the magpies' scolding and sometimes she helped her mothers by chasing away the crows. As the green shoots pushed their way through the ground, these pesky birds liked to pull up the tender plants. Then Turtle or Red Blossom would have to replant, which made them cross. Turtle made a scarecrow of skins to frighten them away. Although Waheenee thought it frightening enough, it only bothered the birds for a little while and they were soon back at their mischief.

Since she was not old enough to spend many hours in the field, she and Cold Medicine found others things to do. They played house, serving meals the boys had "killed," sang their dolls to sleep in their willow bed, played ball, slid down grassy slopes on a buffalo hide and modeled the blue clay of the river bank into little figures.

They spent hours listening to stories. Turtle seemed to have one for everything that happened. If Waheenee cried while in the field, she might turn into a curlew, as a babe

had long ago. If she spilled a few grains of seed corn the gods would be angry; once they'd made a woman search every corn hill in a field for a grain which cried when she left it behind.

She learned how the Hidatsa had first lived at the bottom of Devils Lake until some hunters had climbed a grapevine root up to the earth. She learned how the Mandan had given them corn by shooting pieces of ripe ears across the Missouri on their arrows.

Her Grandfather Missouri River taught her about the gods. He seemed almost a god himself, sitting on the bench before the fire, smoking his black pipe. She knew he was a holy man and held him in awe. He explained that the earth was alive, and that it and all things in it have spirits. Even the lodge they sat in had a spirit and the door was its mouth. The spirits could be good or bad and do help or harm. They spoke to the people through dreams. Good gods sent buffalo and rain for their corn.

How about thunder, she asked, remembering a storm the night before. That came from the thunderbird god, he explained. "He is like a great swallow, with wings that spread out like clouds. Lightning is the flash of his eyes. His scream makes the thunder." Sometimes the gods admired a brave man, for a warrior had once shot a gun at the thunderbird when lightning struck his lodge, and he'd not been punished for his rash act. But it was better not to provoke them. She should never laugh at them or speak of them lightly, he told her solemnly.

Her Grandfather Big Cloud taught her the importance of a good life. She must not quarrel or steal. She must not talk back to her parents or answer anyone with bad words. She must learn to work hard like her mothers so she could feed her family some-day.

One day when she was eight, she went out to a mysterious little tipi her grand-mother had built and discovered one of their dogs had given birth to a litter of puppies. She was allowed to choose one for her own and she loved him dearly, but she discovered he had to be more than a pet. When the pups were ten days old Turtle took them into the lodge and, one at a time, held them in the thick smoke of a green sage fire. The puppies struggled and choked but Turtle assured her it would make them eat meat. Then she held each one in the air and let go. If they held their feet on landing they'd grow up strong enough to pull a loaded travois and would be kept. Waheenee held her breath as her pup, Sheepeesha, dropped to the earth. Though he was still choking from the smoke, his legs stiffened and held. He had met the test.

Two years later she trained him to pull the travois. Feeling very grown up, she hurried to the lodge door with her first load of firewood. She was old enough now to do her share. Daily she fetched water from the river in a bucket made of a buffalo heart skin or a clay pot. The Hidatsa liked the Missouri's water, finding it cool and sweet after the mud had been allowed to settle. It had quenched their fathers' and their grand-fathers' thirst and it satisfied theirs.

She learned to cook and to sew with an awl and sinew, to embroider with dyed quills of porcupines or gulls, to scrape and dress hides until they were soft and pliable. But best of all she liked to go to the cornfields at planting time and later in the summer when the ears began to head and the crows and blackbirds became a real menace to the crop. Then Waheenee and her sister, Cold Medicine, could provide needed help.

Their mothers built a platform in the field where they could sit and look out over the crop and watch and sing. For two weeks or so as the corn ripened they spent the days there, for the Hidatsa believed they should nurture their corn as their children, that the souls of the plants enjoyed their songs. Shaded by a small elm tree, they guarded the fields against birds, horses and their small brothers, who loved the green ears.

Turtle made a small arbor of willows at the side of the field, where they cooked their meals. Often they were there in time for a sunrise breakfast.

Waheenee couldn't imagine ever tasting anything sweeter than the mess of green corn and beans they boiled in the cool morning air. Nor could she imagine a better world. The meadowlarks were singing. The rays of the sun were slanting over the bluff top and bathing their field in glowing amber. In a few years she would be a woman. The gods were good.

ASA BATTLES

Epilogue

For nearly six generations the white man had known about the Missouri River. For more than a hundred years he'd been visiting Waheenee's people. For almost 50 he'd been venturing to the river's source in the Rocky Mountains. Its course had been mapped and its beaver dens mined.

While life on the lower river had changed, the change had come almost as naturally and inevitably as the river carved its bed. Log cabins had replaced earth lodges, towns had replaced tipis, and the river's sailors bent their backs to fireboxes instead of oars.

The people called the Missouris no longer challenged the currents with their sturdy canoes and the Mandan were only a shadow on the waters, but most of the Missouri's native people on the upper river lived lives not much different from their grandfathers.

Waheenee looked forward to the day she would marry and have daughters who'd sing to the corn and train their puppies to the travois. But forces beyond her knowledge were gathering, pressures beyond her understanding were building, and change more violent than the Missouri in the Moon of the Breaking Ice was on its way.

Bibliography

General Background

Athearn, Robert G. *Forts of the Upper Missouri*. University of Nebraska Press, 1967.

DeVoto, Bernard. *Course of Empire*. Houghton Mifflin Co., 1952.

Monaghan, Jay, ed. *The Book of the American West*. Bonanza Books, 1963.

Nagel, Paul C. *Missouri*. W. W. Norton & Co. Inc., 1977.

Neihardt, John. *The River and I*. University of Nebraska Press, 1968.

Primm, James Neal. *Lion of the Valley: St. Louis, Missouri*. Pruett, 1981.

Ramsay, Robert L. *Our Storehouse of Missouri Place Names*. University of Missouri Press, 1973.

Vestal, Stanley. *The Missouri*. University of Nebraska Press, 1964.

Chapter 1 -- Terra Incognita

Munro, William B. *Crusaders of New France*. Yale Chronicles of America Series. United States Publishers Association, Inc., 1974.

Nasatir, Abraham P., ed. *Before Lewis and Clark*, vol. 1 & 2. St. Louis Historical Documents Foundation, 1952.

Repplier, Agnes. *Pere Marquette*. Doubleday, Doran and Co., 1929.

Severin, Timothy. *Explorers of the Mississippi*. Knopf, 1968.

Shea, J. G. *Discovery and Exploration of the Mississippi Valley, with the Original Narratives of Marquette....* J. McDonough, 1903.

Chapter 2 -- King Louis' Banner

Berry, J. Brewton. "The Missouri Indians," *Southwestern Social Science Quarterly*, vol. XVII, no. 2, 1936.

Bray, Robert T. "Bourgmond's Fort d'Orleans and the Missouri Indians," *Missouri Historical Review*, vol. 75, no. 1, 1980.

Chapman, Carl H. and Eleanor F. *Indians and Archaeology of Missouri*. University of Missouri Press, 1983.

DeVoto, Bernard. *Course of Empire*. Houghton Mifflin Co., 1962.

Edmunds, R. David. *The Otoe-Missouria People*. Indian Tribal Series, 1976.

Folmer, Henri. "De Bourgmont's Expedition to the Padoucas in 1724..." *Colorado Magazine*, vol. XIV, no. 4, 1937.

-------------- "Etienne Veniard De Bourgmont in the Missouri Country," *Missouri Historical Review*, vol. 36, no. 3, 1942.

-------------- *French Expansion Toward New Mexico in the 18th Century*. Thesis. University of Denver, 1939.

Giraud, Marcel, ed. "Etienne Veniard De Bourgmont's Exact Description of Louisiana," *Missouri Historical Bulletin*, v. 15, no. 1, 1958.

Johnson, Mary Moyars. *Historic Colonial French Dress*. Ouabache Press, 1982.

Shine, M. H. Letters of "First Visit of Nebraska Indians to Paris in 1725," *Nebraska History*, vol. VI, no. 1, 1923.

Shoemaker, Floyd C. "Fort Orleans: The Heritage of Carroll County," *Missouri Historical Review*, vol. 51, 1957.

Spencer, Joab. "Missouri's Aboriginal Inhabitants," *Missouri Historical Review*, vol. 3, no. 4, 1909.

Chapter 3 -- Seekers of the Sea

Brebner, John Bartlett. *The Explorers of North America, 1492-1806.* Macmillan Co., 1933.

Burpee, Lawrence J., ed. *Journals and Letters of Pierre Gaultier de Varennes De La Verendrye and His Sons.* 1927.

-------------------- "La Verendrye, Discoverer of Dakota," Address. Champlain Society, 1916.

DeVoto, Bernard. *Course of Empire.* Houghton Mifflin, 1962.

Kavanagh, Martin. *La Verendrye, His Life and Times.* Kavanagh, 1967.

Nasatir, A.P. *Before Lewis and Clark.* St. Louis Historical Documents Foundation, 1952.

Smith, G. Hubert. *The Exploration of the La Verendryes in the Northern Plains, 1738-43.* University of Nebraska Press, 1980.

Chapter 4 -- La hameau at the Mounds

Cunningham, Mary B. and Jeanne C. Blythe. *The Founding Family of St. Louis.* 1977.

Chouteau, Auguste. "Narrative of the Settlement of Saint Louis," *The Early Histories of Saint Louis.* John F. McDermott, ed., Saint Louis Historical Documents Foundation, 1952.

Foley, William and David C. Rice. *The First Chouteaus.* University of Illinois Press, 1983.

Chapter 5 -- A Battle Won; A Battle Lost

McDermott, John Francis. "The Myth of the Imbecile Governor Captain Fernando de Leyba," *The Spanish in the Mississippi Valley, 1762-1804.* University of Illinois Press, 1974.

---------------------- "The Battle of St. Louis," *Missouri Historical Society Bulletin*, vol. 36, no. 3, 1980.

Rickey, Don, Jr. "The British-Indian Attack on St. Louis, May 26, 1780," *Missouri Historical Review*, vol. 55, 1960-61.

Chapter 6 -- Prelude

DeVoto, Bernard. *Course of Empire.* Houghton Mifflin, 1952.

Fletcher, Alice C. and Francis La Flesche. *Omaha Tribe*, vol. 1 & 2, University of Nebraska Press, 1972.

Nasatir, A. P. *Before Lewis and Clark*, vol. II, Saint Louis Historical Documents Foundation, 1952.

Nasatir, A. P. "John Evans, Explorer and Surveyor," *Missouri Historical Review*, vol. 25, no. 2 & 3, 1931.

Welch, Roger, "The Omaha and the Ponca," The First Voices. *Nebraskaland Magazine*, vol. 62, no. 1, 1984.

Williams, David, "John Evans' Strange Journey," *American Historical Review*, vol. 54, no. 2 & 3, 1949.

Chapter 7 -- A Fine Morning

Bakeless, John, ed. *The Journals of Lewis and Clark.* New American Library, 1964.

DeVoto, Bernard, ed. *The Original Journals of the Lewis and Clark Expedition.* Houghton, Mifflin, 1953.

Jackson, Donald, ed. *Letters of the Lewis and Clark Expedition.* University of Illinois Press, 1962.

Mattes, Merrill. "On the Trail of Lewis and Clark," *Montana Magazine*, vol. XVI, no. 3, 1966.

Russell, Elizabeth and Clark Kennerly. *Persimmon Hill.* University of Oklahoma Press, 1948.

Satterfield, Archie. *The Lewis and Clark Trail.* Stackpole Books, 1978.

Steffen, Jerome O. *William Clark, Jeffersonian Man on the Frontier.* University of Oklahoma Press, 1977.

Thwaites, Reuben Gold, ed. *The Original Journals of the Lewis and Clark Expedition*, 1904.

--------------------- "William Clark: Soldier, Explorer, Statesman," *Missouri Historical Society Collections*, vol. II, 1906.

Chapter 8 -- That Spaniard Called Manuel

Douglas, Walter B. *Manuel Lisa*. Abraham P. Nasatir, ed. Argosy-Antiquarian, 1964.

Oglesby, Richard. "Manuel Lisa," *Mountain Men and the Fur Trade of the Far West*, LeRoy R. Hafen, ed. vol. V, Arthur H. Clark Co., 1971.

Oglesby, Richard Edward. *Manuel Lisa and the Opening of the Fur Trade*. University of Oklahoma Press, 1963.

Chapter 9 -- Gauntlet at Three Forks

Bradbury, John. *Travels in the Interior of America*. Sherwood, Neeley and Jones, 1817, March of America Facsimilie Series, No. 59, 1966.

Haines, Aubrey L. "John Colter," *The Mountain Men and the Fur Trade*, LeRoy R. Hafen, ed. vol. VIII, Authur H. Clark Co., 1971.

Harris, Burton. *John Colter, His Years in the Rockies*. Charles Scribner's Sons, 1952.

James, Thomas. *Three Years Among the Indians and Mexicans*, 1846 edition. University of Nebraska Press, 1984.

Chapter 10 -- Don Quioxte and Friend

Brackenridge, Henry Marie. *Views of Louisiana*. March of America Facsimilie Series, No. 60, University Microfilms, Inc., 1966.

------------------------ *Views of Louisiana Together with a Journal of a Voyage Up the Missouri River, In 1811*. Quadrangle Books, Inc., 1962.

Bradbury, John. *Travels in the Interior of America*. March of America Facsimilie Series, No. 59. University Microfilms, Inc., 1966.

Dictionary of American Biography, Charles Scribner's Sons, 1964.

Thwaites, Reuben Gold. *Early Western Travels*. vol. 6, Arthur H. Clark Co., 1904.

Chapter 11 -- As Little Harm as I Can Help

Andrae, Rolla P. *A True Brief History of Daniel Boone*. The Daniel Boone Home, 1985.

Bakeless, John. *Daniel Boone: Master of the Wilderness*. William Morrow & Co., 1939.

Brown, John Mason. *Daniel Boone: The Opening of the Wilderness*. Random House, 1952.

Bryan, William S. "Daniel Boone," *Missouri Historical Review*, vol. 3, no. 2, 3, 4, 1909.

Elliott, Lawrence. *The Long Hunter*. Reader's Digest Press, 1976.

Gregg, Kate L. "The War of 1812 on the Missouri Frontier," *Missouri Historical Review*, vol. XXXIII, 1938.

Moize, Elizabeth A. "Daniel Boone, First Hero of the Frontier," *National Geographic*, vol. 168, no. 6, 1985.

Thwaites, Rueben G. *Daniel Boone*. 1911.

Van Noppen, John James and Ina. *Daniel Boone, Backwoodsman*. Appalachian Press, 1966.

Wesley, Edgar B. "James Callaway in the War of 1812," *Missouri Historical Collections*, vol. V, 1927.

Chapter 12 -- Something We Crave

Flint, Timothy. *Recollections of the Last Ten Years in the Valley of the Mississippi*. Southern Illinois University Press, 1968.

Folsom, James K. *Timothy Flint*. Twayne Publishers, Inc., 1965.

Kirkpatrick, John. *Timothy Flint, Pioneer, Missionary, Author, Editor*. Arthur H. Clark Co., 1911.

Chapter 13 -- A Great Distance

Cook, Eliza Hempstead. "Account of Mrs. Manuel Lisa's Trip up the Missouri River," Typescript, Missouri Historical Society.

Douglas, Walter B. *Manuel Lisa*. Argosy-Antiquarian, 1964.

Hempstead, Stephen. "I at Home," *Missouri Historical Society Bulletin*, vol. XIV, no. 1, 3, 1957.

James, Edwin. "Account of the Expedition of Stephen H. Long," *Early Western Travels*, vol. 14, 15, Rueben G. Thwaites, ed. Arthur H. Clark, 1905.

Johnson, Sally A. "The Sixth's Elysian Fields," *Nebraska History*, vol. 40, no. 1, 1959.

----------------- "Cantonment Missouri, 1819-20," *Nebraska History*, vol. 37, no. 2, 1956.

Nichols, Roger L. *The Missouri Expedition, 1818-1820: The Journal of Surgeon John Gale*. University of Oklahoma Press, 1969.

Peterson, Charles E. "Manuel Lisa's Warehouse," *Missouri Historical Society Bulletin*, vol. IV, no. 2, 1948.

Sandoz, Mari, *Love Song to the Plains*. University of Nebraska Press, 1966.

Chapter 14 -- The Breathing Corpse

Alter, J. Cecil. *Jim Bridger*. University of Oklahoma Press, 1950.

Clokey, Richard M. *William H. Ashley*. University of Oklahoma Press, 1980.

Clyman, James. *American Frontiersman*. Charles Camp, ed. California Historical Society, 1928.

Hafen, LeRoy R. *Broken Hand, the Life of Thomas Fitzpatrick*. Old West Publishing Co., 1931.

Myers, John M. *Pirate, Pawnee and Mountain Man, the Saga of Hugh Glass*. Little, Brown and Co., 1963.

Vestal, Stanley. *Jim Bridger, Mountain Man*. University of Nebraska Press, 1970.

Chapter 15 -- An Indignant Soul

Catlin, George. *Letters and Notes on the North American Indians*. Michael MacDonald Mooney, ed. Clarkson N. Potter, Inc., 1975.

Denig, Edwin Thompson. *Five Indian Tribes of the Upper Missouri*. John C. Ewers, ed. Univeristy of Oklahoma Press, 1961.

Ewers, John C. "When the Light Shone in Washington," *Montana Magazine*, vol. VI, no. 4, 1956.

Jackson, Donald. *The Voyages of the Steamboat Yellow Stone*. Ticknor and Fields, 1985.

McCracken, Harold. *George Catlin and the Old Frontier*. Dial Press, 1959.

Chapter 16 -- Where the Saints Dwell

Allen, James B. & Glen M. Leonard. *The Story of the Latter Day Saints*. Deseret Book Co., 1976.

Carter, Kate B. *Our Pioneer Heritage*, vol. 1, 1958, vol. 19, 1976. Daughters of Utah Pioneers.

"Death of Mrs. Emily D. P. Young," *Deseret Evening News*, Dec. 9, 1899.

Lightner, Mary Elizabeth Rollins, "Mary Elizabeth Rollins Lightner," *Utah Genealogical and Historical Magazine*, vol. XVII, 1926.

Parkin, Max H. *A History of the Latter-Day Saints in Clay County, Missouri from 1833 to 1837*. Thesis. Brigham Young University, 1976.

"Partridge Genealogy," *Utah Genealogical and Historical Magazine*, vol. VII, 1916.

Stegner, Wallace A. *The Gathering of Zion*. McGraw-Hill Book Co., 1964.

Young, Emily Partridge. "Autobiography of Emily D. P. Young," *Woman's Exponent*, vol. 13, 14, 1884-5.

Chapter 17 -- To Day I am Wounded

Catlin, George. *Letters and Notes on the North American Indians.* Michael MacDonald Mooney, ed. Clarkson N. Potter Inc., 1975.

Chardon, Francis. *Chardon's Journal at Fort Clark, 1834-39.* Annie H. Abel, ed. South Dakota Department of History, 1932.

Chapter 18 -- The Sparrow and the Crane

Audubon, John James. *The Birds of America.* Roc Lockwood and Son, 1860.

Audubon, John James. *The Life of John James Audubon.* Robert Buchanan, ed. G. P. Putnam's Sons, 1869.

Audubon, Maria. *Audubon and His Journals.* Nimmo, 1898.

Brannon, Peter A. "Edward Harris, Friend of Audubon," Address, Newcomen Society of England, American Branch, 1947.

Chancellor, John. *Audubon.* Viking Press, 1978.

Dock, George, Jr. ed. *Audubon's Birds of America.* H. N. Abrams, 1979.

Ford, Alice, ed. *Audubon, By Himself.* Natural History Press, 1969.

McDermott, John Francis, ed. *Audubon in the West.* University of Oklahoma Press, 1965.

------------------------- *Up the Missouri with Audubon: The Journal of Edward Harris.* University of Oklahoma Press, 1951.

Chapter 19 -- Cries Deep in His Soul

Garraghan, Gilbert J. "Nicolas Point, Jesuit Missionary in Montana of the Forties," *The Trans-Mississippi West,* University of Colorado, 1930.

McDermott, John Francis. "Father DeSmet's Illustrator," *Nebraska History,* vol. 33, no. 1, 1952.

Point, Nicolas. *Wilderness Kingdom, The Journals and Paintings of Father Nicolas Point.* Joseph D. Donnelly, S.J. ed. Holt, Rinehart and Winston, 1967.

Chapter 20 -- Call Me Jane

Godfrey, Kenneth and Audrey. *Women's Voices, An Untold History of the Latter-Day Saints, 1830-1900.* Deseret Book Co., 1982.

Kane, Thomas L. *A Friend of the Mormons: Private Papers and Diary of Thomas Kane.* Gelber Lilienthal, Inc., 1937.

Richards, Jane (Snyder). "The Inner Facts of Social Life in Utah," Manuscript of 1880 interview, Bancroft Library.

---------------------- "Reminiscences," Manuscript of 1880 interview. Bancroft Library.

Stegner, Wallace. *The Gathering of Zion.* McGraw Hill, 1964.

Chapter 21 -- Small Ankle's Daughter

Wilson, Gilbert L. *Agriculture of the Hidatsa Indians, an Indian Interpretation.* University of Minnesota Bulletin, 1917.

------------------- *Waheenee, an Indian Girl's Story told by Herself.* University of Nebraska Press, 1981.

Index

Acknowledgments

In the course of researching *People of the Troubled Water*, I have requested help from many sources and it has been offered with unfailing graciousness. My deep appreciation goes to Laurel Boeckman of the Missouri State Historical Society, Grant Allen Anderson of the Historical Department of the Church of Jesus Christ of Latter-Day Saints, Betty Loudon of the Nebraska State Historical Society and Mary-Ellen Jones of Bancroft Library.

The staffs of the Western History Department of the Denver Public Library, and Arapahoe Regional Library's Castlewood and Christensen branches have been generous with their knowledgeable assistance. I am also indebted to individuals who took time to share their expertise. My thanks to Trinda Myers, Hal Stearns, Alice Rumery, Katherine Murdock, Robert V. Bell and W. B. Spillman.

ABOUT THE AUTHOR

NANCY MAYBORN PETERSON, currently of Littleton, Colorado, was raised along one of the major waterways of westward migration, the North Platte River in Scottsbluff, Nebraska. It was the Platte that served as the impetus for her first book, the very successful 1984 release *PEOPLE OF THE MOONSHELL: A Western River Journal.*

Peterson's interest in the frontier era, particularly in the people who shaped the American West, has spawned numerous historical articles in regional publications. She has also published nature essays and light verse in the *Reader's Digest, Good Housekeeping,* and *The Wall Street Journal. Families, Catholic Digest,* and the magazine supplements of major daily newspapers have given voice to her humor pieces. Winner of numerous awards for both prose and poetry, she is past president of both the Denver Woman's Press Club and the Denver Branch of the National League of American Pen Women.

PEOPLE OF THE TROUBLED WATER is the first portion of Peterson's saga of the settlement of the Missouri River route, the years of discovery along the Missouri. The years of conflict, which followed as the concept of Manifest Destiny became reality, are covered in the second part of her Missouri River epic, *PEOPLE OF THE OLD MISSURY* (Renaissance House, 1989).

ABOUT THE ILLUSTRATOR

ASA BATTLES, also of Littleton, Colorado, specializes in the scratchboard art that graces the pages of *PEOPLE OF THE TROUBLED WATER.* His American Indian (Choctaw) heritage and his extensive study of the Plains Indians culture brings incredibly authentic detail to his work. Battles' illustration and cover artwork for Peterson's earlier *PEOPLE OF THE MOONSHELL* brought high praise from a variety of critics. He previously illustrated *Fodor's Guide to Indian America* and *Ritual of the Wind* by Jamake Highwater, as well as several book articles for major publishers. He has exhibited at many shows throughout the western U.S. and received countless honors and awards.